JEWISH
PERCEPTIONS
OF ANTISEMITISM

JEWISH PERCEPTIONS OF ANTISEMITISM

Gary A. Tobin
with Sharon L. Sassler

PLENUM PRESS • NEW YORK AND LONDON

Library of Congress Cataloging in Publication Data

Tobin, Gary A.
  Jewish perceptions of antisemitism / Gary A. Tobin with Sharon L. Sassler.
      p.   cm.
  Bibliography: p.
  Includes index.
  ISBN 0-306-42877-6
      1. Antisemitism—United States—Public opinion. 2. Public opinion—Jews. 3. Jews—
  United States—Public opinion. 4. Public opinion—United States. 5. United States—
  Ethnic relations. I. Sassler, Sharon L. II. Title.
  DS146.U6T63 1988
  305.8′924′073—dc19   87-37402
                                                                                  CIP

© 1988 Gary A. Tobin

Plenum Press is a Division of
Plenum Publishing Corporation
233 Spring Street, New York, N.Y. 10013

Printed in the United States of America

To Mel Brooks, who has filled the
world with needed laughter

PREFACE

I started thinking about writing this book about four years ago. I kept seeing report after report saying that antisemitism in America was on the decline. The information came from a variety of polls and studies. The news seemed good.

At the same time, my own research in Jewish communities all over the United States showed substantial proportions of Jews, usually at least 20% in each community, saying that they had experienced antisemitism in the year prior to being surveyed. The findings were fairly consistent from one city to another, year after year. To my surprise, Jews under the age of 35 were the most likely to say that they were experiencing antisemitism. These experiences did not seem to fit with all the positive news about the decline of antisemitism.

So I began to look at the subject in greater depth. I examined the available evidence about the actual state of antisemitism in America and was astonished to discover how seldom the topic of "contemporary" antisemitism was actually studied. Instead, impressions, some rather incomplete auditing mechanisms, and occasional public opinion polls were used to measure antisemitism. The methods being used to assess how non-Jews felt about Jews today were not "contemporary" at all. The times and contexts had changed, but the measuring tools were essentially unaltered.

Much of what is written about antisemitism focuses

on the antisemitic beliefs and attitudes of non-Jews as assessed by measuring non-Jewish adherence to antisemitic
stereotypes and attitudes. Interpreting the polls is problematic. We are not sure what they mean. They do indicate that the percentages of non-Jews holding antisemitic
stereotypes or expressing anti-Jewish attitudes have for
the most part declined or remained static over time. In a
few instances, the proportion adhering to certain antisemitic attitudes or stereotypes has actually increased. The
facts remain: substantial percentages of non-Jewish Americans continue to hold negative attitudes and stereotypes
about Jews.

While discriminatory barriers against Jews have been
broken in almost all areas of American life, prejudices remain among non-Jews. These may be expressed in seemingly harmless "Jew" jokes. "Jewish American princess"
stereotypes, caricatures of greed and social parasitism, excessive Israel-bashing, or using American Jews and Israel
interchangeably while condemning Israel's "evils" are all
aspects of antisemitism that remain part of American society today. Antisemitism may erupt in the form of Louis
Farrakhan or the desecration of a synagogue or Jewish
community center. Although a great deal of antisemitism
today may be expressed in attitudes and not behaviors,
Jews continue to sense its presence.

Certainly, the most "objective" measures cannot be
dismissed. Jews have broken the barriers of economic and
political discrimination, and have succeeded in nearly all
aspects of American society. Antisemitic expression does
not negatively affect the economic and political welfare of
Jews today. Still, Jews do not equate this economic and
political success, even the almost universal social acceptance of Jews, with the disappearance of antisemitism.
They are right.

One of the best gauges of current levels of antisemitism is Jewish perceptions themselves. Jews do not have to look far to find antisemitism; the phenomenon remains real enough. The collective intuition, assessment, and examination of antisemitism by American Jews demands a hard look at the current methods of assessing antisemitism.

Jews are concerned about the future because of the past. When prejudice is expressed—and it is often enough to remind Jews of its persistence—Jews try to interpret the signs. Is the antisemitic joke, or description, or anti-Israel news report an aberration, a trend, an important shift in behavior, or an accident? Personal interviews with Jews indicate that most are not sure.

What Jews feel and think and sense provides a useful backdrop for assessing antisemitism in the United States today. The topic of antisemitism cannot be properly addressed without also looking through Jewish eyes, and by exploring Jewish beliefs and attitudes. Clearly, Jews continue to remain wary of antisemitism despite their economic, political, and social successes. Their wariness is demonstrated in their continued support of today's community relations agencies—the "defense" agencies of the past—as well as by the close attention they pay to governmental and legislative affairs and their attempts to influence policy through political lobbying.

These concerns were documented in surveys of Jewish populations throughout the country. Numerous personal interviews were conducted and articles in Jewish newspapers, magazines, and organizational publications were examined. In order to add an element previously missing from assessments of antisemitism in the United States, this book tunes in to the Jewish community's collective view of their fellow Americans' feelings about Jews. Overall, Jewish perceptions are accurate in assessing the amount of antisemitism present in the United States today. While

American Jews see antisemitism as potentially threatening, they also clearly think it is under control.

Social scientists use survey research and other social science techniques to measure and analyze social phenomena. Most of this book is based on surveys of many kinds. What is different about this assessment of antisemitism is the fact that it incorporates Jewish perceptions. The collective perceptions of American Jews may tell much about their external environment and the ways in which they are viewed or treated. Jewish perceptions alone cannot and should not be used to measure antisemitism. However, they can be used as an indicator which mirrors and reflects it. The collective views of American Jews can be used to guide further research and enrich our understanding of antisemitism and other forms of prejudice in the United States.

Gary A. Tobin

ACKNOWLEDGMENTS

This book could not have been completed without the assistance provided by the Cohen Center for Modern Jewish Studies at Brandeis University. Peter Medding, who served as a Visiting Professor at the Center, helped me first conceptualize this topic, and I value my opportunities to spend time with him. Larry Sternberg, Associate Director of the Center, was involved at various stages of the book, from helping design questionnaires for Jewish community relations professionals, to reading and editing drafts. Sylvia Riese, the Center's Executive Secretary, helped in the preparation of the manuscript, including transcribing much of the text and preparing the tables.

Sharon Sassler, who is now a Research Assistant at the Center, assisted in all phases of this book: research design, interviewing, data analysis, drafting text, and manuscript preparation and review. It was a formidable undertaking, and she fulfilled each task with skill and creativity.

I would like to thank all those who agreed to be personally interviewed and those who participated in mail-back surveys conducted by the Cohen Center for their time and their insights. Representatives from a number of organizations were extremely helpful in providing resource materials, including Tom Neumann and Alan Schwartz of the Anti-Defamation League, David Singer of the American Jewish Committee, Jerome Chanes of the National Jewish Community Relations Advisory Council, and Evan Mendelson, formerly with the American Jewish Congress and now with the Jewish Community Federation of San Francisco. Earl Raab also read the manuscript. He is a tribute to the field and an exceptional person.

To all my students from St. Ferdinand Parish in Florissant, Missouri, I send a special note of gratitude for all that we were able to teach each other in a very special year. To Stewart and Judy Colton, I thank you for your hospitality and friendship and the quiet place you so graciously provided me to write this book. To my brother and sister-in-law, Mark and Sharon Tobin, I thank you for the not-so-quiet place you provided. Vicki Ibera proofed and edited the final version of the manuscript, and as always, did a wonderful job.

To my father, who taught me tolerance, and to my mother, who gave me street sense, I give my respect and affection. And to Gussie, Adam, Amy, and Shaina my gratitude and apologies for the missed times while I finished this book. I love you all very much, and next year we will all skip school and go to St. Louis to watch another St. Louis Cardinals' World Series.

CONTENTS

JEWISH
PERCEPTIONS
OF ANTISEMITISM

Chapter One

THROUGH THE JEWISH
LOOKING GLASS

Assessing Antisemitism from the Jewish Perspective

Are Jews safe in the United States? Jews, like other Americans, are concerned about street crime and nuclear war. Most Jews also think about safety in specific terms as Jews: protection from antisemitic discrimination and violence, and the disappearance of antisemitic beliefs and attitudes.

Despite their integration into the fabric of American culture, many contemporary American Jews remain concerned about antisemitism. Jews carry with them a collective knowledge of past antisemitism in other places and other times. Older Jews are aware of the institutionalized antisemitism in the United States of just a generation ago, as are many younger Jews who have not experienced the same barriers. An organizational network has been developed to combat antisemitism, and both the Jewish press and the general press report about it. New forms of antisemitism may develop, particularly in the guise of anti-Israel rhetoric and action. This book documents how Jews currently perceive these issues, and examines the collective efforts of Jews—through institutions, organizations, and political action—to combat antisemitism, against the backdrop of what we know about antisemitism in the United States today.

Some fundamental assumptions underlie the discussion in this book. First, Jews in the United States are rela-

1

tively free of the worst of the expressions of antisemitism that have affected Jews in other countries and in other times. Jews enjoy tremendous access to the social, economic, and political systems of America. Being Jewish, for example, does not keep Jews from elected office. The last decades of the 20th century have become a golden political and economic age for Jews in the United States.

Second, antisemitism still persists in the United States. While overt discrimination has decreased dramatically in the past 40 years, antisemitic beliefs and attitudes remain quite strong and are expressed in a variety of ways. Although public-opinion polls show the decline of antisemitic beliefs, the proportion of non-Jews who still hold such beliefs is quite substantial. Discrimination has not disappeared completely. Furthermore, some groups are increasingly comfortable with expressing their antisemitic beliefs, while a substantial number of small but loud hate groups express antisemitism and racism in attempts to formulate mass movements. Certainly, not all groups are more antisemitic than they were a generation ago, and attitudes have improved among some groups. But antisemitic beliefs among non-Jews remain widespread, even though those beliefs do not inhibit the everyday lives of most Jews.

Third, Jewish perceptions of antisemitism are generally quite accurate. Most Jews are neither overly concerned nor unduly complacent about antisemitism. While some Jews are very fearful about the current state of antisemitism, and others deny that antisemitism is a problem at all, most can be characterized as wary and watchful.

The fourth assumption that provides a framework for the ensuing discussion is that Jews view antisemitism as both Americans and Jews. They have developed a dual identity and see antisemitism through this blended vision. And finally, the fifth premise is that Jews respond collectively to antisemitism through organizations, institutions, the Jewish press, and, in a more general American capacity, through political activity.

Wariness is a sensible response to antisemitism in the United States today. Antisemitic behavior among non-Jews is far from rampant in the United States, and Jews do not perceive it to be so. Furthermore, the overall perceptions Jews have about non-Jewish attitudes toward Jews, and the attitudes expressed by non-Jews, as measured in survey research, are for the most part not very dissimilar. Most Jews realistically assess how they are perceived by non-Jews.

We examine the inadequacies of the uses of current survey research about antisemitism in the United States. Owing to the interpretations of such inquiry, these studies do not accurately present a complete picture of antisemitism today. One of the best gauges of current levels of antisemitism are Jewish perceptions themselves. Jews do not have to look far to find antisemitism; the phenomenon remains real enough. Jews perpetuate their own folklore about antisemitism, but folklore often reflects the real world, even if it cannot be used to measure certain aspects of it. The collective intuition, assessment, and examination of and by American Jews concerning antisemitism creates a composite picture that demands a hard look at the current methods of assessing antisemitism. What Jews feel and think and sense provides a useful backdrop to assess antisemitism in the United States today.

Dual Threats: Antisemitism and Assimilation

As a group, Jews have achieved great economic, social, and political success in the United States. Jews are disproportionately represented in the Congress and Senate of the United States. They sit on boards of hospitals and universities. Jews are well represented in the most prestigious industries and lucrative occupations, and they are visible in the media and the arts. Jews are doing well. Their prosperity and success are expressed in political power, economic power, and social well-being. To be sure, some Jews are not well off. There are many poor Jews, Jews with low occupational status, and Jews who are affected by the same pathologies as other Americans: alcoholism and drug addiction, among others. But as a whole, Jews have settled comfortably into middle- and upper-class modern America.

Although German-Jewish Americans experienced upward mobility and economic success in the mid-19th century, the widespread success of Jews in the United States is a relatively recent phenomenon, occurring primarily after World War II. Overcoming antisemitic barriers that were widespread from the turn of the century throughout the 1920s and 1930s, and well into the 1950s, allowed for much of this success. Education was also a method frequently used by Jews as a means of gaining access to business and professional opportunities available in American society. Jews' high educational status facilitated their economic mobility.

Judaism itself has become an integral part of the national culture. Although only 6 million Jews live in the United States, Judaism is sometimes considered one of the three major religions in the country, along with Protestantism and Catholicism. In most large cities, for example, Christmas time is also Chanukah time. It is not unusual to see a local television station flashing both "Merry Christmas" and "Happy Chanukah" messages to its viewers. Many large city newspapers will carry a story about Rosh Hashanah and Yom Kippur and the arrival of the High Holy Days for the Jewish people in their community. Jewish characters, as well as caricatures, have been part of American radio, movies, and television for decades. Books about Jews and Jewish characters in books have flooded the reading public. Jews have become part of the national consciousness. But many Jews wonder how much all of this really translates into true acceptance by non-Jews.

The melding of Jews into the American culture, and the adoption of American culture by Jews, has been accomplished thus far without sacrificing a distinct and separate religious identity. Jewish identity is both an individual and group awareness of a combination of religious and ethnic beliefs and behaviors that distinguish Jews from the larger Christian majority. In the past, some Jews believed that they had to abandon their separate Jewish identity in order to be accepted as Americans. In the 1970s and 1980s, and in the years to come, Jews will not have to pretend that they are not Jewish in order to "make it." Indeed, just the opposite is the case. Many Jews identify themselves as such, are proud of their culture and their religion, and make it clear to both the Jewish and the non-Jewish observer who they are and what they are about. "Making it" and being part of American culture have not required that Jews become lost in it. Furthermore, like many ethnic and racial groups, Jews have also helped mold the national culture and social structure. Americans have become more Jewish, as they have become more Italian, more Spanish, and at the same time more Protestant. Both ethnic and religious consciousness have risen dramatically over the past two decades.

Integration without total assimilation is a new phenomenon for Jews. Assimilation is the abandonment of traditional religious beliefs and ritual practice. Integration, on the other hand, is the maintenance of one separate and distinct set of beliefs and behaviors and also the adoption of some beliefs and behaviors of the host culture. But popular culture continuously reinforces American values of choice and individualism within a broader American way. Since the 1960s, composite groups have become more acceptable: black Americans, Asian Americans, and of course, Italian, Greek, or Jewish Americans. If Jews abandon their identity in the United States, it is not because they are forced to do so to be part of American society. In other places and other times, Jews had to adopt the religion of the host culture as the price for acceptance. In America, many will argue, it is different. Jews can be comfortable as Jews.

Yet some Jews do *not* feel completely at ease in contemporary America. At first glance, it would seem unnecessary to question the safety and security of Jews, in light of their current status in the United States. Although signs are positive, many Jews are still suspicious about the underlying heart and soul of their fellow Americans. Even in the current "good times," perhaps there is a sound basis for the emotional, institutional, financial, and political attention that Jews give to issues relating to antisemitism in the United States.

It would seem that Jews have more to fear from the threat of assimilation, becoming so comfortable that they lose themselves as a people. Most barriers to full acceptance into American society have been either completely removed or sharply reduced. Total assimilation, the abandonment of a separate religious, cultural, and ethnic identity, poses a different kind of threat to Jewish survival. Total assimilation implies a sort of extinction. External threats, such as antisemitism, have always endangered the continuity of Jews. The *absence* of antisemitism, the lessening of external threats to provide cohesion, makes Jews in America more dependent upon the strength of internal bonds to tie the group together. No discriminatory laws or edicts now force Jews to live together, for example. The removal of terrible barriers leaves Jews to make choices that are less absolute than total isolation or total rejection of one's family and friends.

Although Jews today are concerned about the danger of assimilation, they also remain concerned about anti-semitism. At a time of enormous social, political, and eco-nomic success, many Jews continue to look over their shoulder. They still wonder, either privately or aloud, about the status of antisemitism in the United States and how it will affect them or their children, or their children's children. As secure as they might feel in the American system, antisemitism sometimes occupies the thoughts of many and preoccupies the thoughts of a few.

The continuum of Jewish perceptions about anti-semitism consists of varied concerns, from fear to war-iness to denial. Some Jews believe that there is a great deal of antisemitism in the United States and that Jews are the frequent objects of discrimination and violence. Others believe that most overt expressions of antisemitism have diminished, while latent antisemitism, particularly in the form of anti-Jewish sentiment, remains to some degree. Some Jews do not believe that any antisemitism exists at all in the United States. Both extremes, the inordinately fearful, as well as those denying the continued existence of antisemitism, consist of small minorities. Each group contains about 10% of all Jews.

Some Jews dismiss antisemitism as a serious threat; others deny that it is a threat at all. But the point is, they are still thinking about it and discussing it. Even the pro-cess of dismissing antisemitism requires some thought and consideration. Jews who do not think about anti-semitism are often thinking about how they are not think-ing about it.

Again, opinions about the current state of anti-semitism vary widely. Some Jews believe antisemitism is increasing, while others believe it is decreasing. Many Jews believe that they are experiencing antisemitism. Since Jews are divided demographically and in terms of religious identity, different subgroups view antisemitism differently. A few Jews are "paranoid" and see antisemitism where it does not exist. Others are ostrichlike, determined not to see antisemitism where it is manifest.

Much of what is written about antisemitism focuses on the antisemitic beliefs and attitudes of non-Jews. A vast literature documents antisemitic incidents, discrimination, and violence. Histories have been written on antisemitism, and volumes produced on the psychology of antisemites, authoritarian personalities, and the roots of antisemitic beliefs and behaviors. The topic of antisemitism cannot be properly addressed without also looking through Jewish eyes, and by exploring Jewish beliefs and attitudes. Any complete study of antisemitism must look through the Jewish looking glass.[1]

Defining and Assessing Antisemitism

Antisemitism can be classified into two basic components: The first, attitudes and beliefs, is the most studied aspect of antisemitism in the United States. The second is expression, actual antisemitic behavior. Most research about antisemitism in this country since the 1930s has focused on non-Jewish attitudes and beliefs toward Jews. Some attempts have also been made to monitor antisemitic incidents and movements. But antisemitism has also been examined in terms of its actual expression in individual and group behavior. Researchers base their findings about increasing or decreasing levels of antisemitism in the United States on the results of studies of antisemitic *attitudes* and *beliefs*. The *expression* of anti-semitism, in terms of *behavior*, has not been examined as rigorously or systematically in the past 25 years.

Ben Halpern, in his article "What is Antisemitism?" defines it as "a hostile attitude toward the Jews (regarded as a threat) that develops into a tradition and becomes institutionalized."[2] Halpern notes that the threat can be expressed collectively, socially, economically, or politically. This threat, he states, can vary in terms of intensity, and be expressed by minor fringe groups or through major political forces. Halpern's definition serves as the operating one in this book. Most Jews share this outlook, and their views reflect this definition throughout the book.

Certainly, antisemitic beliefs and attitudes provide the basis for the expression of antisemitic behavior. Therefore, much attention is given to how non-Jews feel about Jews. Recently, the National Jewish Community Relations Advisory Council, a national umbrella organization for many different types of Jewish organizations concerned with Jewish community relations issues, established criteria for assessing antisemitism. In attempting to define antisemitism, the Council created categories to help assess the state of antisemitism in the United States. These include the expression of antisemitism by public figures, official reaction to antisemitism by public officials, the presence of mass movements from the right or the left, and a new form of antisemitism—anti-Israel sentiments. The establishment of these criteria to assess antisemitism reflects the conceptual struggle many Jews have in attempting to filter and sift through all the potential evidence on the character of contemporary antisemitism.

How does one measure discrimination against Jews? What does the antisemitic statement of a public figure represent? Furthermore, even if measurement devices are found, how should the findings be analyzed? Assuming that prevailing attitudes toward Jews can be used as criteria to assess antisemitism, and measurements of those prevailing attitudes can be constructed, what do findings indicate? If 25% of non-Jews believe that Jews have too much power in the United States, what does that mean? Unfortunately, these questions are difficult to answer because systematic study is so rare, or when it is conducted it is incomplete.

Jewish concerns about antisemitism in the United States often focus upon the issue of latent versus expressed antisemitism. Ultimately, the actual expression of antisemitism is much more important than the antisemitic attitudes themselves. Yet latent antisemitism, subtle or unexpressed antisemitism may or may not be the precursors to more overt and dangerous expressions. Since very few Jews believe that no antisemitism exists at all, and proportionately few Jews see widespread expression of antisemitism, the remainder are most concerned about latent antisemitism, reservoirs of anti-Jewish sentiment. They feel that this hidden antisemitism can be tapped and mobilized by active antisemites, or that such secret antisemitism is in actuality indifference or quiet encouragement, on the part of many Americans, to the actions of active antisemites. Thus, Jewish organizations and institutions continuously sponsor polls that measure the attitudes and beliefs of non-Jews, and attempt to assess levels of latent antisemitism and its potential expression.

Antisemitic manifestations take many forms, from the mild—a facial expression or other subtle communication, to others that are severe or dangerous—such as the desecration of a synagogue or a violent demonstration by the Ku Klux Klan. Jews are sensitive to both the mild and extreme expressions of antisemitism. It is common for Jews to detect certain kinds of prejudice simply because they have a "feeling." These feelings should not be categorically dismissed.

Negative remarks directed toward a Jew can also express antisemitism. Stereotype jokes about Jews may not always be intended as antisemitic but may reveal latent antisemitism. The individual making the remark may have had no intention of conveying an antisemitic sentiment; instead, it is the recipient who was "oversensitive." A non-Jew may be completely unaware that he carries and conveys certain prejudices. For example, the use of *pushy* to describe Jews reflects a conscious or unconscious antisemitic feeling; nevertheless, Jews often pick up such code words, in both direct and indirect conversation. Of course, some Jews, especially those who are the most fearful, may indeed misinterpret a comment as antisemitic when it is not.

Antisemitic remarks increase in significance and impact in accordance with the role of the individual who makes them. An antisemitic slur on the part of a fellow employee may be distressing, but it certainly does not have the impact of an antisemitic remark or speech by a public figure. Political leaders, military leaders, church leaders, and other influential individuals are not beyond harboring antisemitic beliefs and attitudes. Their remarks often receive wide media coverage reaching thousands, millions, or tens of millions of listeners. Remarks by public figures may have substantial impact on the public, helping mold values and establish norms, and may ultimately alter behavior. Furthermore, the response or lack of response by other leaders to either challenge or support these statements also significantly influences the attitudes, beliefs, and actions of their constituencies. Just as important, Jews consider the statements and activities of public figures as possible benchmarks reflecting the feelings of their public constituencies. Even more dangerous, to the Jewish population, is the possibility that the antisemitic remarks of figures in the public eye may accurately represent the views of thousands or millions of followers.

Antisemitism is also expressed through discrimination, which may be manifested by the singular action of an individual employer or realtor, or more systematically, as in the collective action of a group of residents on a private street, or the official policy of a country club. Discrimination may occur in the housing sector, in employment, or in a variety of social and cultural organizations. Jews and non-Jews sometimes differ in defining what constitutes discriminatory behavior. For example, is the refusal of an employer to accommodate Saturday, the Jewish Sabbath, as a day off a discriminatory action, or an efficiency measure on the part of that particular firm? Discrimination is difficult to monitor and difficult to prove. Exactly how much discrimination remains against Jews is unknown. Using Jewish success as evidence of the eradication of discrimination, however, is simply illogical. The same arguments are sometimes made about housing discrimination against blacks: Some blacks live in the suburbs—therefore, there is no housing discrimination. The converse for examining discrimination against Jews is true: Just because most Jews find no barriers does not mean that some others are not experiencing discrimination. Levels of discrimination are probably quite low, but there is simply no systematic study.

Violence, of course, is the most severe and dangerous expression of antisemitism, and it is perpetrated against both property and people. Much of the institutional monitoring of antisemitism focuses upon acts of violence to property, such as the desecration of synagogues or the painting of antisemitic slogans in public places. Although antisemites may desecrate Jewish cemeteries or paint swastikas on a Jewish communal building, antisemitism can also be expressed in violent ways against people. The assassination of radio personality Alan Berg in December of 1984 by right-wing extremists serves as an example of this very rare kind of event.

Acts of violence may also be the result of the efforts of groups seeking a mass following for their racial and religious hatred. Organizations such as the Aryan Nations, the Ku Klux Klan, and The Order promulgate antisemitic and racist rhetoric and literature, and indicate their intention to commit acts of violence against blacks, Jews, and others. Such hate groups, even though they constitute a small part of the population, are representative of the ultimate and most feared expressions of antisemitism and often attract the most attention of Jews and other minority groups.

These organizations are vocal, and sometimes swell in numbers, depending on social and economic conditions. They have many sympathizers who are not members. In addition, a large part of the population, while rejecting the groups themselves, remain indifferent to their antisemitism and racism. These extremist groups are monitored by law enforcement agencies precisely because they are potentially dangerous. If ever given the opportunity or power, such groups would make Jews among their first and most concentrated targets. Jews remain wary of these vicious groups and cast a cautious eye upon their activities. While these groups pose no serious threat today, Jews are concerned about the potential growth and danger of these groups in the future.

Jews most fear the adoption of antisemitic rhetoric or action by the more respectable political middle. Therefore, Jesse Jackson, who reaches and appeals to much larger groups of people than do extremists, is of major concern to Jews when he makes an antisemitic statement. While Jews

vigorously monitor the activities and audiences of hate
groups, they remain most wary of any intrusion of antisemitism into the political realm.

How tuned in are Jews to these various forms and
expressions of antisemitism in the United States? We have
determined that they remain aware of antisemitic attitudes
and expression of those attitudes. This awareness may
translate into deep fear, a certain wariness, or in some
cases denial. But denial cannot be equated with a lack of
awareness. When the relatively small proportion of Jews
say that no antisemitism exists in the United States, most
of them mean that they see no *expressions* of antisemitism.
As we will demonstrate, very few Jews believe that antisemitic attitudes and beliefs have disappeared.

Jewish Views of Antisemitism

Jewish perceptions are molded by events of the past,
what is happening now, and how all the information from
both the past and the present is transmitted to them. To a
great extent, Jews teach one another about antisemitism in
all its forms and expressions. An individual's awareness of
antisemitism has its roots in a collective awareness that
was, and continues to be, passed on through a wide variety of mechanisms.

Although Jews are well integrated into American
culture, they have maintained distinct neighborhood,
friendship, and cultural institutions. They operate freely
in two worlds, mixing with non-Jews where they live,
where they work, where they go to school, and in a wide
array of social, political, and economic contexts. At the
same time, there exists a separate world served by Jewish
institutions and organizations, a separate Jewish media,
close friendship patterns, and some clustering of Jews in

particular neighborhoods. Thus, Jewish awareness of antisemitism stems both from their integrated life within
American culture and from their more separate life as part
of the Jewish subculture.

American Jews are positioned along a continuum of
assimilation and isolation. For example, Orthodox Jews
are much more likely than non-Orthodox Jews to live in
densely Jewish neighborhoods, and Reform Jews are
much more likely to marry a non-Jew than either Conservative or Orthodox Jews. Furthermore, Jews are differentiated by class, political beliefs, and many other factors:
They are by no means unidimensional. As a result there is
no single view or single set of perceptions that Jews hold
about antisemitism. Jewish perceptions are a collection of
views.

But along a continuum of varying views, some common perceptions do appear. As this book shows, nearly all
Jews believe that there is some antisemitism in the United
States, and nearly all Jews say that they have experienced
some form of antisemitism in their lifetime. The extent to
which they have experienced antisemitism and their interpretation of those experiences exemplify a wide variety
of views. But there are some commonly held beliefs.

First, it is almost universally believed that antisemitism cannot be completely eradicated. Jews view it as
a constant, a problem that may ebb and flow but that
never disappears. This basic precept colors all other perceptions of antisemitism. Second, even among the few
who believe that antisemitism has almost disappeared,
most believe that wariness is essential. They hold that if
antisemitism cannot be eradicated, then it must be closely
watched, monitored, and combatted.

Contemporary Jewish experience is influenced partly
by a collective history, both modern and premodern. Indeed, the litany of persecutions that Jews have suffered is

an intricate part of their liturgy and their traditional ritual observances. Formal Jewish education, which touches nearly all Jews in the United States at some point in their lives, focuses on the mistreatment of Jews in a variety of contexts, from Egypt through Spain and into the 20th century. Jews are taught about one antisemitic culture after another, and the ultimate expulsion or discrimination that beset Jews in every society in which they resided.

Most first- and second-generation American Jews carry with them a different set of collective memories. In addition to what they have been taught, either through formal Jewish education, ritual observance, or the adopted folklore of the subculture, these Jews experienced first-hand systematic discrimination in the United States. Housing, for example, was closed to Jews in most areas through legally enforced restrictive covenants. These were not declared unconstitutional until the late 1940s. Universities had quotas on the number of Jews that could be admitted, certain employers would not hire Jews, positions of leadership were often closed to Jews in the cultural and political circles of the local and national scene. While the United States was a hospitable environment, it was by no means a completely open system for Jews. Certainly, the United States offered economic opportunity, even where certain avenues were closed. Jews experienced a social and political freedom that they had rarely known elsewhere. Nevertheless, forms of institutional antisemitism were an integral part of the American scene 40 years ago.

The extent of antisemitism in the United States until the coming of age of the third generation of American Jews should neither be overstated nor minimized. On the one hand, antisemitism in the United States was different from antisemitism in Europe. Discrimination against Jews was never part of official government action in this country. The legitimacy of state-sanctioned or -instigated violence never took root in the United States. Furthermore, Jews found themselves enfranchised in the political system in this country. Here they were able to utilize the electoral process to protect their individual and civil rights.]

[But discrimination in schools, housing, and employment were all quite real. Although the government did not promulgate antisemitic rhetoric and action, the government certainly sanctioned, and in some cases enforced, certain forms of antisemitism until the recent past.] [For example, restrictive covenants were supported through the courts, endorsed by the Federal Housing Administration, and enforced by state governments. Until the late 1940s, the imprimatur of federal and state legitimacy was granted to the segregation of neighborhoods by race and religion. Legal protection of many civil rights is a very recent phenomenon in American history.]

[In addition, in the first half of the 20th century many Jews were foreign-born. They carried with them the experiences of Eastern Europe. Primarily from Poland and Russia, these Jews were the victims of systematic discrimination and state-sanctioned violence. Grandparents have relayed to third and fourth generations of American Jews stories of pogroms—sanctioned violent attacks on Jewish settlements. These stories, too, continue to be a part, although a fading part, of Jewish consciousness in the United States.]

More than any other factor, the Holocaust now frames all Jewish perceptions of antisemitism.[About half the Jews in the United States lived through this time period. For them it remains a conscious memory.] Much has been written about the Holocaust and its effect upon Jews in the United States. The Holocaust represents the ultimate expression of antisemitism, a systematic destruction of Jews throughout Europe. Persecution in Egypt and

Spain cannot possibly affect Jewish perceptions as pro-
foundly as the Holocaust.

The Holocaust took place in the modern civilized
world. It flashes on film before Jewish eyes, and people
can still see it, registering as the most horrible event of the
20th century. Furthermore, the meaning of the Holocaust
is now a major component of almost every child's Jewish
education. Children are taught that an assimilated Jewish
community in Germany and less assimilated Jews elsewhere were systematically massacred by a nation at the
height of its scientific and cultural achievements. They are
also taught that most people of other nations did not rush
to help the Jews. Furthermore, questions are raised repeatedly about why the Jews did not resist more, and why
they denied the impending Holocaust. These are questions that haunt first- and second-generation Jews and
perplex third- and fourth-generation Jews. Obviously, not
all questions are answerable. Such unanswered inquiries
leave contemporary American Jews pondering the central
question that was proposed at the beginning of this chapter. Are Jews safe in the United States? The real question
that Jews are asking, of course, is: in the face of the Holocaust, is the current state of Jewish well-being in America
secure, for how long, and what are the warning signs of
impending doom? And most important of all, how can
antisemitism, or its heralding forces, be controlled?

With the Holocaust as a grim standard, the question
of Jewish safety in any society becomes salient to many
Jews. It may be that the answer is a resounding no; however, perhaps Jews are "safe" in the United States, for
institutional, historical, and other reasons. Maybe another
Holocaust or systematic violence perpetrated against Jews
is an impossibility, or so remote that Jews need not be
concerned about it. Nevertheless, the question itself can-

not be viewed as irrelevant, even though the probability is so low.

Clearly, younger Jews have learned their Holocaust lesson. As the generation of firsthand witnesses passes away, the need for many Jews to carefully document and study all aspects of the Holocaust has increased in importance. Formal records can be used to remember and judge the signs of impending danger. Jews have been taught to be wary. The impossible, they discovered, was possible. A tripartite lesson was learned: It is necessary to watch for signs of rising antisemitism; most non-Jews did not stand up to contest what was happening to Jews, leading many Jews to the conclusion that Jews could trust and rely only upon their fellow Jews in times of trouble; and finally, Jews learned that the only way to deal with antisemitism is to face it directly and fight it where necessary. In essence, young Jews in the United States, the baby-boomers and the post-baby-boomers, have been trained to look for and combat antisemitism. First- and second-generation Jews knew extensive antisemitism from firsthand experience. Some tried to pretend antisemitism did not exist, some believed it was their lot to bear it, while others worked in civil rights coalitions to deal with prejudice and discrimination in general.

Many younger Jews, feeling far more comfortable with their dual role as part of the American culture as well as the Jewish one, are more sensitive to, and more outspoken about, antisemitism in any form than were their elders. They have not been taught to bear it. They have been taught as Americans that prejudice and violence are wrong. At the same time, the Jewish subculture has been pounding into them the message of the Holocaust. For Jews under the age of 40, their antennae are up. They are on the lookout for antisemitism both as Americans and as

Jews. Most younger Jews believe what they have been taught. They have no tolerance for intolerance. And since they now operate from a position of greater economic, social, and political status, they feel more at ease in asserting their rights as a minority religious group.

Furthermore, antisemitism is not something that most American Jews of any age are willing to "bear." Even though most Jews do not believe that antisemitism can be eradicated, they do not believe that it should be left alone. The American Jewish community as a whole does not believe that it has to hide its Jewishness or abandon it in order to escape antisemitism. If Jews cannot put an end to antisemitic beliefs, they can still fight to contain its expression. Furthermore, as an expression of faith in both education and the efficacy of social norms concerning racial and religious equality in America, attempts can be made to reduce antisemitic beliefs among non-Jews.

It is much more difficult today for Jews to be unaware of antisemitism in the United States, either in terms of attitudes or behavior. Because Jews have become so successful and integrated into general American society, they have a large number of non-Jewish contacts in their jobs, their neighborhoods, their social circles, and even their families. Increasing numbers of Jews are marrying non-Jews. Paradoxically, because of their free movement in the non-Jewish world, Jews are more likely to come into contact with antisemitic behavior and attitudes where they do exist. As will be seen later, since younger Jews are more likely to have more non-Jewish contacts, they are more likely to say that they are experiencing antisemitism.

Furthermore, an intricate institutional network has been developed to help Jews maintain awareness of antisemitism where it exists. These institutions also lead the way in fighting antisemitism. The Anti-Defamation League, the American Jewish Committee, and many other organizations consider the investigation and combatting of antisemitism to be part of their institutional objectives. This network, much more efficient and powerful than the individual alone, exists to provide concerned Jews with extensive information about antisemitism. In short, the battle against antisemitism has been formalized in such a way that these institutions are constantly gathering and disseminating information about antisemitism in the United States and around the world. Many of those involved in some way with the Jewish community receive information about the current state of antisemitism from a variety of these organizations.

The institutional network addresses issues such as whether or not antisemitism is increasing or decreasing, if the nature of antisemitism is changing, and similar questions. In assessing potential danger, Jews are very concerned with whether or not antisemitic beliefs are increasing or decreasing, in terms of either their intensity or the proportion of Americans who hold them. "Are things better or not?" is a question that community relations professionals ask constantly, in order to determine whether or not Jews are really secure. The current social and economic picture provides the contextual framework for determining the state of antisemitism.

This constant examination of non-Jewish attitudes and beliefs has multiple purposes. The data gathered can make Jews feel either better or worse. But more important, the findings are designed to help determine a plan of action for institutions and organizations. Jews in the United States not only ask how much antisemitism exists and whether things are better or worse than previously, but numbers of Jews also design strategies, create coalitions, and support institutions to implement them in their fight against antisemitism. Even if Jews do not know much about the agencies themselves, they are aware that there is a need to support the ongoing activities and research of these institutions.

Through their public relations offices, lobbying efforts, and access to the press, these institutions are adept at disseminating information about antisemitism to the mass media throughout the United States. The issue of antisemitism is constantly before the public eye because of their diligence in gathering information on antisemitism and monitoring antisemitic events. Major stories about antisemitism are likely to be covered in the general press. Often it is the Jewish institutional network that prepares and disseminates these stories.

Jewish newspapers and magazines are the most likely to run a story about antisemitism. Collectively, these are called the "Jewish" press, Jewish-sponsored English newspapers. In most cities, Jewish newspapers and magazines reach a majority of Jewish households. Editorials, news stories, and features on antisemitism are a familiar and integral part of the Jewish press in the United States. Stories about antisemitism are also included, although much less frequently, in general newspapers. Additionally, Jews read selectively. They are attracted to stories about Jews that appear in general papers, just as other groups are more likely to find stories concerning themselves of particular interest. If a story regarding antisemitism appears in a general paper, it is likely to draw the attention of the Jewish readership. The Jewish reader is the recipient of a constant flow of information about antisemitism in the United States, through both the general and the Jewish press. The institutional network provides the information, the Jewish press and sometimes the general press report it, and the Jewish reader consumes it. Whether affiliated or involved with the Jewish community or not, Jews receive information about the continued presence of antisemitism.

Aside from the mass media and the Jewish press, Jews also have their own organizational networks, neighborhood networks, and friendship groups. Antisemitic acts such as desecration of a cemetery, overhearing an antisemitic remark, or the antisemitic behavior of a fraternity at a university travels through an informal network. Word of mouth, friends telling friends, and stories transmitted by Jewish leadership all spread the news. Several rabbis might give a sermon about a particular antisemitic act and perhaps tell some of their colleagues about it, who in turn might also give a sermon. Bad news still travels fast, and antisemitism is very bad news. Many antisemitic remarks or events reach Jewish eyes and ears. And yet, as will be shown, most Jewish experiences with antisemitism go unreported. Therefore, the information that institutions disseminate about current levels of Jewish experience with antisemitism may actually underrepresent antisemitic incidents in the United States.

While the coverage of news about antisemitism is quite extensive, it is dwarfed both in the general media and in the Jewish media by news coverage of Israel. The establishment of Israel created another dimension of American Jewish consciousness. The State of Israel now occupies a central place in defining Jewish identity in the United States. A vast fund-raising network exists to support Israel, a political organization has been created to lobby the United States government on behalf of Israel, a third of American Jewish households have visited Israel, and almost as many intend to go. Most American Jews care deeply about Israel. Many carry with them a dual identity, which consists of a strong allegiance both to the United States and to a nation of Jews thousands of miles away.

Israel is constantly in the news. The Middle East, in

general, and Israel, in particular, receive an enormous amount of attention from the printed and electronic media in the United States. Events that take place in Israel are sometimes reported almost as if they were happening in Nebraska or California. The Israeli policy toward the Palestinians, its control of disputed territory captured in the 1967 war, its military efforts in the region, and other facets of Israeli life and geopolitical behavior are under constant scrutiny by the general and the Jewish press. It is news, and important news, in this country.

But the news is not always good, and in many Jewish eyes it is not always "fair." Some believe that the anti-Israel sentiment expressed by some observers is thinly veiled antisemitism. One of the issues that American Jews must now grapple with is the relationship of antisemitism to anti-Israelism. For American Jews, who are so closely connected in many ways to Israel, it is difficult to distinguish someone who is a nonsupporter of Israel, or a critic of Israel, from an antisemite. Yet American Jews attempt to filter genuine criticism of certain Israeli government policies from "anti-Zionist" diatribes that use Israel as a substitute for Jew while borrowing traditional antisemitic beliefs and attitudes.

Since Jewish perceptions of antisemitism turn out to be quite accurate, their concern with anti-Israel/anti-Zionist diatribes is well founded. As will be shown, most anti-Israelism is connected in both rhetoric and deed to antisemitism. Certainly, even among Jews there is serious disagreement about many issues in Israel. And Jews expect the same kind of scrutiny from non-Jews. But the interchangeable use of *Zionist* and *Jewish* in anti-Israel propaganda is not lost upon either its Jewish or non-Jewish recipient. Jews, especially, are tuned in to the subtle and often not-so-subtle question of anti-Israelism and antisemitism.

Furthermore, anti-Israel rhetoric is often tied to overt expressions of antisemitism in word and action in countries around the world, such as the Soviet Union or Libya. News about worldwide antisemitism, often linked to anti-Israelism, is constantly reported through the Jewish press. Whether the antisemitism appears in Argentina, France, or the Soviet Union, or comes in the form of terrorist executions or cemetery desecrations, or is expressed in the language of anti-Zionism, Jews often hear about it and digest it. Feelings about antisemitism in the United States are reinforced by perceptions that antisemitism is alive and well in the rest of the world. The transference is an easy one. Antisemitism is an ancient and persistent problem. If it keeps appearing all over the world, it is certainly logical to assume that it may appear more strongly once again in the United States.

American Jews explore these attitudes, along with other signs of antisemitism. The collective perceptions of a group may tell much about the external environment and the ways that they are viewed or treated. Jewish perceptions cannot be used to measure antisemitism, but they can be used as an indicator, to mirror and reflect it. Jews keep a watchful eye, and that collective vision keeps them justifiably wary.

Chapter Two

THE "REALITY" OF ANTISEMITISM IN THE UNITED STATES

The Reality of Antisemitism

Antisemitism remains part of contemporary American culture. It continues to be expressed in a variety of ways. However, institutional discrimination against Jews in the form of housing restrictions, employment, and education has been sharply reduced since World War II.

Furthermore, Jews are currently enjoying enormous political success. Non-Jews are electing Jews to the Congress, the Senate, and other high political offices in numbers unprecedented and disproportionate to the size of the Jewish population. The United States government is extremely responsive to Jewish concerns about Israel, Soviet Jews, and the protection of Jews against religiously inspired violence. Jews in the United States continue to enjoy and avail themselves of enormous benefits from the declining expression or practice of discriminatory behaviors among non-Jews.

Nevertheless, the following premises are supported by the evidence examined in this chapter. First, some antisemitic beliefs among non-Jews have declined over time, while others are constant, and a few are increasing. Most important, large proportions of non-Jews still hold a number of antisemitic beliefs. Second, expressions of antisemitic belief still occur in organized form, voiced by a variety of extremist groups. These groups are small in size but potentially dangerous to Jews and other minorities. Antisemitic beliefs are also occasionally voiced by more "mainstream" public figures and therefore may have broader appeal and effect. Third, current assessments of levels of antisemitism, both attitudinal and behavioral, are woefully inadequate. Therefore, knowledge of antisemitism is based on incomplete measurements and tests. Levels of antisemitic belief and behavior are underestimated. Fourth, much anti-Israelism is thinly veiled antisemitism. Of course, some anti-Israel sentiment has no connection to antisemitism. Much of the evidence on this point is impressionistic.

The continued existence of antisemitism in American culture and society is a critical component of understanding Jewish perceptions. Antisemitism is not a new phenomenon, nor can it be dismissed as a minor factor in the Jewish experience in the United States. Jewish social and economic success occurred in spite of discrimination in employment and housing, not because antisemitism was absent. The American system was open enough for Jews to make progress within it. But trumpeting Jewish success in any realm cannot be used as evidence to demonstrate the disappearance of antisemitism, or its lack of significance. Certainly the tradition of antisemitism, as defined by Ben Halpern, remains.

Increasing numbers of Jews are succeeding where discriminatory barriers have been removed, and individuals have overcome discriminatory resistance where it still persists. Remnants of more widespread discrimination may still be found today. Of course, it is impossible to know to what extent this is the case, because no systematic examinations of discrimination against Jews are now regularly conducted. Lack of documentation cannot be equated with a lack of discrimination. Indeed, as shown by the data from surveys of Jews, isolated incidents of housing and employment discrimination are reported by small numbers of respondents but are never formally reported to any Jewish organization or government office. It can be concluded that discriminatory behavior has not completely disappeared.

Expressions of antisemitism, or even discrimination should come as no surprise. In 1969 Gertrude Selznick and Stephen Steinberg wrote, "Anti-semitism is widespread and pervasive, but not in dangerous form."[1] They went on to say that there is "a sizeable reservoir of anti-Semitic beliefs and stereotypes in the population. Over a third of Americans are anti-Semitic. . . . Even the nominally unprejudiced—that third of the population free or virtually free of traditional stereotypes—cannot be said to constitute a solid nucleus of opposition to anti-Semitism."[2]

No body of evidence has been produced since that study to indicate any substantial change from their basic summary. Those who do not hold antisemitic beliefs themselves are indifferent to those who do. While certain antisemitic stereotypes are disappearing, other stereotypes remain, and still others have emerged. The picture has not been one of unquestionable progress over the past two decades.

The continued persistence of antisemitism is part of a more pervasive strain of prejudice against minorities in the United States. Prejudice against Catholics, blacks, and Asians has been both widespread and violent in the history of this country. Political parties were organized around anti-Catholicism in the 19th century. The horrible history of American racism is well documented. Wartime hysteria in the 1940s stripped Japanese Americans of their constitutional rights. They were robbed of their property and forced to live in "internment camps" for the duration of the war.

Indeed, compared with the way other minorities in the United States were treated, Jews have escaped relatively unscathed. Expression of anti-Jewish beliefs and behavior never reached the point of race riots or internment, as prejudice against blacks or Asians has. But America, a society that has welcomed Jews more than any other, has also demonstrated a darker side. The ideal of extending civil rights to all minority groups has always been coupled with a deep strain of racial and religious hostility and discrimination. Antisemitism, to varying degrees, has been part of this history. Jewish perceptions of antisemitism have always been influenced by this reality.

Despite the many conceptual and methodological problems that are discussed in this chapter, an overall picture of current levels of antisemitic beliefs and stereotypes held by non-Jews can be composed. Evidence of the persistence and consistency of certain antisemitic beliefs and attitudes indicates that the vast majority of Jews are neither paranoid nor oversensitive in their assessment of non-Jewish sentiments. In most areas, anti-Jewish feelings demonstrate that the collective Jewish sense is close to the mark.

Measuring Antisemitism

Current levels of antisemitism can be assessed by analzying public opinion data, available audits of antisemitic incidents, and the rhetoric and behavior of extremist groups. Measuring discriminatory practices against Jews is very difficult, since no systematic study of this phenomenon has been undertaken in the United States. The role of anti-Israelism as a form of antisemitism is also a topic that has not been systematically studied.

Telephone polls are the tool used most frequently to judge the state of antisemitism: how widespread it is, whether or not it is increasing or decreasing, and which groups are most likely to be antisemitic. Gallup, Yankelovich, Harris, Roper, and other polling organizations and market research firms periodically conduct polls that focus exclusively upon attitudes either about Jews or about various racial and ethnic groups including Jews. On rare occasions, the polls are quite extensive and are conducted as major social science research projects in conjunction with teams of scholars at various universities. But most often, the polls consist of a few questions, with little detailed analysis. Most of the polls are commissioned by the American Jewish Committee or the Anti-Defamation League, but individual Jewish newspapers and the Simon Wiesenthal Center have also commissioned polls.

Audits of antisemitic incidents produced by the Anti-Defamation League are the second source of information about antisemitism. These audits, which began in 1979, include aggregated counts from individual states of incidents of vandalism against Jews and Jewish institutions. They also include counts of assaults, harassment and threats against Jews. Since their initial publication in 1979, these yearly audits have received extensive coverage in both the general and the Jewish press. They are often viewed by the public as the definitive measuring device for antisemitic actions in the United States.

These two sources are supplemented by individual social scientists', community relations professionals', and Jewish community leaders' impressionistic accounts of other events and trends. Statements of public figures, the strength and activities of extremist groups, political developments and activities, as well as trends occurring across the country, combine to formulate a frame that lies under and upholds the results of these polls and audits. Both anti-Israel behavior and support for Israel are also included as items that help determine assessments of antisemitism.

The tools used to assess antisemitism are limited by methodological and theoretical constraints, and the measurement devices that are currently used are exceptionally limited. At best, they leave many questions unresolved. At worst, they provide an incomplete picture of the character of antisemitism in the United States. Clearly, the current methods used to assess antisemitism raise far more questions than they adequately answer.

Polling Data

Survey research, in the form of personal interviews and telephone polls, can be extremely useful tools in measuring attitudes and beliefs. Pollsters can accurately predict election results or consumer behavior. The techniques of survey research have become quite sophisticated. Certainly, the results of polls are a better barometer than people's hunches or best guesses.

Survey research techniques are used extensively to analyze behaviors and attitudes, both for Jews and non-Jews alike. Using survey research to study antisemitism is a vital part of our analytic approach. Often, however, the polling data are misinterpreted, or the wrong questions are asked. Poor methodological use of polls may result in distorted pictures.

Polling techniques about antisemitism, and other forms of prejudice, require the most sophisticated and careful scrutiny. While polls are very useful, they must be interpreted with a critical eye. For example, year after year a substantial proportion of non-Jews, about one-third, say that Jews are more loyal to Israel than to the United States. But what does this mean? Is it a statement that Jews are capable of treason? Or is it a statement that Jews have a strong (and desirable) attachment to their "homeland"? Without further probing, the data are subject to many interpretations. The results of the polling data are often consistent, but the use of these data is limited by exactly what is meant by the findings. Just as importantly, how do we interpret the data about those who say "no" or "don't know" to the question of Jewish loyalty to the United States and Israel? Much may be hidden in those responses.

Unfortunately, much of the polling data about antisemitism are subject to severe limitations. As with all survey research, we must be concerned about whether questions are being asked which measure what is intended. Are the questions answered honestly, or do the respondents provide acceptable, normative responses? And are the results interpreted correctly and consistently?

The current survey data about antisemitic attitudes and beliefs among non-Jews are suspect on all three accounts. First, attitudes cannot always be equated with behavior. The measurement of antisemitism in polls consistently probes how non-Jews think or feel about Jews. They rarely ask questions about how non-Jews behave toward Jews. Occasionally, questions are asked about intended behavior, such as hypothetically voting for a Jewish candidate for president. But interactions in social groups, employment, and neighborhoods are not studied extensively. Therefore, the survey data form a picture of how non-Jews say they feel, not what they do.

Second, questions are asked over the telephone, with little probing or follow-up. The subtleties of the complex phenomenon of prejudice are likely to be lost. A few questions about attitudes toward Israel, whether or not someone would marry a Jew, and other questions result in a picture composed of broad, general strokes. A rigorous study and analysis of antisemitism requires survey techniques that pay more attention to subtle shades and lighting. Personal interviews would help, as would more open-ended questioning. Interviewers should be able to probe more carefully in certain areas. Telephone interviews, especially those that are brief, with closed-ended questions, simply do not allow enough latitude for careful inquiry.

Telephone interviews about antisemitism may be subject to normative responses. Statements of antisemitic beliefs may be less forthcoming because many people know that they are *supposed* to say that they would vote for any candidate, for example, regardless of race or religion. Positive statements may be hidden under a layer of what the respondent believes he or she *ought* to believe, and not translate into reported beliefs. These problems might be addressed more effectively in personal interviews.

Third, the data collected in polls about antisemitism are subject to widely different interpretations. There is more than one way to construct the statistical standard through which polling data may be understood. How the data are aggregated makes a big difference. For example, if the non-Jewish population is being classified as "prejudiced" or "nonprejudiced," how many antisemitic beliefs must be held in order to place an individual in either category? Such decisions have a dramatic impact on the overall findings, and the way the research is presented to other scholars and the public. Are all statements of prejudice equal in strength? Belief in one stereotype may be more strongly linked to antisemitic behavior than another. Interpretive decisions largely determine how the polling data are presented to the reader.

Because of these limitations we have reason to question what the polls tell us about antisemitism. Still, there is a need to look at these data, since they represent a critical component in the information that currently exists about antisemitism. Such a review enables us to gain some understanding of certain trends in antisemitic beliefs and attitudes, and points us in a new direction for further research. Despite all the methodological problems, a composite picture can be formulated. Some clues are consistent, and present a general profile of how non-Jews currently feel about Jews.

Polling data about antisemitism in the United States have been compiled into comprehensive essays on two occasions. First, an essay by Charles Herbert Stember in *Jews in the Mind of America* constitutes a thorough examination of the existing data on non-Jewish beliefs about Jews.[3] Published in 1966, Stember's article summarized polls from Roper, Gallup, National Opinion Research Center, and others. His article traced changing attitudes toward Jews and the declining negative perceptions of Jews by non-Jews from the peak negativism of the Second World War. Stember provided data revealing that most antisemitic beliefs, as measured by these polls, dropped significantly over a generation. His essay provides the single best quantitative compendium of available data on antisemitism before 1962. While this critical essay offered an excellent background by which to compare data collected in later studies, it did not create new methodological avenues to explore these issues, nor did it provide new frameworks to analyze antisemitism.

The data indicated that non-Jews were much less likely in the 1950s than in the 1930s to say that Jews have objectionable traits, are unscrupulous, or that Jewish neighbors are objectionable. Substantially fewer non-Jews also said that colleges should limit the admission of Jews. Attitudes about Jews having too much power declined less precipitously between 1938 and 1962. In all, 10% of the non-Jewish population still believed 5 of 12 widely held antisemitic beliefs of the 1930s. The data indicated that the old stereotypes as measures of antisemitic beliefs were declining.

But Stember does not provide an analytical framework to understand these polling data. Were non-Jews more or less antisemitic? Stember erred in his assessment of the decline or disappearance of antisemitism because he analyzed instruments that were appropriate in one period of United States history but woefully inadequate for another. Old stereotype images had passed away, but new ones had emerged. By focusing only on the old stereotypes, he made it seem apparent that antisemitic attitudes had declined. But if antisemitic beliefs took the guise of new stereotypes, these trends would not be discovered unless different questions were devised and probed more extensively. These interpretations could not be made because of the limitations of the data.

A second, less comprehensive essay was completed by Geraldine Rosenfield and published in 1982.[4] This essay looked at a more limited set of variables and attitudes, using some comparative data from 1964 and public opinion polls in the 1970s. Primarily concerned with attitudes toward Israel, the essay offers little interpretive comment but serves rather as a reference tool for some limited questions about non-Jewish attitudes.

Nevertheless, Rosenfield concluded that the data from 1960 to 1981 indicated that "such evidence as the polls provide from the 1960s to the present seems clearly to point to a sharp decline in prejudice against Jews and a marked increase in their social acceptance as individuals and as a group. Although Jews are less than three percent of the American population and are concentrated in major metropolitan areas, their religion is acknowledged as one of the three principal faiths in the United States. . . ."[5]

Rosenfield did go on to note that some negative stereotypes persist. She acknowledged, for example, that a "small but varying proportion see Jews as being more loyal to Israel than to the U.S., as unscrupulous, aggressive, or too powerful."[6] What is a small proportion? In 1964, 30%, or nearly one out of every three Americans, believed that Jews were more loyal to Israel than to America. In 1981 the same proportion, 30%, still held this belief. Just as important, only 32% said that the statement was probably false, while almost two of every five were not sure (see Table 2-1). Even examining only those who stated that this belief was probably true, 30%, translates into tens of millions of individuals. Furthermore, Geraldine Rosenfield, in an analysis published by the American Jewish Committee in 1982, discussed the results of the July, 1981, Y.S. & W. poll. The data, she wrote, indicated that non-Jews see Jews, to a higher degree than other groups (black Americans, Italian Americans) as having "too much power."[7] One of the oldest and most powerful anti-Jewish canards continues to be held by millions of Americans.

In-depth analyses of non-Jewish beliefs about Jews have been most systematically analyzed in two major national studies. Rather than compilations of a variety of polls such as the Stember and Rosenfield analyses, the two major national studies used wide-ranging survey instruments and drew national samples of non-Jewish households for in-depth interviews.

The first of these works was commissioned by the Anti-Defamation League in 1964. A University of California, Berkeley, research team of Gertrude J. Selznick, Stephen Steinberg, Charles Y. Glock, and others undertook the construction of measures of antisemitic beliefs of non-Jews. A number of publications resulted, most notably *The Tenacity of Prejudice*[8] by Selznick and Steinberg, and *Anti-Semitism in America*[9] by Harold Quinley and Charles Glock.

The core of the Berkeley studies was the development

of a scale of antisemitic beliefs of non-Jews. This scale consists of 11 variables that were used to measure attitudes and beliefs and is reprinted in Table 2-2. The following antisemitic beliefs, grouped by negative stereotypes about Jews, constitute the antisemitic index: that Jews are power-hungry, unscrupulous in money matters, irritating in manner, aggressive, clannish, and disloyal to the United States. In short, the following guidelines were used, with respondents classified according to the number of antisemitic beliefs they held: *prejudiced*—accept five or more antisemitic beliefs; *neutral*—accept four or fewer antisemitic beliefs and give "not sure/no answer" responses to four or more items; *unprejudiced*—accept four or fewer antisemitic beliefs and give "not sure/no answer" responses to fewer than four items.[10]

A better understanding of the opinion poll data can be attained by looking at the sentiments they reveal. How many antisemitic beliefs does an individual have to hold in order to be classified as "high" or "low" on this antisemitism scale? And in the adherence to certain antisemitic beliefs, are certain sentiments more likely to lead to antisemitic behavior than others? Are antisemitic feelings to be assessed by the nature of the sentiment, or by the quantity of antisemitic feelings held? These questions are left unanswered. The intensity of certain beliefs may cause us to recalculate the proportion of the population today classified as highly or mildly antisemitic, as compared with a similar population body of 1964. Further experimentation is necessary to explain the increase of some antisemitic beliefs. Certainly, the assertion, based largely on this scale, that antisemitism in the United States has decreased, must be rigorously challenged.

Using this scale without assessing it periodically brings up a more profound, troubling aspect of the polling data. Selznick and Steinberg pointed out this dimension in 1969:

It is not at all certain that data from other countries or from another period in history would yield the same result. During the Hitler era many Germans may have accepted the belief in excessive Jewish power without also accepting beliefs in Jewish dishonesty and clannishness. Indeed, this probably occurred in the United States during the same period. As mentioned earlier, polls during the 1940s found that almost 60 percent of Americans believed that Jews had too much power in the United States. While no evidence is available, it is possible that many held this belief without holding other, less extreme beliefs. This is not an unimportant observation. If people who would ordinarily score low on antisemitism can suddenly take on extreme beliefs when they become current, it is not surprising that antisemitism has often flared up after periods of decline.[11]

Acceptance of extreme beliefs at different times must cause us to define what constitutes "neutral" or "mild" antisemitic beliefs. Are people "mildly" antisemitic if they do not accept extreme negative beliefs most of the time? Or are they "mildly" antisemitic if they only hold one extreme belief most of the time? The increase in antisemitic beliefs about Jewish power during times of Israeli conflict may be interpreted as an aberration during times of stress or as a true barometer when the normative barriers are less severe. Little is known about this phenomenon, and it requires much more extensive study.

We cannot interpret the fact that some items on a scale have declined to mean that antisemitism is on the wane, especially if the questions themselves need revision and the context for more forthright answers is colored by expected responses. If anything, the level of antisemitic beliefs may seriously underrepresent the "true" feelings of a more sophisticated population that knows it is wrong to say that Jews are "too pushy."

The major findings of the Berkeley studies were as follows:

1. Some traditional antisemitic beliefs had diminished significantly since the 1930s and 1940s, particularly those related to Jewish stereotypes.
2. Antisemitic beliefs were strongly linked to age. They were also influenced by education. The higher the education level, the less likely non-Jews were to hold antisemitic beliefs.
3. Despite both the effects of education and a younger generation, some antisemitic beliefs continued to persist in a significant minority of the population.

A wide range of other attitudes and perceptions were linked to political, religious, and other beliefs and behaviors.

The Berkeley research provides both the theoretical and quantitative base by which later studies have been constructed and compared. Scholars and community relations professionals asserting that antisemitism is increasing or decreasing often utilize these findings. Not until 17 year later, when the American Jewish Committee commissioned Yankelovich, Skelly & White, Inc., to conduct a follow-up study in 1981, were additional data gathered to create another comprehensive picture of the antisemitic attitudes held by non-Jews. Using the baseline questions from the Berkeley research, the 1981 study repeated many of the initial questions and added new questions about Israel and other issues. A sample of Jewish households was also drawn to compare the responses of Jews and non-Jews. The research was published in 1982 as a monograph by Gregory Martire and Ruth Clark.[12] Using the 1964 data as a base, this study reported sharply decreasing levels of antisemitic beliefs among non-Jews. Although the study authors noted that antisemitism remained a problem in the

United States, their emphasis was clearly on the decreasing levels of antisemitic beliefs and the dissonance between non-Jewish and Jewish beliefs about antisemitism. But the conclusions reached in this study in both areas are faulty. The data appear reliable. The use of the data is subject to rigorous challenge.

Martire and Clark's primary thesis in their interpretation of the 1981 Yankelovich data is that "while there are worrisome signs, there are also solid reasons to believe that antisemitism may be on the wane in the United States."[13] They state, "antisemitism has declined significantly in the United States since the mid-1960s." [14] The decrease, they argue, is generational, resulting from the passing of an older, more antisemitic generation and the introduction of a more tolerant, less antisemitic generation—the baby-boomers. Martire and Clark are even more hopeful for the future. "The baby boom generation can be expected to raise a generation of children and young adults who are, like themselves, more tolerant of Jews and other minorities than were previous generations," they assert.[15] Martire and Clark acknowledge throughout their analysis, however, that antisemitism continues to be a serious problem in the United States.

The authors base their conclusions solely on their analysis of non-Jewish beliefs about Jews. Behavioral questions are scarce. Questions first used by the Berkeley team in 1964 were asked again of a new sample, and several new questions were added. The data were used to measure the growth or decline of certain beliefs in the two-decade period. The primary tool for assessing such changes is the 11-item index developed for the 1964 Berkeley study and used again to classify the antisemitic beliefs held by the 1982 respondents. Comparing the data in this fashion shows a decline in those classified as "highly antisemitic" from 37% in 1964 to 23% in 1981. But the Martire and Clark analysis repeats the same errors that Stember made in 1966.

The 1981 study conclusions are faulty for a number of reasons. Identical questions should be asked for comparability purposes, but new items must be added. The Yankelovich study did not go far enough. The study should have probed changing normative responses to prejudice and the linkage between behaviors and beliefs. It should have also created new measures of stereotyping, as well as devising more in-depth indicators of potential antisemitic behavior. In the absence of such innovation, what the 1981 study shows, for the most part, is that some 1964 stereotypes have declined. It tells little about anti-semitic beliefs that may have emerged.

Yet even with these problems, the data show the continued adherence to old stereotypes. Table 2-3 shows that some antisemitic beliefs, as measured by Martire and Clark, have declined since 1964. Indeed, 8 of the 11 items on the scale decreased, as have most other items. Some concepts, such as the belief that "the movie and television industries are pretty much controlled by Jews," declined by 24%; the proportion of non-Jews adhering to the belief that "Jews have a lot of irritating faults" decreased by 19% from 1964 to 1981. However, four items on the scale, those with perhaps the most antisemitic intensity, *increased:* "Jews are always stirring up trouble with their ideas" by 1%, "Jews have too much power in the business world" by 4%, "Jews are more loyal to Israel than to America" by 9%, and "Jews have too much power in the United States" by 10%. Some of these increases are well within the confines of the sampling error, so little can be made of them. Nevertheless, no precipitous or even significant decline was noted on these items.

The data show persistent levels of high antisemitic beliefs, whether measured by the portion of the population holding at least one antisemitic belief or by the proportion of the population holding some highly antisemitic beliefs over two generations or more. For example, the belief that Jews have too much power in the business world was held by 19% of the non-Jews in 1940, 33% in 1964, and 37% in 1981. While some stereotypes about Jews have diminished, some remain consistently strong. Statements such as "Jews have too much power in the business world" are inherently negative. Jews may have a great deal of power in the business world. But the questions are designed with negative implications, and not to elicit simple factual evaluations.

Antisemitic beliefs remain widespread among non-Jews as a whole and are clearly rising among certain subgroups, most notably blacks. Table 2-4 shows that most antisemitic beliefs of the black sample increased from 1964 to 1981, including some of the more highly antisemitic beliefs. Blacks are more likely than whites, for example, to believe that Jews are more loyal to Israel than to the United States. Just as important, Martire and Clark report:

> While generational change and increased education have led to lower levels of antisemitism among whites, among blacks, age and antisemitism are not highly related ($r = .07$), and the effects of education are significantly less powerful among blacks than among whites ($r = .14$ among blacks versus .25 among whites). As a result of the weak correlations among blacks between age and antisemitism and education and antisemitism, increased education and generational change have not led to lower levels of antisemitism.[16]

Among blacks, then, age and education play less of a mitigating role than with other groups. Several surveys conducted in the 1980s corroborate the findings about blacks.[17]

It would appear that generational change and increased educational attainment are no longer reliable factors for predicting a continuous decline in antisemitism. The persistence of antisemitism among younger people can be seen in Table 2-5. While younger people are less likely than older people to hold antisemitic beliefs, a significant proportion of those under 30 years of age still hold antisemitic beliefs. Indeed, in 1981 those under 30 years old were more than twice as likely to believe that Jews have too much power in the United States than they did in 1964, 16% in 1981 compared to 7% in 1964. The proportions of younger non-Jews who expressed the opinion that Jews are more loyal to Israel than to the United States also increased significantly, by 21%, rising from 30% in 1964 to over half of all 18- to 29-year-old respondents in 1981, 51%, voicing this belief. Martire and Clark note this trend but dismiss it, stating that as today's young people grow older and displace today's older adults, the process of generational change can be expected to continue.[18] This same hypothesis was put forward in 1964 and was not substantiated by the 1981 study. Similarly, those with higher educational attainment were also more likely to hold antisemitic beliefs in 1981 than in 1964. Again, the proportions expressing beliefs regarding Jewish power and loyalty increased.[19]

The effects of age and education are not as strong as they would appear at first glance. This is certainly not the case among Blacks, for example, where younger, better-educated Blacks are no less antisemitic than their elders, despite their educational attainment. Furthermore, if the antisemitic statements about power and loyalty are a better indicator of either the growth or decline of antisemitism, it may be that antisemitic beliefs have actually increased since 1964. In the absence of better and more detailed questions, and a clearer understanding of the changing normative milieu and the way it has affected these questions, we know only that a strong reservoir of antisemitic beliefs remains.

Widespread adherence to antisemitic beliefs among non-Jews is well documented in the 1981 study. Nearly one out of every two non-Jews still believe that the movie and television industry is pretty much controlled by Jews, 43% still believe that international banking is also controlled by the Jews, 22% still believe that Jews don't care what happens to anyone but their own kind, and 33% believe that Jews are more willing than others to use shady practices to get what they want.[20] These percentages represent very large numbers of people and indicate the widespread continuance of antisemitic beliefs among non-Jews.

Other Polling Data

A 1985 Harris Poll indicated that 37% of the non-Jews sampled believe that when the choice is between people and money, Jews will choose money. Another 25% believe that Jews are irritating because they are too aggressive. The proportions holding these beliefs have declined since 1978.[21] However, substantial shares continue to express agreement with these statements.

The normative responses make it difficult to analyze these and other data. Recent polls indicate that there is, to a certain degree, a greater acceptance of Jews. For example, a Gallup Poll conducted in 1981 indicated that 40% of the non-Jewish respondents had a highly favorable opinion of Jews. Furthermore, nearly seven of every ten said that they approved of marriages between Jews and non-Jews, and only 2% said that they had had unpleasant experiences with Jews.[22] Even among groups where antisemitic beliefs are rising, such as blacks, a 1985 poll showed that 54% of the respondents were favorable toward Jews. Clearly, no subgroup, or the majority of any subgroup, say that they view Jews unfavorably.[23] But the flip side of the coin, of course, is that 60% of the non-Jews surveyed do not regard Jews very highly. This is not to say that negative opinions were elicited. The glass may be more full than it used to be (given the limitations of the data), but it is still more than half empty.

Many Jews express the belief that antisemitic sentiment increases whenever the economy is bad. This rise in antisemitic attitudes may be nationwide, or restricted to certain groups. Specific groups of non-Jews have been polled recently. Both rural dwellers in the Midwest and evangelical Protestants have become of interest and concern to American Jews. Rural residents are experiencing economic hardship, which often serves as a precursor of increased antisemitism. Evangelical Protestants are of concern for several reasons: their growing influence in the political realm, as well as the intricate relationship between their support for Israel and feelings and attitudes about Jews.

Difficulty in the farm belt provides an opportunity to examine the relationship between economic adversity and antisemitism. Because of the economic troubles faced by many farmers, extremist groups have attempted to exploit the situation by placing blame for the farm crisis on "international bankers," the Federal Reserve, and Jews, among others. Pollster Louis Harris, who was commissioned by the Anti-Defamation League to conduct a study of antisemitic beliefs among rural dwellers, called it a "mass movement."[24] Interestingly enough, a press release from the Anti-Defamation League presented the study in such a way that it was reported that "only" 50% of those surveyed had heard about, or were familiar with, the National Agricultural Press Association, a "group combining do-it-yourself help to hard-pressed farmers with anti-Jewish propaganda."[25] It is rare in survey research to describe half of the population as "only."

Yet another recently released poll commissioned by the Anti-Defamation League examined antisemitism among evangelical Protestants. The study, which was released in 1987, indicated that 5% of those polled admitted having unfavorable views of Jews, while four out of ten had a neutral view, and about half had a favorable view. About one of every five indicated that they held at least one antisemitic belief. Furthermore, younger evangelicals were more likely to hold antisemitic beliefs than those over the age of 55. Of those aged 18 to 34, nearly half agreed with at least one antisemitic belief.[26] The findings were portrayed in the most upbeat light possible. While noting that the 22% who agreed with one of seven antisemitic beliefs was "troubling," the report indicated that there was no strong evidence to suggest that "most evangelical Christians consciously use their deeply held Christian faith and convictions as justification for anti-Semitic views of Jews."[27]

Again, such evidence raises questions as to how anti-Jewish sentiment is assessed. In the study of evangelical Protestants, respondents who thought that God might view Jews less favorably than other non-Christians were asked to explain why they felt this way. One Fundamentalist Baptist, who supposedly held a somewhat favorable opinion of Jews, answered: "Because they nailed Christ to the cross. . . . They will be dealt with later. That's all."[28] While such respondents might refrain from consciously using their convictions to justify antisemitic views, to classify them as neutral is deceptive.

A substantial proportion of the evangelicals hold at least one antisemitic view of Jews, and younger evangelicals, those under the age of 35, are almost twice as likely as those over the age of 55 to hold antisemitic views.[29] Again, this demonstrates that age and education are not as mitigating factors as assumed by some observers. Findings from the evangelical study mirror the results of studies conducted among blacks, which also indicate that antisemitic attitudes do not decline with age and increased education.

Among the most prevalent antisemitic stereotypes held by the evangelical Protestants surveyed was that of the Jew as too powerful and too wealthy. Many respondents indicated that they felt Jews had too much power in the country and, when asked what should be done about this, offered responses that are far from comforting. One female southern Baptist said, "I don't think there could be anything done. Perhaps to vote some out of office."[30] Another respondent, a man between the ages of 18 and 34, commented that "Jews are too wealthy. We should diffuse their wealth."[31] Such antisemitic stereotypes and sentiments are mentioned repeatedly in this study. While respondents frequently comment on positive traits, the strength of certain stereotypes persists. Sentiments such as the following, offered by one older southern Baptist male, indicate the tenacious nature of such opinions. His comment, that Jews "own the wealth of the U.S. They own the leading stores"[32] was echoed in various ways by several other respondents. This common stereotype was associated with Jewish stinginess and greed. While results from the evangelical study reveal positive findings in some areas, antisemitic sentiments do continue to be held by significant proportions of the surveyed population. Although their Christian faith and convictions may not justify such sentiments, many continue to hold antisemitic beliefs, regardless of this. The comments of one Pennsylvania woman demonstrate this. Asked to name the first trait of Jews that came to mind, she responded with a derogatory phrase. "The only thing that comes to my mind is 'cheap as a Jew,' " she said. "It is what my son always says to me."[33]

Attitudes about Israel

A question about Jewish loyalty to the United States and Israel has been periodically asked by the Gallup organization. The findings between 1979 and 1982 demonstrate that about one-third of the non-Jews surveyed believe that Jews are more loyal to Israel. This finding remained consistent from year to year.

Again, many of the findings are of the half-empty, half-full configuration. Gallup also discovered that 49% of non-Jews would sympathize with Israel if a war between Israel and the Arab nations broke out, while only 12% would sympathize with the Arab nations. About 39% did not know with whom they would side.[34] While the proportion sympathizing with the Arabs is small, less than half of the population responded that they would sympathize with Israel. Non-Jews have consistently favored Israel over the Arabs. But do these data indicate a pro-Israelism or a greater anti-Arab sentiment? In the absence of more in-depth probing, the data may be accurate, but not very informative. In some ways the data reflect a growing indifference on the part of the American public, which finds it difficult to choose between two sides, for neither of which they feel much sympathy. Such indifference may lead to nonsupport of Israel in times of real crisis. Similar results were found in a 1987 Roper Poll conducted for the American Jewish Committee.[35] The same poll data found one out of every four non-Jews believing that most Jews are more loyal to Israel than to the United States. As might be expected, the authors concluded that the results of the 1987 Roper Poll "reveal positive attitudes toward Israel and American Jews on the part of the American public."[36] They went on to say that these findings "are consistent with previous Roper results, suggest that recent events, including the Iran-Contra affair, the Ivan Boesky insider trading scandal, and the Jonathan Pollard spy case have had little negative fallout as far as attitudes toward Israel and American Jews are concerned."[37]

High support for Israel among non-Jews may be used to argue that antisemitic beliefs are declining or that anti-Israel beliefs do not represent a new form of antisemitism. Yet of the total population, almost as many non-Jews, 27%, are highly unfavorable toward Israel as the proportion, 32%, who are highly favorable. Furthermore, younger non-Jews are more likely than older people to be highly unfavorable toward Israel.[38] Less than half of the non-Jews, 46%, said that they would sympathize with Israel if there were a war between the Arab countries and Israel. Most, 51%, favored neither side or were not sure. A bare majority of non-Jews, 51%, believe that the continuation of the State of Israel is important. Only about one out of three non-Jews, 35%, believe that most Jews would side with the United States if Israel and the United States broke off relations.

The data can be said to show that the non-Jewish public is split in terms of attitudes toward Israel. Very strong support of, and hostility toward, Israel are about equal—while favoring the Arabs is virtually nonexistent. While many Americans favor Israel, a large proportion of non-Jews are indifferent or not sure. These two sets of attitudes may be correlated with negative attitudes about Jews. Those who are critical of Israel are more likely to hold antisemitic stereotypes. Some anti-Israelism may represent new forms of antisemitic expression.[39] But if the scale is weighted improperly, as it may be, these assertions are meaningless. Indeed, anti-Israelism may represent a new form of antisemitic belief.

Louis Harris said in an interview in 1986 that "support for Israel is high despite all the controversies, just as it's always been. At present, 78 percent of Americans feel very warm to Israel. The only time it's been lower than that was during the height of the Lebanon War and then support only went down to 69 percent."[40] He went on to say: "That's the good news. The other news is that anti-Semitism is alive and well and living in the United States."[41] But the positive attitudes toward Israel, he went on, may not carry very far in terms of people's feelings toward Jews, if they are both pro-Israel and antisemitic. He said: "We need to beware of such gifts. . . . Because if it comes down to it and they have to choose between their latent anti-Semitism or their admiration for Israel, they may very well go where their emotions are."[42]

Support for Israel is strong but not really as universal as is sometimes perceived. Furthermore, there seems to be a strong connection between anti-Israel and antisemitic beliefs. Support for Israel may remain strong among non-Jews as long as it is perceived that such support is in the United States' best interest. But if this perception changes, then support for Israel may drop. The perceived dual loyalty of Jews to Israel may take on more negative intensity, and with it increased expression of antisemitism. Such speculation points to the need for much more rigorous examination.

Assessing the Polls

Collectively, the polling data, whether about the non-Jewish public at large or subgroups such as blacks, rural dwellers, or evangelicals, indicate the continued accep-

tance of many antisemitic beliefs by substantial proportions of the non-Jewish population. Certain stereotypes
are declining. But even where the proportions decrease,
some of the waning stereotypes persist in 10 to 20% of the
American population. Furthermore, and more troubling in
nature, other antisemitic stereotypes have increased. In a
number of cases, younger non-Jews are more likely than
older non-Jews to hold these stereotypes. The hope voiced
by the Berkeley researchers in 1964—that education and
generation promised the gradual disappearance of antisemitic beliefs—has not held true in some cases. Better
educated blacks, younger and better educated evangelicals, and the younger population in general are more
likely than their less educated and older counterparts to
hold certain antisemitic beliefs. Perhaps the remoteness of
the Holocaust for younger non-Jews provides fewer normative constraints than older non-Jews on the expression
of some antisemitic beliefs, or the differences on affirmative action or other issues may influence educated Blacks'
views of Jews. The hope for the disappearance of antisemitism over generations is certainly not borne out by
contemporary polling data.

The normative milieu for some may still prevent individuals from stating openly blatant prejudiced beliefs of
any kind on the telephone. One editor of a Jewish newspaper wrote in 1986, "A major flaw in the Harris poll on
farm belt anti-Semitism is that no midwest farmer is going
to give that type of information on his thoughts and activities to a stranger on the phone."[43] While this view
overstates the case, the telephone polls, as previously
noted, may not be the most sensitive measuring device.
Therefore, antisemitic beliefs are probably underestimated.

While at least a fourth of those polled did indeed reveal their antisemitic prejudices to a telephone interviewer, the editor may be quite accurate in assuming that

levels of prejudice are underestimated through these polling techniques. This question is raised as well in a 1982
article in *Current Opinion* entitled "Is the Public Lying to
the Pollsters?"[44] The authors further raise the question of
tieing attitudes to behavior. When a Harris poll indicated
that 63% opposed a cutoff of military aid to Israel if an
Arab oil embargo threatened our supply and the only
way to get enough oil was to bow to such pressure, the
authors ask the question: "Isn't the correct answer to reject
the blackmail threat?" Normatively, few Americans may
wish to acknowledge that they are susceptible to such
blackmail.

Ultimately, it is the relationship between beliefs and
behavior in terms of assessing antisemitism that is most
important to Jews. Since antisemitism is much more than a
set of beliefs, but a set of actions as well, the hard questions, the interesting questions, and, from a Jewish perceptual standpoint, the most critical questions have to do
with the way certain beliefs translate into certain behaviors and how non-Jews will react to social, political, and
economic situations. Most important of all, what proportion of the population has to be antisemitic in order to
pose a threat to the Jewish population? The notion that
only 25% are highly antisemitic does not offer much comfort or security in a system that may not completely control the actions of those 25%.

The polling data, even with their misuse and their
likely misrepresentation of prejudiced beliefs, are clear.
Most non-Jewish Americans are not highly antisemitic.
But a substantial proportion are, and equally generous
proportions are either mildly antisemitic or neutral. As
will be seen in the following chapter, this truly represents
a situation that is at best half empty, when viewed
through American Jewish eyes. Given the number of non-
Jews who hold some antisemitic beliefs, it should be ex-

pected that many Jews encounter these sentiments, both directly and indirectly. Jewish perceptions are tied to the reality of widespread antisemitic beliefs. A "mildly" antisemitic person may hold many or a few antisemitic beliefs, but a Jew may encounter them. If antisemitism is expressed, even mildly or infrequently, a Jew coming into contact with it is likely to notice. Even with the decline of certain antisemitic beliefs (as currently measured), there is a large enough reservoir of antisemitism to be perceived and felt by Jews. The feelings are reinforced by the actual experiences of antisemitism through remarks, and the more violent incidents monitored by the Anti-Defamation League and others.

The ADL Audits

Certain behaviors indicate the transfer of the expression of these antisemitic beliefs into action. Certainly, the ADL *Audit of Anti-Semitic Incidents* offers some evidence. They noted about 600 such incidents in 1986, and 638 such incidents in 1985. The number had grown from just under 400 in 1980 to almost 1000 in 1981, and then dropped back down again. The 1986 *Audit of Antisemitic Incidents* reported nine cemetery desecrations, four arsons and three arson attempts, a number of arrests, and antisemitic incidents on college campuses such as the painting of antisemitic graffiti on campus buildings.[45]

These reports are of value because they attempt to monitor, in some way, antisemitic incidents. Some communities may have better recording mechanisms than others. Clearly, the count is by no means definitive. In many ways it documents only the most obvious and most easily identifiable acts of antisemitism. As the next chapter illustrates, nearly all the antisemitic experiences that Jews say they have go unreported to anyone. These include experiences with discrimination, as well as harassment. The ADL audits, while incomplete both in the total count they represent and in the evenness of the data-gathering mechanisms throughout different communities, nevertheless confirm that antisemitic beliefs do find their way into a variety of expressions throughout the United States.

Are cemetery desecrations or acts of violence against synagogues actually antisemitic or merely acts of random violence? While an individual may commit an act of violence against a Jewish institution without connecting it to specific antisemitic beliefs, a Jewish institution was nevertheless chosen. In some cases, of course, an individual may have selected a cemetery, not knowing what religious denomination was being desecrated, or drawn Nazi symbols on a synagogue, not understanding the symbolism of a swastika or that the institution was a synagogue. Such combinations must be rare, and the connectedness of violence to things Jewish, while not always well thought out in terms of political philosophy, nevertheless constitute, for the most part, acts of antisemitism. For the victims, such distinctions are hard to draw.

Senator D'Amato, introducing Senate Bill 2816 on June 28, 1984, argued that it was necessary to "stem the tide of anti-Semitism which has swept across this nation." The bill, modeled after those in effect in 16 states, enacted stiff federal penalties for those "who commit acts of religious violence or vandalism."[46] At least in terms of the law, the nebulous distinction between antisemitic intent and random violence becomes irrelevant.

It may be argued, of course, that in a nation of over 240 million people with a very wide variety of ethnic groups and a large expression of racial and ethnic violence being found throughout the country, a few hundred acts of violence or vandalism against Jews is not extreme. This, like the argument that violence may be random and not antisemitic at all, is a spurious one. What is known is discerned without any systematic investigation of discrimination. Only the most blatant incidents are compiled and reported. Levels of antisemitism, as measured by discrimination in the workplace, school, or neighborhood, are not systematically analyzed. Some may assume that there is no need. Of course, a tautology emerges: If there is no demonstrable evidence, then no evidence needs to be gathered. While one would not expect to find widespread discrimination against Jews, the backdrop of antisemitic beliefs could hardly lead one to conclude that discrimination is now extinct. But the Anti-Defamation League audits, incomplete as they are, offer some "evidence" of continued expression of antisemitic behavior.

Extremists and Hate Groups

Antisemitic behavior is expressed also through activities and rhetoric of extremist groups. They represent the ultimate behavioral expression of prejudice against Jews and other minorities. Given the Holocaust as a background, they are of special concern to Jews. After all, in Jewish eyes, the Nazis began as a small fringe group. Therefore, "small" and "fringe" are not qualifiers that would allow Jews to dismiss the potential danger of hate groups.

Extremist groups such as the Ku Klux Klan, antidemocratic organizations like Liberty Lobby and the Aryan Nations, and a multitude of pseudoreligious groups such as the Covenant, the Sword and the Arm of the Lord, and the Christian Patriot's Defense League promote antisemitic literature and propaganda. Exact membership figures for such organizations are difficult to obtain. In 1985 the Center for Democratic Renewal, which works closely with the American Jewish Committee, attempted to assess the impact of the farm crisis on the strength of such groups. They arrived at an approximate figure for the membership and following of far-right and racist as well as antisemitic organizations and individuals engaged in the rural Midwest:

> Because it is difficult to develop a strict quantitative analysis of a movement that operates essentially in secret, exact numbers on the various organizational efforts do not exist. It is our estimate that the racist and anti-semitic movement has between 2,000 and 5,000 hard-core activists in the Great Plains-Midwest, and between seven and ten sympathizers for each activist. While the potential for this cancer in the democratic fiber of our country to grow is great, a very real danger already exists.[47]

The objectives and tactics of most of these groups are similar, even if their philosophies are drawn from opposite ends of the political spectrum. Their common goals threaten the American democratic system, in general, and Israel and "Zionist supporters" specifically. Because of their potential danger, such groups continue to be monitored by the Anti-Defamation League and the American Jewish Committee, as well as by various law enforcement agencies such as the FBI. Law enforcement agencies have acted to control some of the most extreme right-wing groups by bearing down on their criminal activities. As a result, both the Aryan Nations and the Covenant, the Sword and the Arm of the Lord have lost leaders and members.

The Ku Klux Klan has also been damaged by successful lawsuits that held the Klan financially liable for actions of its members. In September 1983 the Anti-Defamation League estimated "the combined strength of the various Klans at 8,000–10,000."[48] An ADL special report

produced in May 1985 indicated the decline of Ku Klux
Klan membership. "The KKK's membership has fallen off
to some 6000–6500 nationwide, and the neo-Nazis today
number no more than 500. Both figures represent significant losses over the past several years."[49]

The Posse Comitatus, founded in 1969, has been
known under a variety of names: the Sheriff's Posse Comitatus, the Christian Posse, and other similar derivatives.
In a report issued in 1976, which provided background
material for the Center for Democratic Renewal, the FBI
described the Posse as "a loose-knit national organization."[50] "Investigation has determined," the report continued, "that there have been 78 known SPC chapters . . . during the last two years . . . in 23 states. . . .
Generally speaking, the Posse appears to draw rural people . . . the movement does not appear to be declining . . . the movement will, in all likelihood, increase in
certain sections of the country."[51] The Posse Comitatus is
an antisemitic, racist organization composed of loosely affiliated groups of armed vigilantes residing in several midwestern and western states. The "posses" of which the
organization is composed seek the return of vigilante justice. They are considered dangerous and violent by law
enforcement authorities. The FBI considers the Posse "a
terrorist organization."[52] Membership figures for the Posse vary widely. According to a 1983 ADL Handbook, "the
Posse claims to have a national membership exceeding
two million, but a realistic assessment indicates that figure
to be a gross exaggeration. ADL estimates that they have
perhaps two or three thousand members nationwide."[53]
Many Posse Comitatus members have also founded or are
members of "Identity" churches, while some have run for
public office.

In the summer of 1982, a 100,000-watt country music
station in Dodge City, Kansas (KTTL-FM), began broad-
casting rabid antisemitic recordings provided by Posse

Comitatus leaders. Some of the messages openly advocated violence against Jews. One recording provided the ADL with a foothold with which to petition the Federal Communications Commission for an order forbidding these broadcasts, on the grounds that they constitute "incitement to imminent lawlessness":

> You better start making dossiers, names, addresses, phone numbers, car license numbers, on every damn Jew rabbi in this land, and every Anti-Defamation League leader or JDL leader in this land, and you better start doing it now. And know where he is. If you have to be told any more than that, you're too damn dumb to bother with. You get these road-block locations, where you can set up ambushes, and get it all working now.[54]

Similar messages are spread by the Liberty Lobby, a self-proclaimed "pressure group for patriotism." The right-wing Washington-based group is a prolific source of antisemitic and extremist propaganda. An ADL Facts report issued in the winter of 1982 records the Liberty Lobby's account of itself: "According to Robert M. Bartell, . . . Chairman of Liberty Lobby's Board of Policy, the annual income of the Lobby itself now approaches $4 million. The organization's daily radio broadcast is now heard over a claimed 400 stations, and its short-lived television program was seen in 20 areas. . . . The weekly Liberty Lobby newspaper, *The Spotlight*, can boast more than 300,000 readers."[55]

Sometimes, these groups undertake political activities. For example, the Populist Party was formed in the spring of 1984. It centers around the Liberty Lobby and the remains of the American Independent Party. In 1984 the party attracted almost 64,000 votes in the 14 states in which it appeared on the ballot. "Within the ranks of the marginal third parties, their showing was very respectable," Leonard Zeskind states.[56]

The techniques used are very sophisticated. *The Spotlight* serves as the major voice of the Populist Party. "Literally tens of thousands of *Spotlights* are mailed into the Midwest from the Liberty Lobby's Washington, D.C., headquarters," a report prepared by Leonard Zeskind, research director of the Center for Democratic Renewal, revealed.[57] In its official circulation statement of October 1, 1981, *The Spotlight* claimed an average paid circulation of 315,102 per weekly issue. Running from 28 to 32 pages, Liberty Lobby packages its weekly message in a slick, upbeat format. Its reading audience is the largest of any antisemitic publication in America.[58]

The presence of these hate groups cannot be ignored. Nor can they be taken lightly. Certainly, the murder in 1984 of Alan Berg, the Denver talk show host, and the murder of a Missouri State trooper in 1985 by right-wing extremist groups are only two acts of violence, but the most serious expressions of extremism. Paramilitary trainers, using a cutout figure of a state trooper with a Star of David drawn on his chest, demonstrate the linkage between planned violence and antisemitism.[59] It is well known that these right-wing organizations "focus on Jews."[60] Publications such as *Instauration* spout typical antisemitic diatribes about "Jewish domination" in the United States.[61] Even the most outlandish of antisemitic ploys find an audience. Among the latest, of course, are the Holocaust revisionists, using the argument that the Holocaust never took place as another means for asserting antisemitic rhetoric and actions.[62]

Antisemitic rhetoric and behavior, of course, are not solely a manifestation of the right. The Farrakhan phenomenon is an excellent case in point. Louis Farrakhan appeals to large crowds. Significant numbers of blacks embrace some of Farrakhan's message. Farrakhan, like extremists on the right, represents nascent mass movements with serious antisemitic underpinnings. The exact influence of these mass movements or their potential long-term threat is unknown. Nevertheless, in whatever form and to whatever extent, they are real, and they express their antisemitism in extreme form.

Jewish fears of these groups rest in their continued use of the most virulent antisemitic ideologies, coupled with their advocacy of violence. As long as such groups remain on the political fringe, Jews, like other Americans, tend to view them as "crazies" who need to be monitored and contained. However, most Jews feel that they currently constitute a minimal threat.

The danger in these groups lies in their potential to influence the political system, either through elected candidates or by the more widespread acceptance of their antisemitic ideologies. The extremist groups in this country are viewed as nascent political forces that require constant exposure and opposition. While the activities of extremist groups are rejected by the vast majority of both Jews and non-Jews alike, it is not necessarily because the antisemitic rhetoric itself is rejected.

The most extreme expressions of antisemitism, therefore, are likely to be checked because they come in political or social packages that are simply unacceptable to the vast majority of Americans. If they are tuned out and controlled, and their influence minimized, it is not necessarily because the majority of Americans are interested in controlling antisemitism. For extremists not only shoot Jews, they also shoot state troopers.

The Constraints on Antisemitism

As the Holocaust becomes a more distant event in time, the social restrictions against antisemitic statements and thinking seem to be eroding. Antisemitic rhetoric is creeping into "respectable" places. It may come in the form of a Gore Vidal essay in a national magazine, an actress condemning "Zionist thugs" at an Academy Award ceremony on national television, or an editorial in a Jefferson City, Missouri, newspaper opposing the purchase of Israeli bonds and condemning the Jewish lobby.

While the idea of antisemitic rhetoric and attitudes in everyday life seem far-fetched to some, they continue to emerge in locations that, by their very nature in public forums, seem to legitimize their presence. The Jefferson City, Missouri, *News & Tribune* editorial, which ostensibly sought to point out what the paper perceived as the shortcomings of a candidate, was really an anti-Jewish diatribe that disparaged the candidate because of her relations with "Senator Howard Metzenbaum—uncle of Missouri Lt. Gov. Harriet Woods nee Friedman." After drawing that nefarious connection, the editorial proceeded to imply that electing Harriet Woods would only give additional strength to an unsavory group: "the powerful Jewish lobby in Washington might get the United States to back the [Israel] bonds. It has organized all the left-wingers and liberals in Congress, which last year delivered nearly $4 billion in U.S. aid to Israel."[63] The editorial was never retracted, nor was an apology issued. It simply stood on its own questionable merit.

All of these isolated examples do not constitute evidence that antisemitism is increasing or decreasing in the United States. They merely illustrate that the introduction of antisemitic and anti-Zionist rhetoric in the public arena has become not infrequent in the 1980s. When Louis Farrakhan sprinkles his addresses on the economic ills of blacks with antisemitic rhetoric, these sentiments gain some legitimacy through their continued expression in the public arena. They are not condemned by a sufficiently large number of non-Jews to cease their repetition.

Collectively, current sources about the state of antisemitism raise more questions than they answer. Examining the record in total begs for more systematic exploration of the phenomenon of contemporary antisemitism. Until that time, it can be concluded that antisemitic beliefs still persist and are expressed through different avenues. Discrimination has obviously declined: Jews live in neighborhoods, go to schools, and have jobs they could not have held 40 years ago. To say that nothing has changed would be frivolous. To say that everything has changed ignores the available evidence. But the normative constraints may be lessening, even as the legal constraints increase. This is the reality that most Jews perceive.

Chapter Three

LIVING IN TWO WORLDS
BEING A JEW AND AN AMERICAN

The Dual Identity of American Jews

American Jews live in two worlds. Most Jews are increasingly well integrated into the fabric of American society and culture, while at the same time maintaining a separate Jewish identity, although often marginal and vague. America's Jews are clearly just that: products of the general society. In many fundamental ways American Jews behave and believe much as do other white middle-class Americans. Yet distinct differences remain. Most Jews still adhere to enough minimal religious activity to separate them from the Christian majority.

As a result of their dual identity, the Jewish looking glass through which antisemitism is examined is really more like a pair of bifocals. The vision changes depending on whether or not the Jewish lens or the American lens is used. And as with bifocals, until the wearer adjusts to them, objects tend to blur, unless the view through the lens is perfectly balanced. The vision of antisemitism seems less threatening when viewed through the American lens: security, acceptance, and success characterize the American experience. The Jewish lens offers something different: marginality and a collective history of persecution. Jewish perceptions of antisemitism are molded by the tension of living with a multiple personality.

Jews are simultaneously mainstream and marginal,

like other Americans but also different, accepted but accepted reluctantly, and so on. Their contradictory feelings reflect those of the real world. There is no singular set of perceptions of antisemitism because there is no singular set of Jews, and no neat and simple classification of where Jews fit into contemporary American society.

The dual character of American Jews can be conceptualized along a continuum of identity, with greater and lesser degrees of assimilation. A relatively small proportion of Jews behave only as Americans and not as Jews, while the proportions who would identify themselves only as Jews, and not Americans, are even smaller. The vast majority find themselves somewhere between these two extremes.

Nor is an individual's identity permanently fixed in time. Each identity is buffeted and moved by external events, both personal (life cycle) and more global. While the Six-Day War affected the consciousness of an entire generation of Jews, a college course, the death of a parent, or the birth of a child may alter the religious consciousness of an individual.

A certain kaleidoscopic quality characterizes the identity of American Jews, both individually and as a group. This amorphous identity shifts with time and events, sometimes dramatically and sometimes subtly. Colors combine differently with each turn of a kaleidoscope, and the picture changes if it is passed from one person to another. No matter how one might try, the colors shift ever so delicately with the slightest movement.

Indeed, the American Jewish community, as a descriptive phrase, is something of a misnomer. America's six million Jews hardly constitute a monolithic entity. Occupation, geographic distribution, recreational patterns, and other dimensions of American life are substantially

different within the Jewish population. Jews are very likely to hold white-collar positions, to have high levels of
education, and to live in large metropolitan areas. But not
all Jews are professionals, not all Jews have Ph.D.s, and
not all Jews live in Los Angeles, Chicago, and New York.
Too often, disproportionate differences between Jews and
non-Jews are somehow exaggerated into false stereotypes
believed by Jews and non-Jews alike.

Differences among Jews in terms of religious profiles
are even more pronounced. One of the more troubling
aspects of Jewish life in the United States is the ever-deep-
ening rift occurring along denominational lines. Contemporary Jews in the United States are segmented by differences in levels of ritual observance and belief, as well as
relative assimilation into the greater mainstream of American society. A Jew can be at one end of the assimilation
continuum, a largely observant Jew in terms of ritual practice and observance, and be well integrated into most aspects of general American culture, in terms of social, political, and economic activities. An Orthodox Jew can make
sure his head is covered at a mainstream American activity, such as a major league baseball game, by simply
donning a baseball cap.

On the other hand, one can be a largely nonobservant
Jew and yet have relative isolation from mainstream
American life, in terms of neighborhood, friends, and social life. It is often assumed that the most observant Jews
are also the most geographically or socially isolated. Such
is the case for clusters of Orthodox Jews in sections of New
York. However, even the least observant, those who consider themselves "just Jewish," practicing few if any Jewish rituals, exhibit tendencies to remain within the Jewish
realm. Many say that the majority of their closest friends
are Jewish, live in neighborhoods where Jews constitute

substantial minorities, and in a multitude of other ways remain within the Jewish world, although they certainly do not remain religiously observant.

Data collected in survey research over the past few years verify the dual character of Jewish identity. Jews maintain their separate identity but are also becoming like other Americans. They are Jewish, but not "too Jewish." The changing identity of American Jews is expressed in various ways. Jews are far less likely to live in exclusively or predominantly Jewish neighborhoods. Outside New York even Orthodox Jews, while living in geographic clusters, do not have exclusively, or even predominantly, Jewish neighbors. Jews of the first and second generation lived in urban ghettoes where Jewish neighbors, friends, organizations, and institutions were all concentrated. While by no means distributed at random, Jews today are more dispersed throughout neighborhoods in America's cities. The geographic patterns of American Jews reflect their bifurcated identity. They still live where there are other Jews, but often within a large Gentile presence, and most often with a non-Jewish majority. Such residential patterns are determined more by housing price, school quality, and other factors than by a decision to live among non-Jews. Geographic patterns reveal neither the abandonment of Jewish residential ties nor the high density of the past.

Without geographic density, the ethnic ties are harder to keep, and the religious boundaries become more problematic. As might be expected with rising intermarriage rates and changing neighborhood patterns, the friendship patterns among American Jews are also changing. The basic measure of in-group cohesion and the strength of ethnic bonds—friendship patterns among Jews—show that most Jews, no matter what their age group, still tend to have Jewish friends. But differences by age group can be seen. In Kansas City for example, 95% of those over the age of 65 say that all three of their best friends are Jewish, while about one of every four Jews between the ages of 25 and 34 in Kansas City say that none of their best friends are Jewish (see Table 3-1). Clearly, the association with Jews continues on a large scale. But among third- and fourth-generation Jews, there is a substantial cohort who have moved along the continuum to the point where none of their friendship circles include Jews. Obviously, there is an interrelatedness between those who live outside clusters of Jewish population and intermarry, and those who have no Jewish friends.

Intermarriage rates are one indicator of the extent to which Jews have assimilated into American society. While most Jews continue to marry other Jews, there is also evidence that intermarriage rates, particularly among third- and fourth-generation Jews, especially in the West, have risen dramatically over the past 15 years and continue to do so. Many of these households may indeed adopt something of a Jewish identity. However, it is more likely that each successive generation will see increasing proportions of Jews with fewer and fewer ties to the Jewish community. The most basic of ethnic ties, in-marriage, is weakening with each successive decade and each successive generation. While most Jews may not take the active step of ceasing to be Jewish, that is, converting to another religion, when they intermarry their children are more likely to also marry non-Jews. And some who choose to remain nominal Jews will call themselves Jews more from inertia than affirmation.

The connection between intermarriage, geographic proximity, and friendship patterns is evident in New York City. A study of the Jewish population of New York City found 70% of respondents saying that all of their three closest friends are Jewish. Patterns of intermarriage vary by borough. Brooklyn, the Bronx, Queens, and Nassau have the highest rates of in-group friendships, and a comparatively lower rate of intermarriage. Between 71 and 82% of respondents in each of these counties said that all three of their closest friends are Jewish. Westchester County reported a moderate rate of in-group friendship, with 63% claiming that all three of their best friends are Jewish, and exhibited a moderate rate of intermarriage.[1]

Except for those Jews who completely abandon their Jewish identity, some separateness for Jews remains a reality. No matter how much Jews dress like other Americans, have the same recreational patterns, adopt white middle-class values and accept white middle-class cultural norms, participate in the political system, or advance economically, they continue to adhere to a minority religion. While Judaism has been accorded status as one of three of America's "main" religions, this status does not imply "sameness."

Whether Jews define themselves as "just Jewish," "ethnic Jews," "nonreligious Jews," or some other phrase that classifies them as more assimilated, most know that they differ from other Americans. Furthermore, when Jews say that they are not religious Jews, in terms of their self-definition, they are usually indicating that they are not ritually observant Jews and do not attend synagogue or temple very often.

Synagogue membership and attendance are obviously a key indicator of continued Jewish identity. The proportion of people who belong to a synagogue varies widely by community. Age and marital status are highly correlated to synagogue membership. The Cleveland population study of 1981, states that "it is an accepted fact that the membership of a temple or synagogue is made up of two kinds of families: the permanent ones and those who belong only during their children's religious education."[2] In select cities, such as Phoenix and Washington, D.C., far fewer than half of all the households have a current membership with a synagogue. (See Table 3-2.) Synagogue affiliation tends to be lower in the West, Southwest, and South, and in larger cities. It is somewhat higher in Midwestern cities, and in Jewish communities of 5000 to 50,000. Orthodox Jews are most likely to be affiliated with a synagogue, followed by Conservative and Reform, and affiliation is low among those who identify themselves as "just Jewish" or "other."

Since synagogue membership is largely determined by life cycle, membership is highest among those over the age of 35 and then drops again for those over the age of 65. When asked if they intend to join a synagogue in the future, a high proportion of those under the age of 35 indicate that they will do so. Together with those who have belonged to a synagogue, or currently belong to a synagogue, about 80 to 85% of all Jewish households intend to have some affiliation with a synagogue at some point in their lives. Obviously, not all Jews will fulfill this intent, but nevertheless some marginal affiliation with a synagogue or temple at some point is likely.

The great majority of Jews do attend religious services at various times throughout the year, for the High Holy Days and special times such as weddings and Bar/Bat Mitzvahs. Relatively small proportions, between 10–20% in most cities, attend services once a month or more per year. Even smaller proportions say that they attend weekly, usually 5–10%. (See Table 3-3.) Younger Jews are far less likely to attend services than older Jews. For example, over half of the Jews aged 18 to 24 in Rochester never attend services. In communities like Washington, D.C., those under 35 years of age are most likely to say that they never attend services.

But even if individuals define themselves as ethnic Jews with no religious connotations, they are still differentiated by their nonadoption of the dominant religious culture. In the absence of observing Jewish rituals, or attending synagogue or temple, they have not, for the most part, adopted the religious practices or beliefs of Christianity. Nor, with rare exceptions, would they do so. They do not think of themselves as Christians; they think of themselves as Jews. The adherence to Judaism, even at the most minimal level, constitutes a marginal religious activity in the context of widely practiced Christianity.

Antisemitism and Marginality

Jews, as long as they remain Jews, are *different* from most Americans. While Polish Americans, Irish Americans, and German Americans may maintain some sentimental ties to their country of origin and may have developed sociocultural patterns that define them as differentiated subgroups of Christian Americans, they remain part of the religious majority. Italians and other white immigrant groups have gradually lost or will lose their more distinguishing characteristics. But Jews, although well integrated as white middle-class Americans, maintain a singularly separating characteristic, their religious identity, which keeps them apart. Jews are certainly free to practice their religion, and in some ways they are even encouraged to do so by the general culture. Such acceptance and tolerance do not negate the reality of the distinctiveness and minority status of Judaism within the Christian society.

Nearly all Jews are aware of this marginality. Some may believe that it is insignificant. Others may feel that the schisms between American Jews and other Americans are deep. Some Jews assert that they are neither like nor different from other Americans: They are Jewish Americans. Others see the differences as all-encompassing. Yet it is the recognition of this difference, for most Jews, coupled with the collective histories of the Jewish place in other host cultures, that keeps Jews wary. Most Jews still practice religion differently from nearly all other Americans, and these practices are part of a set of religious beliefs that are fundamentally different from those of other Americans.

The sense of marginality, coupled with the history of Jewish marginality in other times and places, strongly influences the way Jews assess antisemitism in the United States. For most Jews, there continues to be a "them" and an "us," even though the "us," is in some ways part of the "them." As Americans, Jews believe that their non-Jewish neighbors should protect them as equal Americans. At the same time, a level of mistrust remains about how their Christian neighbors really feel about them and whether or not they can be relied upon during times of political or economic crisis to protect their minority rights. American Jews, when thinking as Americans, can hardly believe that racial and religious intolerance or discrimination are possibilities. As Jews, they cannot believe that discrimination is not a possibility. With the Holocaust looming in their collective memories, Jews are convinced that the ultimate threats of discrimination and even violence are lingering possibilities. It is no wonder, then, that the complex feelings with which Jews view antisemitism have resulted in the development of institutions and organizations, and philosophies for dealing emotionally and intellectually with antisemitism.

As Jews become more and more like other Americans, the issue becomes: When do they stop being Jews? Is it possible to stop being Jews? For some Jews, antisemitism may cease to be an issue because they have become so assimilated that their Jewish identity is close to being lost, or they have adopted another religion. On the other hand, a small portion of the Jewish population, as it maintains the most traditional sets of Jewish observance and ritual

practice, remains apart from the large majority of integrated and more assimilated American Jews. As a whole,
Jews have become more unified with the general society.
But within the whole, the divisions within Judaism have
become more severe.

The majority of American Jews continue to struggle to
maintain their separate identity. As early as the late 1950s
Arthur Cohen wrote that the fear of antisemitism is no
longer an effective reason for "holding on to Jewish identity. Fear has waned. . . ."[3] While antisemitism remains a
potential threat lurking sometime in the future, most Jews
are more concerned with the disappearance of Jewish
identity via a slow but gradual disintegration through assimilation. Antisemitism, while terrible and destructive,
has also bound Jews together. As overt antisemitism de-
clines, Jews face the problems of remaining a distinctive
group within a most hospitable climate.

There has been much debate on what it means to be a
Jew in American society. In such a welcoming country,
maintaining separateness is difficult, and, it is argued by
some, unnecessary. Nathan Glazer, a prominent so-
ciologist of American Jewry, has written: "The strongest
and potentially most significant religious reality among
American Jews . . . is that the Jews have not stopped
being Jews. I do not now speak of the fact that they are
sociologically defined as Jews; this is of small significance
from the point of view of Jewish religion. I speak rather of
the fact that they still *choose* to be Jews. . . ."[4]

Most Jews maintain a marginal attachment to traditional observance and ritual life. They still choose to be
Jews. In some ways, Jewish religious life has adopted
some Christian norms. As Michael Rappeport has pointed
out in his study of Morris and Essex counties, New
Jersey, Jewish ritual observance can be classified as a fol-

lowing of the "American ritual."[5] Just as seasonal observances of Christmas and Easter are followed by Christians, Jews have their highest observance pattern with the
corresponding holidays of Chanukah and Passover. Passover and Chanukah are the most widely observed rituals.
In most communities, more than three-quarters of Jews
always or usually observe a Passover Seder. (See Table
3-4.) But it must be pointed out that in Washington, D.C.,
for example, which has a younger, singles population,
30% of the Jews observe Passover only sometimes, while
26% never do. In each community, even among the most
widely observed rituals, a substantial cohort of about 20
to 30% only sometimes or never observe Passover or
Chanukah.

Obviously, lower proportions of Jews observe many
other rituals. Younger Jews are far less likely to keep
kosher or observe the Sabbath. At least for now, Jews
under the age of 35 maintain the most marginal attachment to Jewish ritual observance. Most Jews are far less
likely to "practice" their religion than Protestants and Catholics, in terms of weekly service attendance. Ironically,
as Jews have become more like other Americans, they are
becoming less like them in terms of religious practices.
Being less Jewish, then, with the absence of practicing
some religion, is less American.

The transformation of American Judaism from a religious group to an ethnic group to something new is ex-
pounded by Jonathan Woocher. He argues that Judaism in
the United States has developed for some into a civil religion. In Woocher's book *Sacred Survival: The Civil Religion
of American Jews*,[6] a new theory regarding the influence of
the activity and ideology typically thought of as "secular"
is set forth. According to Woocher, the most influential
religious ideology in American Jewish life today is not

denominational. It is what he calls "civil Judaism."
Through this polity, American Jewry has expressed its
self-conception as a moral community with a special destiny and purpose to fulfill among worldwide Jewry.

"Civil religion" is defined as the system of beliefs,
values, and rituals through which America relates itself to
its destiny. According to Woocher's thesis, American Jews
have created their own "civil Judaism." The ideology that
originated as a value system emphasizing philanthropy
and Jewish adjustment to American life has developed
into one that encompasses a set of beliefs promoting Jewish survival and activism in modern-day America. The result is the achievement of a unity of purpose and identity
as a moral community, which receives expression in a
characteristic set of beliefs, myths, and rituals. Therefore,
ritual has not been abandoned but transformed into a different set of activities.

"American Jewish civil religion plays a unique and
important role in defining the character and self-under-
standing of American Jewry today," Woocher states in the
preface to *Sacred Survival*. "It helps American Jews to
achieve their most notable aspiration: to survive and to
thrive precisely as *American Jews*, as loyal members of an
ancient people with a proud tradition, and as full participants in a great new society- and nation-building endeav-
or."[7] Because of this role, and its apparent success,
Woocher argues for the acceptance of the importance of
civil religion, because it occupies an important place in the
Jewish struggle to validate and to direct Jewish existence
in America. By this definition, Jews are no longer defined
as either a religious or an ethnic group but as some manifestation of religion, through organizational and institutional ties and networks. In this way, Judaism becomes
both a local and a national member organization.

Civil Judaism, as expressed by organizational and institutional behavior, is by no means universal. Indeed, it can be argued that civil Judaism is an expression of religious commitment for those who are already somehow attached in other ways. For those who are most assimilated, whose religious identity is not expressed through any mechanism, civil Judaism has disappeared as well. Those who practice civil Judaism are also likely to have some attachment to traditional Jewish ritual observance in some form.

In most communities, between 50 to 60% of the households have someone in them who belongs to at least one Jewish organization. (See Table 3-5.) However, membership levels vary by age, with younger respondents, those under 35, less likely to be dues-paying members of any Jewish organization. For example, while 75% of the Kansas City respondents over 65 years old are members of one or more Jewish organization, only 33% of respondents aged 25 to 35 belong. This trend is parallel in each and every community for which there are data.

Households with all Jewish members—where intermarriage has not occurred—are far more likely to belong to Jewish organizations than are mixed households, as seen in Denver, Phoenix, and other Jewish communities. In Milwaukee, for example, intermarried households have minimal contact with Jewish organizations: Only 15% have a current affiliation, compared with almost 70% of all Jewish households in Milwaukee.[8] In Denver, Jews married to Jews are most likely to belong to Jewish clubs and organizations (65%), followed by Jews married to converted Jews (42%), while born Jews married to non-Jews are the least likely (14%).[9] Over the span of life cycle, some younger Jewish individuals who are not currently affiliated may develop organizational ties when they are married or when they have children. At any rate, a majority of Jewish households have a current affiliation with a Jewish organization, or will in the future. Along the identity continuum, it is those who are intermarried who are least likely to have such institutional and organizational ties, just as they are the least likely to have Jewish friends or to live where there are other Jews. As other binding influences decrease, the role of organizations and institutions becomes more critical. But these bonds may prove to be much more tenuous. They can hardly substitute for neighborhood, ritual observance, and in-marriage among Jews.

If one were to characterize synagogue attendance, synagogue membership, and organizational membership, approximately 10 to 20% of the population would be found to be highly affiliated and active, and about 10 to 20% to be completely inactive and almost totally detached. The vast majority of Jews lie somewhere in between, in terms of synagogue attendance, synagogue membership, and organizational membership patterns. Those who are least affiliated are most likely to be younger, third and fourth generation, and intermarried.

Wrestling with issues of assimilation for American Jews has changed dramatically. Prior to the Second World War, assimilation was equated with abandoning Jewish identity as well as the accoutrements of religious observance and distinctiveness. For some, becoming an American implied rejection of Judaism and becoming less Jewish in name, dress, or neighborhood. One analyst wrote in 1942 that "there are persons who are unconscious assimilationists, who, having lost interest in Judaism are drifting out of it unwittingly. In other instances, that drift is accelerated by desire, recognized or unrecognized, to escape the penalties of a minority identity. And in still other instances impetus is lent to the movement by those emotions of inferiority, self-contempt and self-hatred which have infected the personalities of many American Jews."[10] Before the Second World War, being Jewish was considered by some a liability, unnecessary baggage that had to be discarded in order to benefit fully from opportunities offered in America.

As overt discrimination waned in the post-World War II period, third-generation Jews were the first to experience a relatively open society. It is they, according to another scholar, Ben Halpern, who were the first to struggle with the issue of assimilation outside of the ghetto experience.[11] Because this departure from the ghetto is still relatively fresh, the American Jew, now an "integrated" member of American society, typically native-born, is coping with the problems of increased assimilation. "The problem is a totally new one; it presents the first challenge whose creative mastery might establish a continuous American Jewish historic tradition."[12] Only in the years since World War II has American Jewry been compelled to face its own unique situation and create its own history. Halpern draws the conclusion, then, that "American Jewish ideological development may still not really have begun."[13]

Many American Jews now struggle with this development, and how comfortable they have become in the general society. They fear disappearing through assimilation. For example, a survey of Rochester Jewish leadership completed in 1986 found that 70% feel that Jews are losing their separate identity. When asked whether or not losing a separate identity was a good thing or a bad thing, not surprisingly, 58% perceived it negatively, and, interestingly enough, another 40% said it was both good and bad. Only 3% said that it was a good thing that Jews are losing their separate identity. Separate identity is seen as the means of preserving Jewish culture and values, ensuring the identity of Jews as a people, and maintaining the Jewish religion. One respondent indicated that a separate identity is necessary "to keep Judaism alive. We must know who we are and why we are different."

When Jews were asked, in a series of personal interviews for a national study of leadership, what the most important problem facing Jews today in the United States was, the issue of assimilation was clearly foremost on people's minds. Jewish continuity and the survival of distinct Jewish groups within the general culture were the issues described most frequently. At the same time, the growing schism among Orthodox, Conservative, and Reform Jews was also mentioned as another source of concern. Obviously, as certain elements of the Jewish population move toward one end of the assimilation continuum and others move in the opposite direction, the potential for true conflicts between Jews becomes more real. But the issue of assimilation remains most critical for most Jews.

No consensus exists among scholarly observers about how Jews will resolve the conflict of living in two worlds and maintaining a separate identity. Even the titles of their work reveal the dilemma. *The Ambivalent American Jew*[14]; *Jewish Continuity and Change: Emerging Patterns in America*[15]; *The Masks Jews Wear: The Self-Deceptions of American Jewry*[16]; and Jacob Neusner's *Stranger at Home*[17] all indicate a struggle between two conflicting worlds for American Jews. Most Jews continue to maintain a separate identity, defined by marginal ritual practice and worship, continued ethnic ties as expressed through neighborhood and friendship patterns, and organizational and institutional affiliation, a "civil Judaism." The strength of those collective ties is debatable. How many of America's six million Jews will become more strongly identified with Judaism, how many will drift away from Judaism, and how many will adopt a religion other than Judaism is unknown. Certainly, the character of the next generation is more of a mystery. But for now, most Jews have managed to delicately balance their lives as both Americans and Jews.

Jewish Identity and External Forces

In the absence of religion as a set of symbols and guides for daily activity and thought, Judaism in America is reinforced and identified with external events and structures to help provide continuity, meaning, and cohesiveness for American Jewry. Antisemitism answers this need, playing each of these roles, but to a much lesser extent than ever before in American life. Obviously, the place of the Holocaust in this identity formation plays a second and more crucial role for American Jews. The Holocaust is not so far removed from fourth-generation Jews that they do not understand its import and significance. The experience of the Holocaust continues to unite Jews, whether positively or negatively, in some common understanding and fear of what it means to be a Jew.

The state of Israel, both its establishment and its continued existence, remains a third central focal point for American Jewish identity. As Charles Liebman, author of *The Ambivalent American Jew* and other scholarly works, points out, "Israel has not replaced religion as the focus of Jewish identity; rather, it has increasingly become the content or the expression of Jewish religious identity."[18] In other words, Israel has become a central component of how American Jews think of themselves as Jews. Israel has become for American Jews not only a country, a religious dream fulfilled, but also an expression of identity and its focal point. Marshall Sklare wrote that "the most significant aspect of the impact of Israel concerns its effect on the Jewish self-image, on the psychological make-up of the American Jew, on the feeling of the American Jew toward his Jewishness."[19] Even with some of the magic worn off by the war in Lebanon, defining who is a Jew, and other divisive issues, Israel remains a central positive

force in Jewish identity. In some ways, it mirrors the contemporary Jewish experience in America. Israel corroborates, as a nation, what Jews feel as a minority in the
United States. In the aftermath of the Holocaust, the ultimate experience of being victims, a simultaneous expression of economic, social, political, and military power
is exhibited in varying ways in both America and Israel. In
some ways, for many American Jews, Israel is a vicarious
expression of Jewish pride and success.

These feelings were most accentuated by the Six-Day
War. One observer wrote that "Israel's military victory
brought elation and pride, but, even more, release from
tension, gratitude, a sense of deliverance. Of course, the
pride was one of being victorious, a new kind of pride in
being Jewish, in the aura that radiated from General
Moshe Dayan, his ruggedness, vigor, determination.
Many Jews took pride in the changed image of the Jew, no
longer seen as victim or the historic typification of a per-
secuted people."[20] For a whole generation of American
Jews the Six-Day War marked a watershed in the definition of American Jewish identity. The fledgling sense of
independence, growth, and security that American Jews
were feeling at home was intensified and corroborated by
the Israeli victory in 1967. While the Israeli victory did not
create a sense of pride and accomplishment and power—
Jews had already begun to feel that in the United States—
the Six-Day War was an external verification for American
Jews of what they were experiencing at home.

But recent data illustrate that while most Jews remain
firmly committed to the idea of Israel's continued existence, and still feel a sense of support and deep emotional
commitment to Israel, the character of that support may be
changing, especially among younger Jews. The glory of
the Six-Day War has been tarnished by the conflicts inherent in acquiring new territories and overseeing a large

minority population of Palestinians. Evidence from recent survey research indicates that younger Jews are less likely to feel obligated to support Israel financially, and feel less of a sense of personal commitment to Israel. But this change should come as no surprise. Since Israel remains an external embodiment of Judaism, it is subject to varying degrees of loyalty and belief. Furthermore, in the absence of crisis, less attention is required and therefore given. At this point, Israel is not at war, is militarily secure to some extent, and has the support of the world's most powerful nation as its major ally. American Jewish attitudes toward Israel in many ways parallel the current mood of American Jews about their Jewishness. Jews have not stopped being Jews, but participation, for a large number of them, is marginal. The same can be said for American Jewish support of Israel. Very few are nonsupportive, while a substantial proportion remain highly committed. In the middle are many who care about Israel, who rally to its support in times of crisis, but who otherwise have no outlet for expression of their support. Nor can this support be tapped without considerable effort.

The threat to Israel is viewed as vague. It is a threat at some point in the future, as opposed to a more imminent catastrophe. Since most Jews feel relatively safe in America, they also feel that Israel is relatively safe as well. Indeed, in the Yom Kippur War of 1973, that sense of serenity was shattered, and Jewish fund-raising efforts for Israel skyrocketed in response. Without such crisis, concern has no equivalent means of attaining expression. Jews feel about Israel's safety much the way they feel about antisemitism in the United States. Vigilance is required, as well as continued support and effort, but American Jews believe that things are generally under control.

While Jews are most concerned about assimilation, and the threat of Jewish continuity and survival in the face of an open society, there remains an uncertainty concerning the continued marginality of American Jews. Antisemitism remains a concern, but a more distant one. An inherent contradiction exists. Jews are worried about the potential of persecution or random violence or worse as a consequence of being different. At the same time, they are most concerned about maintaining characteristics that differentiate them from the general population.

A generation or two ago, some Jews were wondering how to shed their distinctive Jewish identity in order to avoid discrimination. In the 1980s, they are worried about maintaining their separate identity and distinctive character, even while recognizing that the threat of more active antisemitism is a possibility. In essence, prior to the Holocaust and the establishment of Israel, some Jews felt that the burden of their religious identity was more than they wanted to bear if it meant risking exclusion or the experience of antisemitism. That burden seems minimal in the United States today.

In contemporary America, the diminution of discrimination has allowed Jews to feel more free about proclaiming their Jewishness. While living in two worlds, American Jews want the best of both. They want what they see as the uniqueness and richness that comes from being Jewish, and also the diversity and sense of belonging to a great and varied populace that comes from being an American. Most American Jews are acutely aware of the threat of disintegration from within but also are plagued by a sense of the threat of an external assault, both here and in Israel. In both cases, Jews continue to struggle with the issues of continuity and survival. Because signs of antisemitism around the world and at home are still exhibited, Jews both desire and fear their marginality.

CHAPTER FOUR

DENIAL, WARINESS, AND FEAR
WHAT JEWS SEE

Living in two worlds produces a complicated set of feelings about antisemitism. Looking through American eyes, signs of economic, social, and political success indicate very low levels of discrimination against Jews. Such an assessment might lead some to deny that antisemitism exists at all. However, looking through Jewish eyes may produce feelings of fear. Signs of antisemitism in the United States, both behavioral and attitudinal, continue to be present in one form or another. For most Jews, this results in wariness, the large middle ground between denial and fear.

Sometimes the interpretation of what is seen through American and Jewish lenses is reversed. The bitter history of antisemitism, viewed through Jewish eyes, causes some Jews to deny the continued presence of prejudice, hostility, or violence. Coping is facilitated by denying the problem. Yet American Jews, as Americans, have an almost obsessive concern with individual rights and freedoms, and abhor potential infringements upon those rights. Such an obsession may produce fear, and this fear may in turn result in obsession, mutually reinforcing one another. American Jewish responses to antisemitism are clearly a combination of their hyphenated identity. But neither response, whether it be fear or denial, is the sole product of identity as either Americans or Jews.

The wariness response is the most common blending

of the dual identity. Ties to collective Jewish history cannot be disengaged, but neither can the collective experiences and acculturation of Jews in American society. Combining the two identities, Jewish Americans or American Jews, separate and blended, results in a broad perceptual view of antisemitism, both as a group and as individuals within the group.

Social scientists, community relations professionals, and the general Jewish public respond to antisemitism in many ways. Most Jews are not at either extreme in their views of antisemitism; nevertheless, some are. At the denial end of the continuum is complacency. Since antisemitism is not, for those who deny its existence, a reality—that is, overt, actions against Jews never take place, or when they do are random and trivial—there is no need for concern, and certainly no need for action. Jews at the denial end of the continuum are most likely to see their fellow Jews as "paranoid," looking for enemies that do not exist. Often, they believe that organizations that fight antisemitism are self-perpetuating, fostering myths of antisemitism in order to serve their own bureaucratic and institutional ends. Antisemitic acts are somehow explained away by those denying its presence. If a swastika is painted on a synagogue, they produce explanations as to why it is not an antisemitic act. The denial response is usually most prevalent and strongest among the most assimilated Jews.

Fear of antisemitism centers around issues of acceptance, social and political power or lack thereof, and concern for physical safety, individually or for all Jews. Such fear itself may result in several responses: withdrawal, the need for collective isolation within the larger society, or combativeness, the need to fight back, either as individuals or collectively through organizations and institutions. Again, most behavioral response will be between the two extremes. Sometimes, a combination of fear and denial may cause organizations and individuals to downplay the threat of antisemitism, while simultaneously calling for strategies to combat it. The rhetoric of community relations agencies frequently reflects this perceptual conflict. They play a balancing role, taking these disparate beliefs into account in their program planning. The results are often programs characterized by caution and wariness, sometimes aggressive, sometimes timid.

Those who want to feel that they are fully assimilated Americans are particularly likely to be a part of the denial contingent, generally supporting less emphasis on programs to combat antisemitism and advocating very careful assessment of a "Jewish" response to particular political and social issues. At the most extreme end of the fear continuum are those who have translated the combativeness that comes from fear into a more aggressive seek-and-destroy mode. Feeling that only Jews can take care of Jews, these individuals, or groups such as the Jewish Defense League, even advocate violence if they perceive it as necessary to protect Jewish interests.

Interestingly, at both ends of the continuum, both groups are so comfortable as Americans that neither questions their freedom within the larger society to state their views. In either extreme, both underplaying and overplaying their hands may be the result of a distorted view of how accepted, integrated, and "safe" they are within the American context.

The Experts' Views

Most social scientists and other scholars are unlikely to be found at either extreme of the fear and denial continuum. Few would argue that antisemitism no longer exists in the United States. Nor would many argue that Jews are immediately threatened by any large-scale antisemitic behavior. Most rest in the large gray area in between, wary and concerned. The primary evidence used by those on the denial side that antisemitism is not a problem is the widespread success of Jews in the United States and various polling data. As noted, these data have been interpreted as showing a rapid decline in antisemitic beliefs among non-Jews. For experts in the gray area, the same polling data are used, but the proportions of non-Jews still holding antisemitic views are interpreted to show the continued existence of antisemitism. For those most fearful of antisemitism, bits and pieces of information, including the rhetoric of extremist groups, isolated acts of discrimination, the ADL audits, and their own personal experiences are utilized in order to draw the conclusion that antisemitism is dangerously active in the United States. Those most afraid of antisemitism also link trends in the United States to those of other countries, particularly the Middle East and the Soviet Union, to corroborate their view that much of the world, including the United States, remains hostile to Jews.

Many scholarly observers agree on some issues relating to contemporary antisemitism in the United States. First, most agree that antisemitism in the United States is different from antisemitism in either Western or Eastern Europe. Jonathan Sarna, a historian at Hebrew Union College in Cincinnati, lists four differences. He argues first that Americans have always fought antisemitism freely in the United States. Jewish leadership has often publicly combatted American antisemitism. Second, antisemitism has been one, and usually not the major, form of racial and ethnic prejudice in the United States. Certainly, periods of anti-Catholicism have been more forceful, and the persecution of blacks is deeply ingrained in American so-

ciety. The third difference, Sarna states, is that antisemitism is foreign to American norms and can be properly labeled as un-American. Fourth, Sarna argues that
American politics "resists antisemitism." Seeking to build
broader-based political coalitions, American political parties cannot afford what he calls "the politics of hatred" of
alienating a block of Jewish voters.[1]

Most observers look at the American context and de-
note obvious differences. There have never been pogroms,
and antisemitism has never been part of a successful political ideology that has achieved any appreciable power at the
national level. Furthermore, there has never been any established Church in the United States. Even though America has been similar to other societies, with widespread
social and economic discrimination, sprinkled with large
reservoirs of antisemitic beliefs, structural antisemitism has
been the exception rather than the norm.

Along with the view that America is different, most
scholarly observers agree that antisemitism does not constitute a current threat in the United States. Still, observers
believe that antisemitic attitudes continue to be prevalent
in America to one degree or another. Many feel that vigilance remains necessary.

But the denial philosophy has its adherents. Recently,
Charles Silberman argued that "antisemitism is no longer a
significant factor in American Jewish life."[2] He cites the
economic, social, and political success of American Jews
since the 1960s as evidence in arguing that the old antisemitism is dead (old stereotypes and discrimination) and
that there is no possibility of a new antisemitism in the
future. Silberman states that Jews "have difficulty distinguishing between reality and their own worst
imaginings."[3]

Silberman's attitude is representative of those who

deny that antisemitism is at all significant in the context of modern-day Jewish success. To this contingent many Jews are victims of their own paranoia. In an article by Arthur Magida supporting this opinion, aptly entitled "Jewish Paranoia," Rabbi Eugene Borowitz was quoted as saying that Jews have a "special talent for discovering threats in even the best of circumstances. They are quick to see anti-Semitism lurking everywhere—in jokes about Jews, in criticisms about Israel, in pranks and vandalism that may choose Jewish targets more because they are handy and close than because they are Jewish."[4] But antisemitic jokes may reveal some level of prejudice, criticisms of Israel are often antisemitic in nature, and Jewish targets of vandalism may not be the random selection of misguided youths.

Some of those at the denial end of the continuum are actually responding to what they perceive to be the hysteria of other Jews. They seek to be a calming influence, placing any particular act of antisemitism into a broader context. Individuals who play this role attempt to determine the *motive* of perpetrators of antisemitic acts, in order to assess whether or not an act, such as painting a swastika on a synagogue, is "ideological" or just an activity of adolescent hostility. Of course, to the victims of such acts, the trauma may be deep, regardless of the perpetrator's motives.

Nevertheless, some of those who deny the existence of antisemitism may state the need for moderate response, careful analysis, and measured examination, expressing through actions rather than by statements their belief that antisemitism has not disappeared. But a few refuse to acknowledge the presence of antisemitism. Milton Himmelfarb has been one of the leading proponents of the denial philosophy, using polling data to substantiate his view. In an article on Jewish voting patterns, Himmelfarb argued that Jews do not even vote in their own self-interest because they have a paranoid view of antisemitism in the United States. He presented data showing that 47% of Jews believed that antisemitism is still a serious problem, alongside data from the same study showing that Jews believed by a very wide majority, 83% to 6%, that the United States has offered Jews more opportunities and freedom than any other diaspora country. Juxtaposing these two sets of polling data, Himmelfarb flippantly comments about what he obviously views as Jewish paranoia. In combination, these data, he states, "evoke a kind of pity for the poor little rich girl."[5] He is essentially mocking the Jewish public that holds these seemingly conflicting beliefs, when he himself believes that "prejudice and discrimination are lower than ever before."[6]

To those furthest along the denial continuum, all important discriminatory barriers are now gone. Any exhibitions of antisemitic behavior or attitudes are viewed as aberrations, and therefore trivial. Or they are not even antisemitic. Painting a swastika on a synagogue is usually explained away by such adherents as an adolescent prank, even though the adolescent chose a swastika for the symbol and a synagogue as the target. The effect on the victims is almost dismissed, because they should "recognize" the irrelevance of the act. All antisemitism is ultimately explained away. For example, rising black antisemitic beliefs are described as antiwhite and therefore somehow not anti-Jewish by those asserting that antisemitism is no longer significant. Antisemitic statements couched in anti-Zionist diatribes are viewed as third world philosophy, and again not antisemitic. It is odd that these Jews, who believe that other Jews are looking for antisemites under every rock, could be hit over the head by an antisemite (with the same rock) and either deny it took place or find a logical and rational argument for why the perpetrator was not really antisemitic.

Milton Himmelfarb, in a forum sponsored by *Present Tense* magazine that featured Charles Silberman and Marvin Schick, a columnist for the *Long Island Jewish World*, defended Silberman's thesis. Schick had challenged Silberman's optimistic premise that antisemitism is no longer a major factor shaping the lives of American Jews. Himmelfarb, the third panelist in the forum, supported Charles Silberman's book, saying that Jews "attack the messenger that brings them good news."[7] He believes that most American Jews are paranoid, and that "quite simply, we do not allow the facts to invalidate our logic."[8] Clearly, the same can be said for those who are so adamant about dismissing the antisemitism that still persists in the United States.

On the other hand, there are numbers of Jews who see antisemitism in every act, deed, and word of the gentile world. Like those at the denial end of the continuum, they account for only a small proportion of all Jews. Meir Kahane, founder of the Jewish Defense League (JDL) and a prominent spokesman for this group, argues vociferously against relying on non-Jews or on the American system alone. "Nor will all the efforts to mingle with the gentile, to prove to him our melting-pot qualities, succeed in our winning favor in his eyes in time of crisis," he stated in 1971. "At best we are tolerated; the tolerance, sooner or later, wears thin. All our attempts to compromise and tailor our Jewishness so that it may prove acceptable to a modern world are foolish, self-hating moves that, properly, earn us nothing but the contempt of the gentile."[9] In this view, the world has a clear delineation, a "them" and an "us." Some may not view Kahane as an "expert," but he speaks for Jews at the fear end of the continuum.

Whatever real progress American Jews have made in developing intergroup cooperation is trivialized by these views. To some, the United States is merely another society waiting to exploit the Jewish minority as a scapegoat in times of economic or social crisis. Individuals who are the most concerned about antisemitism existing everywhere use the isolated incidents of antisemitism coupled with the rhetoric of either the right or the left, but usually the right, as their primary evidence of antisemitism's prevalence. The collective history of Jews, along with continued antisemitic rhetoric from around the world, corroborates the composite picture. Furthermore, there is a continuous barrage of information about the danger of antisemitism, coming primarily from the Anti-Defamation League and, more recently, the Wiesenthal Center. The ADL consistently publishes information on the radical left and right, which finds its way into both the Jewish and the general press. Each release of one of these documents is used by those who are most fearful to substantiate their views.[10]

Each antisemitic incident is viewed as part of the ultimate move toward another Holocaust. This fear, the ultimate expression of antisemitism, is incorporated into this group's view of America as simply another temporary good time for Jews. An article in the *Baltimore Jewish Times*, which looked at antisemitic literature spread by hate groups, noted: "Those who say 'It can't happen here' should be reminded that not very far from Baltimore—only a 45 minute drive from the White House—at Loudon, Virginia, Lyndon H. LaRouche Jr., has recently established on a $2.3 million property the national headquarters of his well-read anti-Semitic, neo-Nazi organization which lists as its enemies 'narcotic gangsters, liberals, Zionists, agents of Moscow, the Rockefellers, the Trilateral Commission, the Queen of England and international terrorism."[11] The article concludes by saying, "Not only *can* it happen here; it *is* happening here."[12] For example, Sylvia Mandelbaum, writing from Safed, Israel, warned American Jews that they must leave the United States for Israel. In describing all sorts of antisemitic incidents, she says: "These are signs of the times . . . can we see them? Can we hear them? Do we understand them? Jews are guests in their host country for as long as the host pleases. It appears that Jews have outworn their welcome."[13] After raising the specter of discrimination and, ultimately, the Holocaust, she argues that a safe climate exists only in Israel.

For those at the most extreme end of the fear continuum, antisemitism is not assessed solely in terms of levels of discrimination, or the rise and fall of antisemitic attitudes, but rather whether or not American Jews will be subjected to mass violence or murder. While most Jews classify the Holocaust as a unique historical event within the context of societies that are unlike those of the United States (even though they are wary about potential signals), those at the fear end of the continuum cannot distinguish between the United States and other societies at all. Therefore, the Holocaust is not just a threat that can happen at almost any time, it is just around the corner.

Most observers take the middle road, neither oblivious nor fearful. An article by one Jewish author, Rochelle Wolk, which analyzed Jewish perceptions of antisemitism, was entitled "Prophecy or Paranoia?"[14] The title alone represents the more extreme views of Jewish perceptions of antisemitism: prophecy of another Holocaust, and paranoia about unreal enemies, the myth or reality of the levels of antisemitism in the United States today. Abraham Foxman, of the Anti-Defamation League says that the Jewish community may be affected by "schizophrenia."[15] We live, he says, in what we might call the other "promised land," and yet, he continues, there is "uneasiness, a tension, and an anxiety."[16] Most Jewish observers neither predict nor fear another Holocaust, but neither are they sanguine that antisemitism is no longer a potential threat in the United States.

Those who study antisemitism are far from unified in their assessment of, reactions to, and proposals for combatting antisemitism. Additionally, the messages professionals and experts relay to the Jewish public are frequently contradictory. Jews are told of the need to be vigilant, often at the same time as community relations professionals are reassuring the Jewish community of their safety. If the Jewish public is unsure of how to realistically assess antisemitism, they are only mirroring the contradictions inherent in the opinions and strategies of their experts and leaders. Earl Raab, the former executive director of the San Francisco Jewish Community Relations Council, offers an insightful summary of the nature of this dilemma. He notes that "American Jews have been supplied evidence that antisemitic attitudes are decreasing while antisemitic incidents are increasing. In their innocence, many Jews believe that these two signals are incompatible. They are not. Jews perceive no real growth in economic or social discrimination against Jews, nor Neo-Nazi groups; but public expressions of antisemitism seem more common, along with warnings about growing antisemitism from their non-Jewish friends. Complacency derives from reliance on one set of signals; despair derives from reliance on another set. Neither mood is warranted."[17] Raab is most concerned not with a growing cadre or reservoir of antisemitic beliefs, or the growing ranks of antisemites, but rather with the "loosening of constraint for those who are already in the anti-Semitic ranks, and a spurt in commodity anti-Semitism around specific issues."[18] Anti-Israelism is one such issue. For

Raab, a keen observer of the state of antisemitism in the United States, unpleasant signs in the 1980s point to the need for action on the part of the Jewish community, measured action commensurate with both the degree and the nature of antisemitism in the United States. His views are shared by most American Jews.

Jews remain sensitive, and sensibly so. But those who see no antisemitism and those who see only antisemitism everywhere represent minorities, relatively small ones, of American Jewish experts and commentators and the constituencies whose views they reflect. What scholars, leaders, and other experts see, as well as the divergent views they represent, is mirrored in the perception of the Jewish community at large.

Views from the Grass Roots

What can be seen from the evidence gleaned from community studies, as well as from personal interviews that follow, is that Jews do not see a great deal of active antisemitism in the United States. Yet they are worried about its latent potential. Their overall assessment is neither alarmist nor overly pacific.

Interviews conducted in cities across the country demonstrate that Jews are much more concerned with issues of assimilation and internal division within the Jewish community than with antisemitism. In a 1984 national poll of Jews, 40% of the respondents agreed that antisemitism in America is currently not a serious problem for American Jews. However, 46% disagreed with this statement, viewing contemporary antisemitism in the United States as problematic, while an additional 14% were not sure whether or not antisemitism poses a serious problem for today's American Jews[19] (see Table 4-1). Furthermore,

77% of those surveyed in 1984 agreed that antisemitism in America may become a serious problem in the future. While some analysts use the high proportion of Jews who say that antisemitism is a serious problem as a sign of a "paranoid" populace, they misunderstand the meaning of the evaluation. The vast majority of Jews do not believe that there is a great deal of antisemitism, either in their own communities or in the United States today. Since Jews view antisemitism as a potential threat, they would naturally label it serious. Such an analysis does not indicate that most Jews see antisemitism as very "active" in the United States.

Samples of Jewish populations in seven cities were asked a series of questions, in both community studies and personal interviews, about how much antisemitism they believe exists in their local community. Antisemitism was not defined by the interviewer as actions or attitudes of non-Jews but was left to the self-definition of the respondent. The vast majority of Jews see little or a moderate amount of antisemitism in their communities. For example, nearly three out of every four Jews in both Baltimore and Kansas City saw little or a moderate amount of antisemitism in their communities, compared to about four out of five in Worcester, Massachusetts, and Washington, D.C. At the same time, relatively small proportions believe that a great deal of antisemitism exists in the community, or that none exists at all. Generally, 10% or less of the population believe that no antisemitism exists, and around 10% or less in most communities believe that a great deal exists, as do 17% of the Jews in Baltimore (see Table 4-2). Additionally, in the personal interviews conducted in 1987 with Jews from all over the country, nearly all of the respondents answered that little or a moderate amount of antisemitism existed in the United States, while one respondent said a great deal, and no one said none.

Collectively, Jews do not believe that antisemitism has disappeared, nor do they believe that it is pervasive in their communities. Examination of these data by age, sex, occupation, and other factors does not reveal widespread differences in perceptions.

Lifetime experience with antisemitism is also used as a measure that may shape perceptions. Respondents in many communities were asked how much antisemitism they had experienced in their lifetime. Generally, the proportions that had experienced a great deal of antisemitism in their lifetime range from just below 10% to a high of 15%. At the same time, between 10 and 20% indicated that they had experienced none. In nearly all cities, nearly one out of every two Jews said that they had experienced little antisemitism in their lifetime, with the remainder saying they had experienced a moderate amount (see Table 4-3).

Interestingly, respondents over the age of 65, those who lived during the days of Father Coughlin and other forms of antisemitism prevalent at the time, do not for the most part believe that they have personally experienced a great deal of antisemitism in their own lifetime. Rather, younger Jews in many communities are more likely than those over 65 to say that they have experienced a great deal or a moderate amount of antisemitism. Thus, even among those generations that would have been subjected to more overt antisemitic attitudes and discrimination, the vast majority do not believe that they have personally experienced a great deal of antisemitism in their own lifetime.

Similar results were found in the personal interviews. Nearly all of the respondents said that they had experienced either little or a moderate amount of antisemitism in their lifetime, with most saying little. As noted in the previous chapter, issues relating to assimilation and factionalism within the Jewish community are viewed by most respondents as the single most important problem facing Jews in the United States today. In the late 1980s, the vast majority of Jews, when asked about a multitude of issues facing the Jewish community, do not place anti-semitism at the top of their list of concerns. Given percep-tions of how much antisemitism currently exists in either their communities or the United States, or how much per-sonal experience individuals have had with antisemitism, this answer should come as no surprise.

The problem of antisemitism, while not perceived as the foremost difficulty facing the Jewish community, is nevertheless of continued concern. Almost all of the re-spondents in the personal interviews conducted in 1987 answered that programs to combat antisemitism are very important, as did large proportions of respondents in all community studies. Eighty percent of respondents in community studies in San Francisco, Essex and Morris counties, New Jersey, and Worcester, Massachusetts, view such programs as very important. Other issues of concern included the separation of church and state, inter-marriage, and Jewish education.

As a minority religious group, Jews are highly sen-sitive to church–state issues and consistently support the necessity of maintaining clear distinctions. In a 1984 sur-vey of the political attitudes of American Jews, most re-spondents opposed lowering barriers between church and state, voicing opposition to tax credits for private or paro-chial schools and school prayer.[20] Church and state sepa-ration, particularly concerning its bearing on Jews, is also seen as very important by the majority of those personally interviewed in 1987. Indeed, when asked which they viewed as more important to the Jewish people, the sepa-ration of church and state or programs to combat anti-semitism, nearly all the respondents in the personal inter-views indicated that separation of church and state was more important. As Joel Reck, president of the Jewish Community Relations Council of Boston, stated: "The separation of church and state provides Jews with governmental support for the proposition that people can be Jews and be treated equally under the Constitution, and with equal protection under the Constitution. If that breaks down, and if, for example, the country were to become a Christian country, then in a whole host of ways it would be second-class citizen status to be a Jew. That would, in fact, undoubtedly lead to antisemitism, number one. Number two, it would lead to subtle forms of discrimination which, even if they don't rise to the level that you would call antisemitism, wouldn't be able to be eliminated as a matter of law."[21]

Martin Stein, the current National Chairman of the United Jewish Appeal, echoed this sentiment. The breakdown of church and state separation, he said, is "the forerunner of visible antisemitism. Once there is a state church, once you don't belong, once you're not a part, you can lose your citizenship. Eventually it provides great opportunities for antisemites. As long as church and state are separated, obviously you have a barrier that is good for all minorities. . . ."[22]

Nearly all the respondents saw an obvious connection between the breakdown of church and state and the increased possibility of uncontained antisemitism. In that sense, as far as Jews are concerned, the greatest program or set of programs to combat antisemitism rests in the legal framework provided at all levels of government. The respondents, reflecting the majority view of American Jews, recognize that maximum protection is provided by laws and statutes, as opposed to attempting to control antisemitism through other mechanisms. While other programs are deemed important, the legal framework is seen as most critical. But in most Jewish minds, the separation of church and state and the issue of antisemitism are inextricably linked. Therefore, Jews equate a theoretical constitutional issue such as church–state separation as an institutional bulwark against antisemitic actions.

On occasion, some individuals see the relationship in reverse. For example, Rabbi Mark Cooper of Temple Israel, Natick, Massachusetts, said that antisemitism would "directly affect our lives and our circumstances and our ability to freely engage in the practice of Judaism in this country. The separation of church and state would not necessarily affect that, though I see the two as interrelated really, ultimately."[23] Whether the respondent views antisemitism as a threat leading to the breakdown of church and state or vice versa, the ultimate result, persecution of Jews and other minorities, is seen as inevitable.

Antisemitism over Time

Nearly all of those surveyed in personal interviews agree that there is less antisemitism in the United States today than there was before World War II. Generally, individuals believe that the war and the immediate postwar period ushered in a new era of greater knowledge among and between ethnic and racial groups, and, consequently, a greater tolerance as well. However, respondents are not as unified when asked whether antisemitism has continued to decrease in the years following the 1950s. More specifically, many respondents question whether antisemitism has continued to decline since the 1970s, while others assert that it is and has been steadily diminishing.

Frequently respondents, when asked to assess levels of antisemitism over time, stated the difficulty of this undertaking because of the changing nature of antisemitism. The nature and expression of antisemitism, they pointed out, adapt to the times. Some of those interviewed believe that the war and the Holocaust, coupled with rising Jewish affluence and influence, served to change the norms of antisemitic expression among non-Jews. For example, Mitch Orlik, the associate director of the Columbus Jewish Federation, believes that there is "less overt antisemitism because there is more overt Jewish strength. There are a larger number of Jews identified by non-Jews as 'influential,' people with influence, people who can induce change. Therefore there is less 'overt' antisemitism."[24] However, this does not mean that antisemitism has necessarily decreased. "I'm not sure there is less antisemitism *overall*," he went on to say, "there is just less overt antisemitism."[25] Most people believe that a combination of less antisemitism and less overt expression characterizes the change from the prewar period.

While respondents are not quite as unanimous in their belief that there is less antisemitism today than in the 1950s, the great majority do feel that the level has declined. For the most part, respondents say that discriminatory barriers have broken down, a great deal of progress has been made, and, as one respondent noted, there is "a much greater ethnic tolerance today than the 1950s generally." Much of the perception that expressions of antisemitism have decreased since the 1950s is tied to this increased acceptance and greater intergroup tolerance. In other words, improvements for Jews are linked in many people's minds to the general improvement in racial and ethnic attitudes. Clearly, Jews examine their positions as one ethnic group within the larger framework of American society. Along with other minority groups, Jews are the beneficiaries of clear progress in civil rights legislation.

However, some Jews are beginning to believe that the best times may be over, or at least temporarily in jeopardy. For example, the survey of the Jewish community in

Rochester, New York, asked respondents whether they believed there was more or less antisemitism than there was ten years ago. A total of 36% felt there was more, while 20% said there was less, and 37% felt that the level of antisemitism was about the same. Younger Jews were more likely to say that there is more antisemitism than there was ten years ago, when most were in their early 20s or late teens. A combination of factors may account for these findings. First, recent events, particularly as they relate to Israel and the rhetoric of extremist groups on the right, have made Jews more sensitive to antisemitism once again. Furthermore, younger Jews have only the benchmarks of periods of lower amounts of antisemitism in the 1960s and 1970s, as opposed to the 1940s or 1930s, with which to compare.

The personal interviews echo these assessments and premonitions. Arguing that things are about the same in the 1980s as they were ten years ago, one respondent said that there are ''events that come up that affect how people feel for the short term. I'm sure that a good example is 1973, the era of the oil embargo which caused a rise in antisemitism when Americans had to wait in line for gas and had to pay higher prices for oil, and then there were gas rationings and things like that. And you saw bumper stickers: 'Burn Jews Not Oil,' 'When You Run Out of Oil, Burn Jews.' You saw pretty ugly things because people made the connection between the Arab oil embargo. . . .''[26] Other respondents feel that certain incidents calculated by the Jewish community to cause an increase in antisemitism, such as the Pollard spy case, the Israeli role in the Iran–Contra affair, and the Wall Street insider trading scandal, have not resulted in appreciable rises in antisemitism. However, they continue to be watchful of such events.

All respondents were unified on one point: An increase in antisemitism will inevitably occur, to some degree, during times of economic crisis. For all their security in America, this, they believe, is a constant. A variety of events, such as the war in Lebanon or public events that involve Jews, are watched in order to determine their effect on the economy, and the resultant behavior of the non-Jewish public. Some Jews are particularly sensitive about each and every issue that involves Jews and the relationship of these issues or events to antisemitism. As one respondent noted, even isolated incidents may produce "backlash". "If someone is arrested for child molesting, I want to know, 'Is he Jewish?'" she said, "because I am always afraid that somehow that will reinforce the stereotype that someone might have that Jews are bad people, and therefore bring down more antisemitism, so I'm sensitive to it."[27] Others mentioned fear of antisemitic "fallout" from the widely publicized insider trading scandals, which involved several prominent Jews. Many respondents were demonstrably uneasy over the potential influence of such negative publicity. Polls showed that no such fallout, at least of a measurable sort, occurred.

Anti-Israel sentiment and propaganda are also seen as one of the factors affecting perceptions of increased antisemitism in the 1980s. As a president of a federation in a major metropolitan area stated, "I think the Arabs are getting more sophisticated in their public relations, stronger lobbies. Latent antisemitism projects itself in lobbying against Israel."[28] The frequency with which Israel appears in the news, and the nature of such news coverage, influences the Jewish outlook.

Wariness about the present and the future are an integral component in the Jewish psyche in dealing with antisemitism. While Jews assess antisemitism in the past and the present, their feelings are also colored by attempts to assess how antisemitic attitudes and behaviors will affect

Jews in the future. When respondents were asked whether or not they foresee more or less antisemitism in the United States ten years in the future, answers were thoughtful and well qualified. Not a single respondent optimistically said that antisemitism would disappear. As Ruth Fein of Boston stated: "I don't think there will ever be a time in which there is no antisemitism. I think we have probably reached a good low point with which we can live as Americans and as Jews. But there will always be outcroppings, incidents, people who for one reason or another need to use antisemitism as a tool, and that's when I think you begin to see a reprise. And we will have that."[29] When further asked whether or not antisemitism might threaten the security of Jews in the American society of the future, she went on to say that "I will never be one to say it can't happen here because I believe it can happen anywhere, given the proper set of circumstances. . . . At the moment it's good, as long as America remains the kind of society that it is it will be okay. But that can change. It can change with a change of party. It can change with a horrible, horrible depression—worse than we have seen in the past. It could change with a real military defeat. There are all kinds of ways in which it can change."[30]

Neil Kominsky, a rabbi at Harvard-Radcliffe Hillel, when asked about his prognosis for ten years from now, said that he held two differing views of what the future might hold. "I have optimistic and pessimistic scenarios," he said. "My optimistic scenario says that the New Right has shot itself irretrievably in the foot, between the Iran–Contra business and the collapse of a couple of major evangelical empires, and in consequence there will be a return to a more middle-of-the-road suspicion of absolutist ideas which will, I think, result in less antisemitism. An alternative model says that the lower middle classes in the great American heartland, as well as the black and Hispanic underclasses, are going to experience more economic pressure, more technological displacement, and more sense of powerlessness. And that would, I think, potentially result in an increase in antisemitism."[31] The reluctance of many respondents to assess future levels of antisemitism demonstrates that, although Jews may be able to examine present circumstances and be assured about their present security, they are unable to believe that this level of security is unalterable. The specter of future antisemitism looms.

Personal Experiences with Antisemitism

A majority of Jews said that they have *not* personally experienced antisemitism in the last 12 months. In community surveys, whether conducted in the early 1980s, in the mid-1980s, or toward the end of this decade, about 17 to 28% of those asked said that they experienced antisemitism in the 12-month period prior to being surveyed. This included, for example, 22% in Worcester, Massachusetts, 21% in Baltimore, 17% in Morris and Essex counties, New Jersey, 23% in Kansas City, and 28% in Washington, D.C. (see Table 4-4). It is difficult to assess whether or not the time period or the community accounts for the differences in the proportions of those who say that they experienced antisemitism in the 12-month period. Nevertheless, a substantial proportion say that they have experienced antisemitism in some way.

Given the continued prevalence of antisemitic sentiment shown in Chapter Two, it should come as no surprise that appreciable proportions of Jews, especially since they are attuned to potential threats, should encounter antisemitic attitudes and actions. While antisemitism has declined in its overt expression since the 1930s and 1950s, both the ADL audits and the public opinion polls show that these attitudes, while diminished, are still widespread. Therefore, it is quite logical that substantial proportions of Jews should come in contact with expressions of antisemitism, since Jews operate freely within their own subculture and American culture as well.

Younger Jews, those under the age of 35, are far more likely to say that they have experienced antisemitism in the 12-month period. Well over half of the 18- to 24-year-olds in Kansas City and Atlantic City, for example, said that they experienced antisemitism in the 12-month period, as did over 40% of those between 18 and 35 in St. Louis and 46% of the 18- to 35-year-olds in Washington D.C. Jews over the age of 65 are the least likely to say that they experienced antisemitism in the 12-month period. Two explanations for the disparate results among age groups may be offered. The first is that younger Jews are much more likely, through school, work, and a proclivity to live in non-Jewish neighborhoods, to have contact with greater numbers of non-Jews. Therefore, the prospect for an antisemitic encounter is much greater than for Jews who might have more exclusively Jewish contacts. At the same time, those over the age of 65 are far more likely to live in Jewish neighborhoods, be retired, and have all Jewish friends. The opportunity for contacts with non-Jews, and therefore an antisemitic experience, is greatly reduced.

A second explanation may lie in the perspective that comes from different generational experiences with antisemitism. Older Jews have the context of overt discriminatory behaviors in housing, employment, and other dimensions of American life. What may seem to be overt antisemitism to a younger person in the 1980s may be completely passed off by someone who is older. On the flip side, younger Jews who have had little experience with employment or housing discrimination may be more alert to antisemitic remarks. Furthermore, they have been fully acculturated as third- and fourth-generation Americans with a normative rejection of racial and religious exclusion. Therefore, actual experiences with discriminatory behavior may be more quickly noticed and noted by younger Jews.

Those who say that they experienced antisemitism personally are not as a matter of course predisposed to search it out. Interestingly, those who believe that there is a great deal of antisemitism in their community or in the United States are not necessarily the ones who say that they have experienced antisemitism. Therefore, there does not appear to be a predilection to look for antisemitism where it does not exist. This distinction must be drawn. A predisposition to manufacture antisemitic experiences because of the belief that a great deal of antisemitism is prevalent has not been demonstrated. In many cases, those experiencing antisemitism are people who are alert to and reject racial and ethnic prejudice, including jokes, rather than people indulging in some "paranoid seeking out of antisemites," as one respondent put it, "under every rock."

What kinds of antisemitic incidents do respondents in community surveys report experiencing? Most of those reporting experiences with antisemitism say that they have heard an antisemitic remark in their neighborhoods, in social gatherings, or at work. The vast majority of them occur at work. Some hear remarks, statements of anti-Jewishness from in-laws or friends where there is an intermarried couple. The kinds of antisemitism that Jews report experiencing are consistent with the evidence available from public opinion polls among non-Jews and the monitoring efforts of Jewish community relations agencies. Most stated experiences of antisemitism do not involve physical attacks or blatant discrimination.

In each case where these interviews were conducted, the antisemitic remarks or experiences of other kinds were recorded. Examination of what people say indicates that most remarks were antisemitic in nature. For example, one respondent tells the following story: "My roommate owed me a lot of money for a long period of time. I asked her when she'd be able to return it and suggested maybe she could borrow it from her father. My roommate's father is Jewish, her mother isn't, and she herself doesn't think of herself as Jewish. Anyway, my roommate's boyfriend said about her father: 'Oh, that Jew—he'd never give her a penny!' I got very upset, told him that if he ever said anything like that again, I'd throw him out of my apartment. A while later it happened again. This boyfriend, Rick, was talking about some kind of bargain he had made and he said, 'Boy, I really jewed him down.' I said, 'Where did you get that expression?' and he said, 'Oh, it's the truth. That's what they're like.' He thought it was a statement of fact. I think that it's dangerous to have people who, even after you have explained that it is offensive, believe it's a statement of fact."

Stories like these were routinely recorded by the interviewers. Most of those who said that they experienced an antisemitic remark heard expressions such as "kike" or "jew him down," or negative references to characteristics of Jews. Almost none of the respondents reported hearing anti-Israel expressions and interpreting them as antisemitic. On occasion, some of the incidents are more difficult to interpret. For example, one respondent with a Jewish surname tells the following incident: "I was going home for the break but had to change my flight time. I knew that the fares would be different, but the travel agent said I could take care of it at the ticket counter. I got to the ticket counter for Air Canada and explained to the agent behind the desk what the travel agent had said. The agent behind the ticket counter, a young woman, asked me how I planned to pay for the difference. 'By credit card,' I told her. 'I should have known by your name,' she said. I didn't know how to respond. I just thought, all those years of Hebrew school and I can't even think of what to say." The meaning of this incident is less clear. Much of it would depend on the intonation, facial expression, and other attributes of the ticket agent. Even then, one cannot be exactly sure that an antisemitic slur was being made.

Furthermore, some of the other comments that are recorded as antisemitic by the interviewers are clearly not antisemitic. These are more rare, but they do appear. Therefore, comments such as these have been removed from the computations of antisemitic remarks, even though they were reported as such by the respondent.

Encountering antisemitism in terms of remarks is experienced by substantial proportions of Jews. When they say they are personally experiencing antisemitism, this is its most common form. However, there are those who claim they have been denied access to certain housing units or who say they have experienced job discrimination because they are Jewish. These claims are more difficult to verify and substantiate. Relatively few of those who say that they experienced antisemitism reported overt discrimination. Rather, they felt and sensed it. Incidents of overt antisemitism are rarely reported and are difficult to prove or disprove. Nevertheless, while they cannot be documented as instances of overt antisemitism, they do influence perceptions about the presence of antisemitism in contemporary America.

The vast majority of those who say they have experienced antisemitism in the previous year do not report it to any organization or institution. They may tell friends or family about what happened. But almost universally they do not report it to community relations agencies, to other Jewish organizations, or to local, state, or federal agencies. Sometimes they report it to an employer and work out the problem internally.

When asked why they do not report it, the vast majority say that they did not know to whom it should be reported, that they could not prove it, that they handled it themselves, that reporting it would do no good, or that they did not want to make trouble (see Table 4-5). "I just let it go," commented one respondent, when asked why she had not reported her experience. "I guess I figured, 'What could they really do?' "[32]

In terms of the Jewish community's collective knowledge about antisemitism, it is critically important that the vast majority of these experiences go unreported. Most antisemitism goes unnoticed and unexamined because these incidents come to nobody's attention, except that of the individual or the immediate family. It can also be assumed that some measure of discriminatory behavior still occurs, as recorded through personal experiences of those interviewed. "It did not occur to me" is a common response of those asked why they did not report their antisemitic experience. Because many of those experiencing antisemitism do not report these incidents, the phenomenon is unknown to community relations agencies and others.

It is no wonder, then, that some dissonance exists between what is perceived to be the grass roots experience with antisemitism and the views of some social scientists and community relations professionals. Part of the dissonance can be explained by the lack of communication between community relations professionals and the Jewish public itself.

Relying only on limited interpretations about the attitudes from polls of non-Jews, and the success of Jews, it is logical that many observers have concluded that discriminatory behavior has all but ceased to exist. Jewish organizations have failed to undertake systematic audits and investigations of discrimination against Jews. But since most Jews do not report such incidents, there seems to be little incentive to do so. This cycle prevents any clear assessment of the true state of discrimination against Jews.

Jewish Assessments of the Antisemitism of Other Americans

Surveys periodically assess the proportions of non-Jews holding specific beliefs and attitudes regarding Jews. However, social scientists have already investigated what proportion of non-Jews it is that *Jews* feel are antisemitic. Several surveys asked respondents to assess levels of antisemitic attitudes and behavior of different non-Jewish groups. The respondents were instructed to classify Americans into three categories: (1) Americans who were not antisemitic at all (that is, those having no antisemitic beliefs and not acting out antisemitic attitudes in any way); (2) those who were passively antisemitic (that is, those holding antisemitic beliefs or attitudes but not acting on them); and (3) those who were actively antisemitic (those Americans who express antisemitic beliefs and attitudes, and act on them). Most of those interviewed believed that less than 20% of Americans, usually the lower end of this range, are actively antisemitic. At the same time, only 1 to 20% of Americans were believed to hold no antisemitic beliefs at all. The vast majority of respondents believed that more than half of all non-Jewish Americans are passively antisemitic, that is, hold antisemitic beliefs and attitudes but do not necessarily act on them. However, while not acting on these beliefs, they may not react against others who do. Much of the uneasiness expressed by the Jewish community focuses on this belief. The proportion of non-Jews who might be expected to make antisemitic remarks or behave in an antisemitic way, given their levels of antisemitic beliefs, is consistent with the proportion of Jews saying they experienced antisemitism in the past year. While neither proportion constitutes a majority, they are not insignificant.

Combatting Antisemitism: Who Is Perceived as Threatening

Despite the rise of antisemitic sentiment among some groups on the political left, Jews continue to believe that the political right remains the greatest potential threat to Jews. A 1984 study commissioned by the American Jewish Committee indicated that Jews are much more likely to think that Republicans and Conservatives rather than Democrats and Liberals are antisemitic. Fundamentalist groups were also viewed with suspicion (see Table 4-6). A survey of Rochester, New York, Jewish community leaders corroborates these findings. Even though some Jews now vote Republican, Jews continue to support Democrats and Independents in greater proportions.

Of all the groups, blacks are most often considered antisemitic by Jewish respondents.[33] But blacks are not identified with the political right. The suspicion of blacks is largely a reflection of the threat perceived as a result of antisemitic statements made by black leadership, including Jesse Jackson and, most recently, Louis Farrakhan. According to findings from Steven Cohen's 1984 study of the political attitudes of Jews, a much higher proportion of Jews answered affirmatively to the question "Is Jesse Jackson antisemitic?" than believed that "most" or "many" blacks were antisemitic.[34] Blacks are also seen as being more anti-Israel than many other groups. However, while blacks are most frequently perceived by Jews as antisemitic, they are not seen as the most dangerous group.

Right-wing extremist groups, such as the Ku Klux Klan, Aryan Nations, or Posse Comitatus, use the most blatant antisemitic rhetoric, are known to commit violent antisemitic acts, and are the most visible to the Jewish public. Respondents in both community studies and personal interviews were asked whether or not these extremist groups pose a threat to Jews. A variety of answers was given. While some respondents feel that their influence is minimal, and that their overall power is relatively small, others say that they pose a threat to individual Jews, and thus are viewed as a problem. Their present influence is not considered to be very great. One respondent in a personal interview indicated that they (extremists) have "no effect on anybody other than their own members. They influence people in the South, maybe, but I think the average guy who doesn't have an opinion isn't going to be swayed by the Ku Klux Klan or the Posse Comitatus." Many view these groups, in the words of another respondent, as "bizarre," going on to say that they are simply not "credible to the majority of the American public."

However, the presence of such groups is far from reassuring. "Anybody who holds guns and commits murder is a threat," stated one respondent. "Are they a threat to the existence of the Jewish community in the United States?" he continued. "No. Are they a threat to the shifting of public opinion? No. Are they a threat to the life, health and happiness of individual visible Jews? Absolutely!" And while nearly all of the respondents in the personal interviews do not consider them a current threat, the opinion that "as long as they are around, they are a threat in the future" is commonly expressed. "There is a potential, a climate may develop in the future for them to grow," the respondent explained.

Concern about extremism, particularly right-wing extremism, is a function of collective Jewish wariness and vigilance. Concern is less focused on the present because it is assumed that the vast majority of Americans will reject extremist views. Most Jews believe that these groups require constant monitoring by both Jewish and governmental groups to prevent extremists from extending their influence.

The fear of right-wing extremist groups is sometimes coupled with a general fear of the religious right and conservative politics in general. Together they are viewed as a collectivity that attacks the fundamental principles of church and state separation. Therefore, they are viewed as a threat because of their attempts to Christianize America. In the 1984 study of American Jews commissioned by the American Jewish Committee, respondents were asked to assess the antisemitic levels of various religious groups. Almost one-fifth of all respondents, 19%, responded that most Fundamentalist Protestants are antisemitic, compared with 12% expressing the same opinion of mainstream Protestants, and 11% stating that they perceive most Catholics as antisemitic. Of all religious groups, Fundamentalist Protestants are viewed with the most suspicion by American Jews. Ultimately, the religious right, in its more mainstream legitimate form, is viewed as more dangerous than the extremist right or the extremist left.

Jewish support for the Democratic Party and many liberal social movements and organizations is well documented. Jews have favored Democratic Party candidates more than any other religious or white ethnic group. Although there has been a decline in the proportions of Jews supporting Democratic candidates (American Jews' identification with the Democratic Party, as determined in the 1981 to 1984 National Surveys of American Jews, declined from 65% in 1981, to 59% in 1983, to 56% in 1984),[35] there has not been a shift to the political right. American Jews continue to endorse liberal positions and to remain suspicious of Conservatives and Republicans. Jews assess most or many Republicans as antisemitic four times as often as Democrats (29 to 7%) while Conservatives outscored Liberals by a proportion of 35 to 8%.

Jews' assessments of political groups are closely related to their sensitivity to antisemitism. Steven Cohen elucidated, in his 1984 study, the correlation between fears of right- and left-wing antisemitism and political orientation. Those who perceive more right-wing than left-wing antisemitism are more often Liberals, while conservative respondents are more likely to perceive a greater threat of antisemitism arising from the left.[36] However, despite all hypotheses to the contrary, the largest proportions of Jews continue to adhere to liberal views and support Democratic candidates.

The extremist left is feared primarily for its attitudes, rhetoric, and behavior toward Israel. For most Jews, anti-Israelism and anti-Zionism are clearly antisemitism. While some of the respondents believe that one can be opposed to the political entity of Israel and still like Jews, most agree with one respondent, who said, "I think that people don't generally make a distinction between Jews and Israel."[37] At the same time, there is general agreement with Alan Goldstein of Boston. "I think that there is a clear connection between Israel and American Jews," he stated, "and I think people relate them in the same period. Non-Jews, I think, look at them as one and the same. It's a Jewish state. There are Jews here. Well, I think that the majority of statements [anti-Israel] are somewhat anti-semitic. That's without the comment of the legislator saying that we spend far too much on Israel compared to what we spend proportionately on the rest of the world. If we take those kinds of things where they are entitled to be criticized out of the picture and deal with the general criticisms, I think that they do have antisemitism in those terms."[38]

Martin Stein, National Chairman of the United Jewish Appeal, summarizes the way many Jews view anti-Israel statements. "People that don't like Jews don't like Jews, and they call it whatever they want," he said. "People who want to be anti-Israel are the more sophisticated anti-semites."[39] Israel is discussed constantly in the media, often in negative terms. Many see the obsession with Israel translated as an obsession with Jews, much of it negative. The intuition of most Jews that much of the anti-Israelism and anti-Zionism rhetoric is linked to anti-semitism seems to be sensibly concluded.

The views regarding which non-Jewish groups are antisemitic have serious implications for Jewish behavior. More than any other factors, these perceptions affect the way Jews organize, which causes they support, and how they vote. These issues are discussed more fully in the conclusion of this book.

Non-Jewish Feelings as a Measuring Device of Jewish Concern

Numerous studies undertaken periodically, which document Jewish and non-Jewish opinions and feelings about each other, demonstrate that while Jews may be more suspicious of non-Jews than survey evidence supports, their fears are not as exaggerated as some analysts profess. The Jewish public is barraged with studies of how Americans feel about them, how Catholics, Protestants, Fundamentalists, blacks, and other groups assess various characteristics of the Jewish populace. Many of these surveys indicate that antisemitic sentiments have declined in the past few decades. Jewish institutions frequently publicize these survey results as a means of demonstrating to the Jewish public the increasing awareness and acceptance of Jews by the non-Jewish population. Yet these numbers sometimes look far from positive to the Jewish public. They demonstrate that a substantial share of the non-Jewish populace continues to adhere to antisemitic attitudes and beliefs.

Some of the dissonance that is evident in Jewish and non-Jewish beliefs is the result of methodologically flawed survey research analysis. This includes not asking the questions accurately, comparing statistics that cannot be compared, and failing to follow up with more sophisticated and sensitive measuring tools in order to explore the subtle differences between what Jews are really expressing and what non-Jews really feel and believe, as well as how they act.

A second point should be considered. Reports such as the 1981 Yankelovich study rely on non-Jewish attitudes and perceptions, rather than using Jewish experiences and perceptions as the barometer. A more logical examination might look at the data the other way around. Why is it assumed that non-Jews are telling the truth and Jews are paranoid? Perhaps non-Jews are not revealing their true feelings and Jews are properly tuned in. Either explanation is reasonable, and neither should be used as the sole standard.

Finally, assessment mechanisms used to measure discriminatory behavior are highly inaccurate. Most Jews do not report their experiences with antisemitism. However, no additional proportion of unreported incidents is factored into reports, such as the yearly ADL audit of antisemitic incidents, to account for the large majority of Jews who experience antisemitism but do not report it. While these reports receive wide coverage and are accepted by the non-Jewish public as authoritative studies, it is easier for the Jewish public to dismiss them as inaccurate. Nevertheless, methodological and analytical shortcomings cannot totally explain the dissonance between Jewish and non-Jewish perceptions. The data reveal a continuing uneasiness, uncertainty, and mistrust among Jews about the attitudes and beliefs of their non-Jewish neighbors.

In 1981 a summary report for the American Jewish Committee conducted by Yankelovich, Skelly & White noted that "the perceptions of American Jews regarding how non-Jews feel about them is consistently more negative than the beliefs actually expressed by non-Jews. Related to this sharp difference which exists between the perception of Jews and non-Jews is the sharp difference which exists in the experience of antisemitism among Jews and non-Jews. Jews are much more likely to be aware of antisemitic incidents in their community."[40] They assume that it must be the Jews who are looking at the "real world" inaccurately. The strong language in this analysis and the data that were produced in the Yankelovich study provide one of the most cited and referred to empirical works to substantiate conclusions that Jews overreact to antisemitism, see it where it does not exist, and are "paranoid."

However, such an analysis is inherently flawed. Of course Jews are much more likely than their non-Jewish counterparts to hear anti-Jewish remarks where they live or work, or see them on television or in newspapers. Jews look for comments about Jews much as blacks look for comments about blacks, or Catholics about Catholics. One would not expect non-Jews to be as tuned in to anti-Jewish remarks. But just as important, what the Yankelovich study failed to acknowledge has been documented by other authorities on the subject, such as Selznick and Steinberg[41] and Quinley and Glock.[42] It is a fact that anti-semitic remarks and feelings, such as "Jews have too much power in the United States" or "Jews use shady business practices," may not be perceived by the non-Jewish observer, or indeed even by the maker of the remarks, as being antisemitic.[43] They may believe them to be statements of fact that do not reveal any prejudice at all. The Yankelovich study, curiously enough, disparages Jewish perceptions by supporting the primacy and accuracy of non-Jewish measures. Indeed, the more reliable benchmark might be the receiver of the antisemitic statement rather than the transmitter.

The sample of non-Jews from this 1981 study is largely unaware of antisemitic incidents. Non-Jews simply tune out or are not very concerned with many antisemitic remarks. When asked about awareness of antisemitic incidents, about 2% of the non-Jews indicated that they knew of workers who were passed over for promotion because they were Jewish, compared with 10% of the Jewish respondents answering in kind. Furthermore, while 6% of the non-Jews were aware of social clubs and groups that restrict Jews, this proportion is more than twice as high, 14%, for Jews.[44] One could logically deduce that these phenomena, while not as widespread as a generation ago, have not been eradicated. Some reservoir of anti-Jewish discriminatory behavior remains and is picked up in varying degrees by both Jews and non-Jews alike (see Table 4-7). Given that 60% of the 1981 Yankelovich sample of non-Jews were aware of no antisemitic incidents over a two-year period,[45] it is hardly acceptable that they are used as the measuring device for determining Jewish accuracy regarding perceptions of antisemitism. Both groups are picking up some levels of antisemitic behavior.

Serious doubts about the questions used to analyze dissonance also emerge. The lack of follow-up does not allow for truly accurate contrasts between the perceptions of Jews and non-Jews. In many cases, the questions asked of Jews by Yankelovich made no attempt to distinguish between *possibility* and *probability*, resulting in very poor measurements of Jewish perceptions and attitudes. The subtleties and the important distinctions in Jewish perceptions are lost. In the Jewish mind, probability and possibility are distinct. The failure to probe this critical difference results in a comparison of apples and oranges: Jews and non-Jews may be describing different phenomena.

When asked whether they thought antisemitism might increase in the future, Jews were much more likely than non-Jews to feel that it could. Forty percent of the Jews sampled in the Yankelovich study believed that antisemitism could increase in their community, compared to only 7% of the non-Jews.[46] Nearly seven out of ten Jews felt that antisemitism increasing in the United States was also a possibility, while this belief was echoed by only 21% of non-Jews[47] (see Table 4-8). The perceptual differences between Jews and non-Jews are quite large. But the comments in the personal interviews show a great deal of difference between Jewish perceptions of *possibility* versus probability. All of those interviewed felt an increase is possible, but not likely or probable. Yet it should be pointed out that in the 1981 Yankelovich study 60% of the Jews sampled were not concerned about the possibility of an increase in antisemitism in their area, and one out of three was not concerned about it elsewhere in the country.

The nexus between attitudes and behavior is very difficult to isolate. The correlation between positive or neutral attitudes and positive actions toward Jews is not so strong as to leave Jews totally confident. This skepticism is well founded. For example, over the past 20 years whites have consistently indicated that they are less reluctant to live in integrated neighborhoods with blacks than in the past. Yet data indicate that integrated neighborhoods remain rare. While other explanations are provided about the continued existence of segregated neighborhoods, prejudice and discrimination continue to play a key role. The stated willingness of whites to live in integrated areas is rarely behaviorally expressed.

Poll data indicate that most non-Jews say that they would vote for a Jew for president if he were nominated. The Yankelovich study of 1981 shows that 59% of non-Jews would not be troubled at all if a Jew were nominated for president. Jews, however, are much more doubtful of the acceptance by non-Jews of such a candidate. Only 7% of Jews believe that non-Jews would not be troubled by such a nomination[48] (see Table 4-9). We see quite a discrepancy between the two perceptions, partially because of the methodological problem of asking the question as a means of measuring majority opinion rather than proportional response. While Jews may be overly doubtful of non-Jewish acceptance of a Jewish presidential candidate, their suspicions are fed, and rightfully so, by the nearly four of every ten non-Jews who said in the 1981 Yankelovich study that they would be troubled, either very much, somewhat, or a little, by the nomination of a Jew for president. Jews are unsure of the accuracy of the measure of how many non-Jews would really not be bothered at all by a Jewish candidate, aware that attitudes and actions are not always unified. Since substantial proportions of non-Jews continue to express attitudes unfavorable to Jews, it is difficult to answer whether positive attitudes will really exhibit themselves.

Although the data reveal a continuing uneasiness and uncertainty among Jews about the attitudes and beliefs of their non-Jewish neighbors, these views are not universally held. In many cases, substantial proportions of Jews do not believe that a majority of non-Jews hold certain antisemitic beliefs. While Jews might be inaccurate about particular beliefs of non-Jews, their assessments of groups of non-Jews are much less negative. Jews do not view the world in the same way as do non-Jews. Yet their vision is not as myopic as some analysts claim. While Jews remain suspicious of the attitudes and opinions of their non-Jewish neighbors, they express the belief that attitudes toward Jews have become increasingly favorable over time.

The Threat of Antisemitism to Jewish Security in the Future

How secure American Jews remain in American society is contingent, according to many respondents, on several factors. The vast majority of those personally interviewed state that levels of antisemitism are much lower now than they were at the beginning of the century. The checks and balances provided by the American system are an important means of ensuring that antisemitism remains under control.

Responses to questions posed about the threat of antisemitism to Jewish security in the future reveal the wariness with which Jews view their present status in American society. Rabbi Neil Kominsky, when asked whether he thought antisemitism could pose a threat to the security of Jews in American society in the future, responded that "anybody who reads Jewish history would be a fool to think that it's impossible. It seems to me somewhat unlikely, but not unthinkable."[49] As might be expected, any discussion of Jewish security in the future immediately brings to many of the respondents' minds the specter of the Holocaust. As Paul Goldberg of Rochester, New York, indicated: "I see a possibility. I don't consider it likely. I have kept my eyes open all my life. I watch for the signs and I wait. And I hope I never see them. There's a lesson once learned. I did not have family in Germany, thank God. I don't come from that background. But they didn't keep their eyes open and they stuck their heads under a cover. . . . It doesn't hurt to keep your eyes open. It doesn't hurt to be a little paranoid."[50]

Philip Cohen, past president of the Cincinnati, Ohio, Federation, responded to the question by saying that he did not think antisemitism would threaten the future security of Jews in American society because of networks established with the non-Jewish community. "We've built some very strong bridges," he stated, "a tie where each has supported the other's way of life."[51] Others are stronger in their assertion that antisemitism will not threaten Jewish security because of Jewish social and political power. As Mitch Orlick of Columbus stated, antisemitism will not threaten us for several reasons. "One, we won't let it. We're aware of it. CRCs, ADL will respond to it."[52] The belief that antisemitism can be controlled is the primary hope held by Jews.

Respondents were asked how antisemitism could be eliminated. A variety of absolutist, desperately humorous, yet serious answers were given. One respondent suggested that all the antisemites be killed. A second said antisemitism would disappear by killing all the Jews. A third said, "Mass murder everybody and antisemitism will be eliminated." Still another said that when we find a cure for the common cold we will find a cure for antisemitism. And finally, one interviewee responded that "antisemitism will disappear when the Messianic age is instituted or the Messiah himself comes." Clearly, Jews assume that in whatever form and in whatever degree, antisemitism will continue to persist in the United States in the future. Security, therefore, is clearly tied to efforts to combat and contain antisemitism by whatever means possible.

A variety of methods for containing and combatting antisemitism were suggested by respondents from community surveys. These efforts include education, lobbying, coalition building, and, some suggest, general integration into American society. As one respondent noted, "living in a way that we are no longer 'ghettoized' in itself helps to remove some of the antisemitism." But most believe that education about "the history of Jews, about the Holocaust," is essential. The education should be targeted, one respondent said, "for non-Jews and Jews, but primarily non-Jews," combined with what he called a "strong, effective network of organizations that have as their primary responsibility education and direct action approaches." Good public relations are also essential, the same respondent stated, "dissemination of how antisemitic attitudes develop, of acts that take place, so that when the public sees them they will understand them." Any support of the combination of education, public relations, and community organizing is tempered by the belief that these are mitigating influences to help contain an essentially permanent problem. Nevertheless, there is much support for activity "behind the scenes." As one respondent explained, working "ahead of time with different groups, building coalitions, building respect between groups will go a long way."

The Effect of Jewish Perceptions of Antisemitism

How much do these perceptions of antisemitism in their totality affect Jews in the United States? Most of the respondents in the personal interviews said that on a daily basis it does not affect their lives very much. Others say that it has had a certain affect, on employment, for example. One respondent said that he left a Fortune 500 corporation because he was "the first Jew that was ever hired. I was not made to feel uncomfortable, but at the same time I was not comfortable. I just didn't feel like being the 'house' Jew." But others say that antisemitism may affect them in more subtle ways—such as in choosing a school for a child. "Antisemitism plays a subconscious rather than a conscious role in their mind," one respondent said. Even if she were not very aware of it, she might send her children to a school where she felt antisemitism would not be too prevalent.

Others affirm that antisemitism has played a more apparent, readily visible role in their lives. "Antisemitism influenced my life a great deal. It has left its mark on me. I have dedicated a good deal of my life to Jewish survival and antisemitism decided my direction,"[53] stated one respondent. Perhaps Paul Goldberg of Rochester, New York, had the most insightful observation. He said, "I suspect it affects us a great deal, even though we don't know it."[54]

The ultimate effect of Jewish perceptions of antisemitism on the ways they lead their lives is unknown, although some assessments are made in the conclusion of this book. However, it is clear that perceptions of antisemitism are neither overly pessimistic nor free from fear and concern. Jews remain uncertain about the exact nature of antisemitism today. They accept the current good times, recognizing relatively low levels of antisemitism. But at the same time they look over their shoulders to make sure antisemitism does not creep up from some unknown corner.

Chapter Five

AN INSTITUTIONAL RESPONSE TO ANTISEMITISM

A well-known fable about the three major national Jewish community relations agencies summarizes the Jewish institutional approach to dealing with antisemitism. A particularly nasty piece of graffiti was found in a public bathroom. Different Jewish community relations agencies were called, and each one rushed over its top specialist. The Anti-Defamation League took fingerprints and, speeding back to their headquarters, compared them with their file of known antisemitic graffiti writers. The American Jewish Committee immediately convened an interethnic, interreligious conference on racist and antisemitic graffiti in bathrooms. And the American Jewish Congress filed a lawsuit against everybody within 20 feet of the bathroom.

While these caricatures obviously do not accurately represent each agency's methods of dealing with antisemitism, they do broadly define basic philosophies. They collectively represent the structured yet varied response of American Jews to antisemitism. Since Jews differ in their views of antisemitism, a set of institutions has developed to represent the wide range of perceptions about antisemitism.

Representatives from the community relations agencies defined their institutional agendas along lines not unlike the exaggerated versions of the above story. For example, the assistant executive director of the American

Jewish Congress noted that the American Jewish Congress acts as "the lawyers of the Jewish community." Representatives from the Anti-Defamation League pride themselves on being the action agency, hard-hitting and aggressive. And Henry Feingold, in remarks made at the 75th Annual Meeting of the American Jewish Committee, used the following sentence to summarize the American Jewish Committee: "In a word, more than any other agency, the Committee acts as the community's think tank."[1] This chapter examines the relationship between Jewish community relations institutions and antisemitism. We analyze what these institutions do, and what they say they do. The attitudes of the professionals of these agencies, as well as their beliefs about antisemitism and other issues affecting Jews, are also discussed.

American Jews combat antisemitism primarily through institutionalized response and initiative. Utilizing the social, political, and legal frameworks of American society, Jews reacted to antisemitism by forming structured defense agencies: the American Jewish Committee in 1906, the Anti-Defamation League in 1913, and the American Jewish Congress in 1920. In 1944 the Council of Jewish Federations and Welfare Funds formed the National Jewish Community Relations Advisory Council (NJCRAC), an umbrella agency for defense and other community relations organizations. These agencies have grown and developed over the years and are now prominent organizations within the Jewish community. Each has developed its own following, agenda, and distinguishing philosophy.

In addition to the three national agencies and the umbrella organizations, local communities often have community relations councils or committees that are sometimes independent but usually attached to or funded by the Jewish Federation. These individual CRCs play a direct role at the local level in dealing with a wide variety of community relations issues, including combatting anti-semitism. The American Jewish Committee, the American Jewish Congress, and the Anti-Defamation League also have regional and local offices, but local CRCs are the most geographically dispersed set of institutions that deal with antisemitism.

The Simon Wiesenthal Center is a relatively new addition to the set of institutions that are involved with anti-semitism. Created in the 1970s, originally as a yeshiva and then as a Holocaust memorial museum, the Wiesenthal Center has more recently adopted antisemitism as a major part of its institutional agenda. It adds to an already formidable institutional presence in the American Jewish community aimed at combatting antisemitism. Of course, none of these institutions is committed solely to issues relating to antisemitism.

Despite their different approaches, all of the major community relations agencies share combatting anti-semitism as part of their institutional agenda. Their styles vary, but all acknowledge to one degree or another the need to combat antisemitism in some way. To a certain degree, the justification for the continued operation, activities, and funding of these institutions rests on the assumption that antisemitism remains a reality in contemporary America. The relative importance attached to antisemitism as part of the agency's operating portfolio, however, and the strategies for dealing with antisemitism are quite different, as are the perceptions of agency professionals as to how much antisemitism exists today in the United States. As these institutions have struggled to define their piece of the bureaucratic turf in dealing with antisemitism and related issues, each has assumed its distinct character.

The transition from "defense" agencies to community relations agencies illustrates this expansion of purposes

and programs, as well as the evolution of Jewish perceptions of Jewish safety, security, and acceptance in American society. At their inception, these agencies were con-
ceived and designed to combat overt antisemitic behavior
in all realms of American life. As Jews became more integrated and also more secure within the larger context of
American society, the concept of "defense" was gradually
transformed into one of "community relations." Because
Jews felt themselves to be equal partners with a multitude
of other groups in a pluralistic society, intergroup and
community relations better described how they perceived
their position. "Defense" agency somehow implied an un-
equal relationship, the need for a victimized minority
group to protect itself from a larger and more hostile society. As Jews increasingly rejected this characterization of
their social and political status, fewer agencies defined
their role as a defense function. Only the Jewish Defense
League, representing those who fear antisemitism, maintains this approach.

But none of the major national organizations that
combat antisemitism now assumes a defensive posture.
Each of them, to one degree or another, assumes a
monitoring function, a lobbying function, a coalition-
building function, an education function. They combine in
their totality to constitute a more offensive strategy to deal
with antisemitism.

Strategies for dealing with antisemitism differ dramatically, however, among the agencies. As noted in previous
chapters, there is hardly unanimity on the part of Jews as
to how much antisemitism exists in American society, or
the best way to deal with it. The multitude of agencies that
have developed to combat antisemitism is more than a
historical artifact. The collectivity of agencies, while in
some sense duplicative, accurately reflects multiple views
of antisemitism. If American Jews are ambivalent about

their security and the feelings of their non-Jewish neighbors, these institutions complement one another to cover differing tactics of strategies and philosophies. Indeed, individual institutions can shift approaches internally where necessary. Therefore, one agency can take one stance on a particular issue and approach a similar issue differently at another time. Since none of the institutions themselves are unidimensional, they can assume different positions, sometimes conflicting with one another, sometimes complementing each other.

The faith and support that American Jews lend to the community relations agencies are in many ways a sound endorsement and demonstration of confidence in the American social and political system, while at the same time expressing fears and anxieties about non-Jewish Americans themselves. The primary vehicles for combatting antisemitism—political activity, coalition forming, education, and exerting political influence—are all mainstream components of the American social, legal, and political systems. Like other social and political groups, Jews support their institutional representatives with their time and dollars as they jockey for positions of security, prosperity, and power within that system. Jewish community relations institutions have striven to make antisemitism socially and politically unacceptable. Yet the need for these activities rests on the assumption that action is still required to deal with issues of Jewish security.

Given the continued presence of antisemitism in American society, in terms of both attitudes and behavior, it is no wonder then that the agenda of the community relations agencies garners strong support from many American Jews. Since Jews do not believe that antisemitism can be eradicated but do believe that it must be contained, the courts, the schools, the media, and political arenas at every level are the mechanisms for achieving this goal. Individual action is supplemented by organizational efforts. Individuals participate in the electoral process with their single votes, and they participate effectively in the decision-making processes with their institutional voices. The well-developed community relations institutional network reflects the collective wariness of American Jews.

Even though these agencies engage in many activities, combatting antisemitism remains a central part of their organizational agendas. For example, a pamphlet published by the American Jewish Committee states, "The Committee . . . fights antisemitism and all forms of prejudice, recognizing that the disease of bigotry is indivisible and that Jews are intimately involved in the problems that affect all minority groups."[2] A recent publication of the Jewish Community Relations Bureau, representing Jewish community relations councils around the country, states that "a primary element of the JCRB is helping Jewish individuals who suffer from acts of antisemitic attitudes. The JCRB receives and investigates allegations of institutional antisemitism and seeks to eliminate any antisemitic policies and practices that may be found."[3] In 1981 the American Jewish Congress published a pamphlet by associate director Phil Baum. He stated that "in one sense, the Jewish community can never properly be accused of overreacting to signs of renewed antisemitic activity. Since the Holocaust, we have in effect pledged to each other that we will not be silent or indifferent to any indication of reticent antisemitism, however remote or incipient. We regard this unspoken pledge as immutable and enduring. And we affirm our readiness to act upon its charge."[4]

Rarely does a piece of Anti-Defamation League literature appear without some reference to antisemitism. And the National Jewish Community Relations Advisory Council, in its joint program plan for 1986–1987 outlined the following strategic goals for the Jewish community relations field.

> The Jewish community relations field should:
> —continue to encourage law enforcement agencies to prosecute vigorously all hate groups, including antisemitic extremists who commit violent crimes;
> —continue to assess the depth and breadth of inroads hate groups, including antisemitic extremists, have made in gaining support among residents in the midwest, south and Pacific northwest;
> —encourage member agencies to convene meetings with local public officials, civic and religious groups, law enforcement agencies, news media and college and university officials to discuss appropriate ways to minimize the effectiveness of antisemitic extremists, consistent with First Amendment principles;
> —encourage development of guidelines regarding campus appearances by extremist spokespersons;
> —encourage passage of federal, state and local legislation to combat acts of racial, ethnic or religious intimidation, violence and vandalism in those states that have not already done so.[5]

Antisemitism is also a clearly defined part of the agenda of the Simon Wiesenthal Center. In an article by Gary Rosenblatt that appeared in the *Baltimore Jewish Times*, the Wiesenthal Center philosophy for combatting antisemitism was stated by Martin Mendelsohn, counsel for the Center. He said, "We see the glass of antisemitism as half full, and they [other defense agencies] see it as half empty—and sometimes they don't see the glass at all."[6] The Wiesenthal Center makes concerted efforts to remind American Jews about the Holocaust and the current dangers of antisemitism in the United States.

Despite their differences, the community relations agencies share a common relationship with the Jewish press. In national conferences, annual plenums, the preparation and distribution of special reports and news releases, these agencies are active collectors and disseminators of information about antisemitism. Through the use of research departments, human relations departments, and other media management techniques, a continual information flow about antisemitism and related issues is relayed to the Jewish public. In their role as monitoring institutions, these agencies report to the general Jewish public any incidents of vandalism, employment discrimination, or antisemitic political activity.

A wide assortment of agency publications distribute information. The American Jewish Committee publishes numerous reports and studies, sponsors survey research and books by scholars, as well as editing the *American Jewish Yearbook* and *Commentary*. *Congress Monthly* is the publicity organ for the American Jewish Congress. The Anti-Defamation League also produces numerous publications, such as the *ADL Bulletin*, but also *Facts*, in-depth reports on antisemitic and extremist movements, *Dimensions*, a journal of Holocaust studies, *Face to Face*, an interreligious bulletin, *International Reports*, and *Nuestro Encuentro*, which targets the Spanish-language population. Many of these publications are directed to the individual agency's membership or supporters. However, more importantly, they go to the Jewish press and the Jewish Telegraphic Agency, as well as to general newspapers. Both the Jewish press and the general media greatly increase their exposure by publishing such findings.

Press releases, regularly submitted to the Jewish and general press, detail study findings or commentary on a particular incident. Jewish community relations agencies also offer educational materials to local governments, schools, and churches and civic organizations. Part of their agenda is to convene gatherings of leaders, both Jewish and non-Jewish, to discuss antisemitism. These conferences are another vehicle used to form intergroup coalitions to deal with antisemitism and other forms of racial and religious prejudice.

Origins

The American Jewish Committee was founded in response to a series of pogroms in Czarist Russia at the turn of the century. Prior to the organization of the American Jewish Committee, no religious or ethnic group in the United States had organized for the sole purpose of defending its rights. The American Jewish Committee was founded in 1906 by a small group of patrician Jews of German descent who believed that quietly exerted influence was the key to achieving rights within the American system. Tactics were characteristically low-key.

A group of volunteers established the Anti-Defamation League of B'nai B'rith in 1913. Its goal was "to stop the defamation of the Jewish people . . . to secure justice and fair treatment to all citizens alike."[7] Since that time, the Anti-Defamation League has referred to itself as the action agency of the Jewish community. The ADL tracks the non-Jewish population by monitoring antisemitic and racist groups and individuals and by bringing legal action against those who discriminate against Jews or other minority groups, as well as through lobbying efforts.

The American Jewish Congress was created in 1920 as a grass roots organization, a representative body for Jews.[8] Congress founders were initially opposed by members of the American Jewish Committee, who thought a select core of elite, established, and successful representatives was more effective in achieving change than attempts by Jewish "masses." The differing philosophies are reflected in the names chosen by the agencies. Henry Feingold wrote that "the very notion and nomenclature of a 'committee' composed of selected members smacked of exclusivity. The opposite presumption, i.e., inclusion of Jewish 'masses,' accounts for the use of the term 'Congress' by the founders of the American Jewish Congress. Founders of the American Jewish Congress sought to democratize Jewish life, by the 'removal of the oligarchy of *shtadlanim* (Court Jews) who controlled it.' That was the rallying cry of the 'illustrious obscure' who founded the Congress movement."[9] The members of the American Jewish Congress purposely selected an approach that was designed to be more representative.

Distinctions can be drawn from the inception of these agencies. Both the American Jewish Committee and Congress directed their efforts to fight antisemitism by dealing with general issues of legal structure and coalition building, with Committee emphasizing the latter. The Anti-Defamation League, on the other hand, operated from the premise that aggressive actions to contain the perpetrators of antisemitism were necessary. Targeting the non-Jewish population redirected the defense approach. It was offensive rather than defensive. Congress and Committee looked inward, at the Jewish population, saw in which ways Jewish rights were being infringed upon, and projected these concerns outward to form intergroup cooperation or use legal channels. The Anti-Defamation League scanned the general population and launched actions more directly at perceived threats.

The membership structure of the American Jewish Committee and the American Jewish Congress, once quite different, have since become quite similar. Members of both the Committee and Congress pay dues, in return receiving mailings and information about the agency. From the original limited membership of 60, the American

Jewish Committee has grown to include over 50,000 associates living in more than 600 communities and organized in some 80 chapters and units. Membership of the American Jewish Congress exceeds 40,000. The Anti-Defamation League is not a membership agency. Financial supporters receive ADL information.

Since each organization has its own focus, redundancy is generally dismissed as a problem by agency representatives. David Gordis, former executive vice-president of the American Jewish Committee, when asked to differentiate agency responses, replied that "when a job has to be done, we try to do it. If it's being done by someone else and we don't feel we can contribute, we won't do it. We believe in pluralism, in a variety of approaches and styles and emphases, we think that's good."[10]

A summary of selected programs and budget of the American Jewish Committee, presented at the Large City Budgeting Conference in 1986, addressed the issue of redundancy: "In some instances, where special coordination is deemed necessary and appropriate on behalf of the Jewish community, the three community relations agencies—American Jewish Committee, American Jewish Congress, and Anti-Defamation League—voluntarily and mutually agree upon individual assignments that allow each of the agencies to operate in those areas which best utilize their special abilities and strengths."[11]

Perceptions of the Community Relations Professionals

In the spring of 1987, the Cohen Center for Modern Jewish Studies contacted community relations professionals in Jewish agencies, surveying them on their perspectives about antisemitism. A questionnaire was distributed to branch offices and headquarter locations of Federations, Community Relations Councils, the Anti-

Defamation League, the American Jewish Committee, and
the American Jewish Congress. A total of 73 surveys were
returned of 215 sent, a response rate of about 34%. Individual survey respondents are not identified. However,
the organizations for which the respondents worked are
named. Findings are presented for the total sample, and
also by agency.[12]

Overall, some fascinating anomalies appear in these
findings. First, only about half, 51%, of the community
professionals consider programs to combat antisemitism
as very important. This is considerably lower than most
community studies, which indicate that a much larger proportion of the general population consider programs to
combat antisemitism as very important. Obviously, the
community relations professionals see their tasks as much
broader than only fighting antisemitism.

Like the general public, however, Jewish community
relations professionals are most concerned about assimilation issues. When asked to select the single most important problem facing American Jews, 34% listed Jewish education and 18% named Jews marrying other Jews. The
Jewish education issue is really a concern about assimilation, since most Jews believe that Jewish education can be
a deterrent to assimilation. Only 10% considered programs to combat antisemitism as the single most important issue. Community relations professionals who were
most concerned with assimilation and education outnum-
bered those expressing the greatest concern for programs
to combat antisemitism by five to one.

Basically, community relations professionals assess
the amount of antisemitism in their communities along
lines similar to the general public. Very small proportions
see either a great deal or no antisemitism. Most see either
little or a moderate amount.

On the other hand, Jewish community relations professionals are almost twice as likely as respondents in community studies to say that they have experienced anti-semitism themselves in the past year. Obviously, they are more active in areas where they may experience anti-semitism. Age is also a causal factor here. The community surveys indicate that those under the age of 30 are more likely to say that they have experienced antisemitism in the past year, and community relations professionals tend to be younger than the general population. (Almost one-fourth of community relations professionals responding to the survey, 24%, were under 35 years old, while 35% were between 35 and 44.) Nevertheless, Jewish community rela-tions professionals, while arguing that the general public sees more antisemitism than exists, are twice as likely as the general public to say that they are experiencing anti-semitism. Jerome Chanes of NJCRAC, in a personal inter-view, said:

> There seems to be a discrepancy in perception. What we keep hearing is that the grass-roots—*amcha*—may not be in total agreement with the judgements of the leadership on antisemitism. Again, the highest function of communi-ty and national leadership is to convey the message to the grass-roots that we may not all be in complete agreement on what is the state of antisemitism, on what is happening out there, but we truly do hear what you are saying. In fact, you may be saying something, touching upon some-thing, that we are missing. You may be smelling some-thing out there.[13]

In some ways the community relations professionals are denying their own experiences. While they have percep-tions similar to the general public about how much anti-semitism exists, and they are personally experiencing anti-semitism, the real perception gap exists at the professional level. Perhaps because they are more tuned in to polling data which they interpret to show declining antisemitism, or because they hear individual complaints about anti-semitism that turn out to be false, community relations professionals believe that the public feels that there is more antisemitism than really exists. It may truly color the way professionals deal with the Jewish public, and what they may believe to be the "hysteria" of this public in their views of antisemitism.

This is certainly an odd configuration. Agencies consistently reinforce existing concerns on the part of the Jewish public, and at the same time believe that the grass roots Jewish view may be somewhat exaggerated. For example, in the 1985–1986 program guide for NJCRAC, the discussion of antisemitism noted that events had "bolstered the pervasive perception of vulnerability in the grass roots of the Jewish community that has existed in recent years."[14] And in a recent NJCRAC subcommittee that was convened to assess criteria for measuring antisemitism, much of the discussion focused on the perception gap that was supposedly documented in the Yankelovich study of 1981.[15]

Despite the proliferation of organizational newsletters, press releases, and sponsored studies, the Jewish press is the greatest source of news about happenings and events in Jewish life. Even for Jewish community relations professionals, the Jewish press is mentioned most often as a source of news about antisemitic incidents. The primary source of news, however, as opposed to the source most frequently listed, consists of reports telephoned in to the office. Nevertheless, the Jewish press is obviously a vehicle for community relations professionals to share, organizationally and institutionally, information about antisemitism. Awareness comes not only through what is happening in their individual offices but through the shared experience of the Jewish media.

Many community relations professionals view most Americans as passively antisemitic, that is, holding antisemitic beliefs but not necessarily acting on those beliefs. Only 23% of the community relations professionals believe that a majority of Americans, or near a majority, hold no antisemitic beliefs at all. Again, these perceptions are not substantially different from those held by the majority of the Jewish public.

The irony of these findings is that the community relations professionals, imbued with the trust of, and given the charge by, the constituencies that they represent, feel much the same as their constituents in almost every area, except when it comes to the relative importance of programs to combat antisemitism. Perhaps there is an institutional denial about the purposes of the organizations and institutions themselves. Somehow or other, some community relations professionals, while believing on a personal level that antisemitism is real in moderate form, are somewhat less concerned about the relative importance of fighting it. Or, being more sophisticated observers of antisemitism, they see programs for intergroup relations, separation of church and state, or political activity as more important than programs specifically designed to combat antisemitism. In the Jewish public's eyes, there is little difference.

Obviously, there are differences between the agencies, and this will be explored in the following sections. The profiles, agendas, and philosophies of the different organizations account for these differences. Anti-Defamation League, Federation, and Community Relations Council representatives are much more likely to say that they have experienced an antisemitic incident in the past year than are American Jewish Congress or Committee members. Some of this difference results from the nature of agency involvement within communities. ADL and Community Relations Council professionals are most often identified as the agencies that deal with individual incidents and local acts. The nature of their involvement exposes the professionals from these organizations to a variety of antisemitic reactions, ranging from newspaper letters to hate mail and personal threats. However, the orientation of the American Jewish Committee and Congress generally removes some of these agency professionals from the focus of individual antisemites. They are more involved with general issues, coalition building, and political lobbying.

Responses to the survey reflect these differences. Committee members tend to view antisemitism as a threat within the context of other threats to many ethnic groups. Representatives of the Anti-Defamation League, on the other hand, consider antisemitism as a specific threat to Jews. The context differs, and markedly. The American Jewish Congress also approaches the problem of antisemitism through Jewish rights as Americans, working on general civil rights issues. Community Relations Councils, in their role as coordinators of Jewish agencies, maintain their separateness as a Jewish organization working for primarily Jewish causes. The American Jewish Committee and the American Jewish Congress deal more with the American aspect of Jewish identity, while the Anti-Defamation League focuses more on the Jewish side of the identity issue.

The agencies also define antisemitism differently. Representatives from each organization described antisemitism as prejudice, bias, or hatred directed toward Jews solely because of their Jewishness. Professionals from the American Jewish Committee consider Jews a minority group in a nation of other minority groups. Intergroup conflict is not, in their view, necessarily antisemitic. The approach of the American Jewish Congress is much the same. Respondents characterize the American Jewish Congress's philosophy of dealing with anti-semitism as "one of education and the utilization of law and the legislative process to ensure civil rights for all while combatting ignorance and fear." Congress members assert that their organization approaches the problem from within the American system: "Working on American civil rights and liberties issues, we demonstrate our American Jewish community's interest and investment in American traditional values," explained one respondent. The emphasis of the Anti-Defamation League is upon Jewish self-interest. Jewish rights are not held up comparatively to other minority group rights. And, extending their definition of *antisemitism*, members of the Anti-Defamation League have added a new dimension to the word. Antagonism to the state of Israel, or, as one professional said, "unrelenting attacks on Israel's legitimacy," is also incorporated in the definition of antisemitism.

Methods of combatting antisemitism vary, as a result of different institutional ideologies. Like most Jews, community relations professionals view the complete elimination of antisemitism as impossible, or, as stated by one Congress respondent, "unrealistic." However, methods to reduce the impact of antisemitism are employed. Community relations professionals working for the American Jewish Committee often suggest education and coalition building as a means of combatting antisemitism, as well as law enforcement, litigation, and public repudiation. The Congress is most likely to rely on the American legal foundation. The Anti-Defamation League, however, while equally emphatic about the need for education, legislation, and litigation, suggests other, more combative means of fighting antisemitism. Firm counteraction, monitoring of extremists, and communication directed to those outside of the Jewish community are frequently mentioned by ADL representatives. Most significantly, Anti-Defamation League professionals also advocate impressing upon Jews who experience antisemitism their communal responsibility to report it. "It is critical to convince Jews to report and respond to incidents," stated one ADL respondent, advocating participatory counteraction.

Personal experiences bear out these philosophical differences. ADL professionals are the most likely, of all community relations professionals, to have experienced antisemitism within the past year. While 22% of Committee respondents say that in the past year they experienced antisemitism, almost half of all ADL members, 46%, have had such experiences. The majority of attacks against ADL members are verbal attacks and hate mail, with a few mentions of threats and attacks. Committee professionals report verbal slurs and remarks. Regardless of their organizational attachment, however, many of the community relations professionals appear to doubt the representativeness of their own experiences, failing to see that their fears and experiences are often similar to those of the general Jewish public. Their own personal experiences with antisemitism are seen as isolated phenomena, because they work for community relations agencies, not because antisemitic behavior among non-Jews may be more widespread than they like to believe.

Respondents were asked to identify issues of concern to American Jewry. Five factors relating to Jewish life in America were listed: Jewish neighborhoods, the separation of church and state, Jews marrying other Jews, programs to combat antisemitism, and Jewish education for Jewish children. They were also asked which of these five offerings was the single most important. Nearly three-quarters of all respondents, 72%, feel that separation of church and state is very important, while Jewish children receiving a Jewish education is considered very important by 61% of community relations professionals. Slightly more than half of all respondents view Jews marrying other Jews and programs to combat antisemitism as very important, 55% and 51%, respectively. While the proportions of those considering such issues as important vary, church–state separation and Jewish education are clearly predominant issues of concern for community relations professionals (see Table 5-1).

Jewish children receiving a Jewish education was selected as the single most important issue by the greatest proportion of respondents. About one-third, 34%, believe that Jewish education for Jewish children is the single most important issue, compared to 29% indicating the separation of church and state. Eighteen percent feel Jews marrying other Jews is the most important issue, while 10% select programs to combat antisemitism, and neighborhoods where Jews can live with other Jews is considered most important by only 6% (see Table 5-2).

Like the overall Jewish population, Jewish community relations professionals believe that antisemitism is more prevalent at the national level than it is in their own community. Forty-eight percent of agency representatives say that there is little antisemitism in their own community, while an equal proportion say that a great deal or a moderate amount of antisemitism exists in their area. However, when asked to assess the levels of antisemitism in the United States, only 30% feel that little antisemitism exists, and 64% say that there is a great deal or a moderate amount. Generally, community relations professionals state that the amount of antisemitism existing in America is moderate. The majority, 52%, profess the belief that antisemitism affects American Jews only a little. An additional one-third of the responding professionals believe it affects American Jews a moderate amount (see Table 5-3).

Community relations professionals state that they consider the levels of antisemitism in the United States to be relatively moderate, and their own experiences reflect this perception. A substantial proportion of community relations professionals, 46%, state that they have experienced a moderate amount of antisemitism in their lifetime, while only 4% say they have experienced a great deal. *Not a single respondent claimed to have experienced no antisemitism in his or her lifetime* (see Table 5-4). And although most professionals feel that antisemitism affects American Jews a little, a substantial share assert that experiences with antisemitism have influenced their lives a great deal.

The proportions of community relations professionals who claim having personally experienced antisemitism in the 12 months prior to being surveyed are much higher than those of the general Jewish population. Some of this discrepancy results inevitably from the nature of their work. In the general community, between 17 and 32% say that they experienced antisemitism within the 12 months prior to being surveyed, while 38% of community relations professionals cite personal experiences within the past year. Unlike the Jewish public, however, the majority of professional community relations workers reported their antisemitic experiences.

Various channels bring antisemitic events to the attention of community relations professionals. Incidents can be reported directly or through organizational and professional networks. Professionals are most likely to say that they hear of antisemitic incidents through such networks. While almost one-fourth of all professionals, 23%, say that more than 11 instances of antisemitism have been reported directly to them, the majority of respondents say that they have been the initial contact for fewer than 10 actual incidents. However, organizational and professional networks also serve to inform community relations professionals of antisemitic incidents. One-fourth of the responding community relations professionals say that over 21 antisemitic incidents were brought to their attention in this manner in the past year, while another 28% were made aware of between 7 and 20 incidents as a result of such organizational and professional networks (see Table 5-5).

The Jewish press is most often mentioned by community relations professionals as the means by which antisemitic incidents were brought to their attention. Two-thirds of all respondents, 67%, cite the Jewish press as a source of information on antisemitism. Slightly fewer respondents, 64%, are informed of antisemitic incidents through reports made to their offices, while the same proportion credit the general media for their awareness. A variety of other methods also serve to inform community relations professionals of the presence and prevalence of antisemitism. Forty-five percent indicate that professional publications are a means of receiving knowledge about antisemitism, while 41% mention friends and relatives. Organization publications are mentioned by 35% of respondents as yet another method of information dissemination regarding antisemitism, while 20% mention organizational bulletin boards. It is primarily the Jewish press, publicizing information from various agencies, that brings such incidents to the attention of the professionals. Again, in this regard they are not much different from their constituencies.

While many receive the publications of various agencies, Jewish newspapers are their primary means of information. However, despite the fact that the greatest share of community relations professionals say they receive knowledge about antisemitic incidents through the Jewish press, the single most important source of information regarding antisemitic incidents is through office reports.

Almost half of all respondents, 45%, say that their primary source of information consists of incidents reported to their office, while only 13% credit the Jewish press. An additional 13% credit professional publications as their main information source (see Table 5-6).

In order to determine how community relations professionals view non-Jewish antisemitic beliefs, respondents were asked to divide Americans into three categories, according to levels of antisemitism. Active antisemites were defined as those whose antisemitic beliefs influence their behavior, passive antisemites were perceived as Americans holding antisemitic beliefs that do not influence their behavior, and the third category consisted of Americans holding *no* antisemitic beliefs. By far the largest proportion of non-Jewish Americans are considered passively antisemitic by community relations professionals. Ninety percent of respondents feel that active antisemites account for less than 20% of all Americans. Almost three-quarters of all professionals, 72%, say that between one-fifth and four-fifths of Americans hold antisemitic beliefs that do not influence their behavior. As for those who hold no antisemitic beliefs, the largest proportion of professionals feel that less than one-fifth of the American population fits in this category. However, a considerable share of the respondents feel that larger proportions of Americans hold no antisemitic beliefs. Almost one-quarter, 23%, are of the opinion that between 41 and 60% of Americans hold no antisemitic beliefs (see Table 5-7).

Jewish community relations professionals are sensitive to anti-Israel statements, perceiving many of them as antisemitic. As with other Jews, there is a feeling that anti-Israelism is really a new form of antisemitism. Although the largest proportion of professionals, 42%, feel that some anti-Israel statements are antisemitic, over half, 52%, say that many or most are (see Table 5-8). In personal interviews as well as in the survey questionnaire, anti-Israeli comments and feelings were frequently described as antisemitism.

How Each Institution Views Antisemitism

The American Jewish Committee

Combatting antisemitism has been the professed first concern of the American Jewish Committee for over 80 years. In a report prepared in 1981 by Alisa Kesten, Milton Ellerin, and Sonja Kaufer, antisemitism received top billing on the Committee's agenda. "It will always be the primary focus of the American Jewish Committee's activities and program," Ellerin, former head of the Trends Analyses Unit, wrote.[16] The program priorities singled out by the American Jewish Committee during the 1985–1986 year were designed to fulfill the Committee's permanent commitments to combat antisemitism and to protect the civil and religious rights of Jews. Each of the Committee's mission documents seems to reaffirm its chief role in combatting antisemitism.[17]

However, the tenor of this support is colored by statements of key figures in the agency. Former executive vice-president David Gordis stated during a personal interview in March 1987 that the American Jewish Committee largely supports the argument set forth by Charles Silberman in his book *A Certain People: American Jews and Their Lives Today*, which claims that antisemitism is no longer a major problem for American Jews. "We do not view antisemitism in this country as normative, we view it as aberrational," Gordis said. "We don't believe the roof is caving in. And we believe one has to be vigilant about antisemitism, but, as I said before, the principal threat to Jewish life, the principal determinants of Jewish future are going to be the internal questions of the content of Jewish life, not what's going on in the farm belt, not whether blacks are more or less antisemitic."[18]

Harold Applebaum, special assistant for Antisemitism and Extremism Programs, supported Gordis's views. American Jews are pretty well off, he says, and to emphasize or concentrate on the threat of antisemitism is crying wolf.

> We start out not from a position of paranoia, but from a position of saying, 'Hey, our position is pretty good.' Nevertheless, we have to develop a better understanding of those forces which either in actuality or potentially threaten us. And finally, a focus on what is marginal may not help us. The fact that Jews are outraged when a synagogue's window is broken, or when a Jewish cemetery is desecrated, that outrage has to be respected and understood. It doesn't mean that those incidents are essential threats to the security of American Jews. So to the extent that you devote a lot of energy to that may represent the dissipation of our energy. Our resources are not unlimited.[19]

The American Jewish Committee prides itself on being a multi-issue agency, and a narrow focus on antisemitism is looked upon disfavorably. Asked to define the essence of the American Jewish Committee's approach to antisemitism, David Gordis stated, "Our emphases are on coalition building, long-range research, and intervention."[20] The Committee has moved away from a predominant concentration on antisemitism, to an emphasis on establishing coalitions and facilitating intergroup dialogue.

The Committee views itself as low-key, seeking to downplay antisemitism while continuing to combat it. Nevertheless, it can be said that intergroup relations as a means to dealing with Jewish group security is the primary focus, rather than a specific attempt to combat anti-semitism per se. The Committee, in terms of both its published documents and the individuals who work for the organization, prefers to emphasize the strides that American Jews have made, and the need to avoid what they might term "paranoid" responses. The first goal of the American Jewish Committee listed in a 1981 publication was protecting the civil and religious rights of Jews.[21] This is obviously a modification of the goal of combatting antisemitism and other forms of bigotry and discrimination. In the eyes of the Committee, combatting antisemitism and promoting equality are part of a common program. Combatting antisemitism is not viewed as a functional activity in its own right.

American Jewish Committee Professionals

When asked to identify the single most important problem facing Jews in the United States today, American Jewish Committee professionals responded with a variety of answers. The greatest number by far, however, suggested assimilation, or some variation of the difficulty of defining Jewish identity in a welcoming secular environment, as the problem of utmost concern. Among some of the other problems mentioned were antisemitism, threats of a breakdown in the separation of church and state, internal strife, decreasing Jewish affiliation, and the poor quality of Jewish education.

Committee professionals define the same problem in a variety of ways. Assimilation is described as a problem because "people are not continuing to pass the tradition on to their kids." It is also a difficulty because it "causes us to embark on a difficult balancing act between acceptance and assimilation. We seem to look for examples of where we are not accepted/tolerated in society, and then feel equally uneasy at the notion that as Jews we will be absorbed too readily into society and lose our Jewishness," explains one Committee member. Yet another respondent juxtaposes assimilation and tolerance, or in this case, antisemitism. "With the absence of widespread and institutionalized antisemitism, American Jews have few external forces that cause Jews to maintain their Jewish identity."

A need to maintain Jewish identity also seems to fall under the general rubric of assimilation. A number of American Jewish Committee professionals stated that maintaining a distinctive Jewish attitude in American society is the biggest challenge currently facing Jews. As one respondent aptly states, the problem is "finding the delicate balance between particularistic belief and practice, and living in today's world, recognizing the need to be both Jewish and modern." Another Committee professional defines the problem more as one of choice, an either/or decision, rather than a balancing act, asserting that Jews today can choose whether or not they wish to maintain their Jewish identity. As a result, the single most important problem to this respondent is "developing a democratically based, nonpanicked reason for remaining Jewish in a free society, where Jews have a choice of whether or not to maintain their identity." Other suggested problems include internal strife and factionalism between religious blocks, the need for better Jewish education, and decreasing Jewish affiliation.

Several respondents stated that external threats, such as antisemitism or a breakdown in the separation of church and state, were the most important problems. This concern emerges in various ways. One respondent expressed the need to "prevent the erosion of the high level of status, credibility, and security that the community has achieved." Another defined the core difficulty as "perceptions and reality about antisemitism." Other major problems facing Jews today in the United States included resolving difficulties with the United States–Israel relationship, and the importance of establishing intergroup relations with new ethnic populations such as Asians and Hispanics. Antisemitism related to Israel is yet another external problem for the Jewish community to face. However, the largest problems are by and large considered by American Jewish Committee professionals to be assimilation-related threats, rather than danger posed from outside the Jewish community.

The American Jewish Committee's philosophy is revealed in the ways that professionals set priorities. Holding to their belief that Jewish security lies in the strength of American institutions, the great majority of Committee professionals assess a breakdown of the separation of church and state as a greater threat for Jews in the United States than a rise in antisemitism. Those selecting the separation of church and state as the greater concern voice fears of the "Christianization" of America, and state the need for a pluralistic society. Expressing the common opinion, one respondent explains that the separation of church and state "is what allows Jews to participate in America on an equal footing with all others"; challenging this division "would most likely provide the 'breeding ground' required for antisemitism to grow." But many Committee professionals see a breakdown of church–state separation as the precursor for increased antisemitism. "Once that barrier is broken, it opens the door for all sorts of intolerance," explains one Committee professional. The few respondents who believe that a rise in antisemitism is a greater problem feel that, because antisemitism has a more immediate impact, it is more dangerous, and they state that increasing antisemitism will lead to a breakdown of church/state separation if unchecked. However, these respondents were in the minority.

Church and state separation is vital to Jews because, as one member states, "it gives us the freedom of a minority in a democratic society. Less separation would encourage a monolithic culture to impose a homogenous ideology on any minority." Another respondent has a more explicit fear: "Less separation means greater movement toward making Christianity the 'official' state religion." The consequences of less separation are "a tendency to stamp Jews as 'outsiders,'" one Committee member fears, or, in the words of another, "religiously based antisemitism." In many ways, then, the church–state and antisemitism issues are, for many respondents, fused.

Most Committee members, when asked to assess levels of antisemitism over time, believe that it has declined dramatically since World War II. By far the greatest proportion also feel that this trend will continue. Several express the opinion that recent events, such as the Wall Street scandals, the Pollard spy case, and the position of Israel on various issues, have resulted in an increase in levels of antisemitism from the 1970s, but they still believe, for the most part, that the levels of antisemitism will be lower in the future. A third faction agrees that there is less antisemitism now than ever before. However, they are unsure of the future. Some state that there will be more, while others are not so negative. Or, as one member says, "there may well be more, but of a different nature."

Although most Committee members did not feel that antisemitism might threaten the security of Jews in American society in the future, few answered definitively that it would not. "Antisemitism has no acceptance in government, law enforcement, or media. It won't rise to pose a real threat to Jews. Jews are too well positioned to expose and combat it," asserted one respondent, who did not see antisemitism as a potential threat to the future of American Jews. Those holding such an optimistic view were few in number. One professional aptly summarized the uncertainty of the majority. "Based on my sense of America from post-War to the present, no," he wrote. "Based on my reading of Jewish history, who could say no with certainty?"

The American Jewish Committee's approach to the problem stresses a pluralistic approach, tackling the issue through coalition building and dialogue, "reaching out to leaders in ethnic and religious sectors to build trust and understanding," as one member writes; studies and research are also conducted, such as annual polls; media involvement in attacking antisemitism, as well as legislative action and law enforcement, is also practiced where necessary. Several respondents mention that the American Jewish Committee approaches the problem of antisemitism in a "low-key" fashion. "We do not act with alarm, but instead attempt to work behind the scenes to prevent incidents from becoming explosive," explained one Committee member. A large number of respondents cite this ability to work quietly as a distinguishing trait unique to their organization. As one respondent says, drawing distinctions between the American Jewish Committee and other organizations, "We use a low-key approach that does not put others on the defensive." Supplementing this statement, another member writes, "We tend to deal with such incidents more quietly, focusing on coalition-building, research, and prevention."

The research capacity of the American Jewish Committee is also touted as a differentiating feature. "More than any other agency we use research as a tool," one respondent writes. "We are working to improve instruments for measuring and evaluating antisemitism," answered the coordinator for Antisemitism and Extremism Programs. "We distinguish between antisemitism and legitimate intergroup conflict." And, as a result of their coalition-building, research approach, in the words of another Committee member, "our approach is long-range, rather than incident-related."

When asked how the American Jewish Committee influences American Jews' perceptions of antisemitism, several respondents state that the Committee plays a quieting role. "We tend to be a calming influence, not publicizing every 'crisis,'" one member said. Through release of polling and other research data to the media and agency publications, the American Jewish Committee addresses its Jewish audience, informing them of current opinions and attitudes toward Jews. However, one member questions the effectiveness of the Committee's information dissemination, claiming that their work does not really affect the general public's perception of antisemitism. "My experience indicates that the rank and file of the Jewish community believes antisemitism exists as a serious problem, no matter what good news the polls tell us."

Evaluating extremist groups, such as the Ku Klux Klan, Posse Comitatus, and neo-Nazi groups, elicited different reactions from members of the American Jewish Committee. Many respondents felt these groups had a positive effect on the way Americans think about Jews, generating feelings of sympathy for their intended victims. "I think they put this type of raw, unsophisticated antisemitism in sharper focus for the American non-Jewish community, and therefore give antisemitism less credence and validity," answered one Committee member. Others dismissed them as "crackpots" and "crazies." However, despite their feelings that such groups had little effect on Americans, many Committee professionals stated the need for constant vigilance to ensure that their influence does not spread, echoing the sentiments of most Jews. While all respondents felt that such extremist groups pose a minimal threat to American Jews, they also believed that their presence cannot be ignored.

Respondents often described antisemitism through the context of anti-Israel or anti-Zionist statements. When asked if anti-Israel statements are antisemitic, though, many qualified their answers. "I don't believe that an anti-Israel statement is necessarily antisemitic, but I do think some people and groups tend to mask their anti-Jew-ishness by Israel bashing," one respondent wrote. However, defining valid criticism of Israel is problematic. As one member says, careful distinctions need to be made. "Jews need to give more people who are not anti-Israel or antisemitic more room to dissent with Israeli politics. Jews criticize Israel and yet we too often attack non-Jews who do this." No common concurrence emerges among Committee representatives on this issue.

The Anti-Defamation League

In a roundtable discussion with the editors of the *Long Island Jewish World* in April 1983, the former national director of the Anti-Defamation League, Nathan Perlmutter, stated the League's approach: "The core purpose of the ADL is to fight antisemitism. . . . We have learned that the well-being of the democratic process determines the well-being of the Jews."[22] Other high-ranking League officials concur with Mr. Perlmutter in his assessment. "Our philosophy is basically to deal head on with antisemitism, to utilize those mechanisms that are existing in society that allow us to do that," Tom Neumann, director of intergroup relations, explained when asked about the institutional philosophy of the Anti-Defamation League. "We deal with the antisemites, but we also deal with those who are not antisemites but have positions that are contrary to the welfare of the Jewish community, and to this country as a whole."[23] The League's method of dealing with antisemitism involves multiple programming, which includes research, education, and intervention. However, along with its sophisticated techniques and extensive research facilities, the Anti-Defamation League has adhered to its basis. Antisemitism continues to be the Anti-Defamation League's primary issue.

The Anti-Defamation League, according to Mr. Neumann, has "taken the preeminent position in the investigative area of antisemitism. In other words, if you want to know what's going on with the Ku Klux Klan in this country, you can talk to a whole bunch of people, but you're going to find the answers here."[24] ADL's monitoring of changing conditions, part of what its founders called "vigilance work," reveals topics of present or prospective concern for the Jewish community. The Anti-Defamation League has a large professional staff employed in two departments of the Civil Rights Division, Research and Fact Finding. "We are the only ones as sophisticated as that," Mr. Neumann continued. "Others dabble in it. Ours is a very old, entrenched, sophisticated process. Inside the Jewish community, or outside the Jewish community, we are recognized as an authority on antisemites in this country. We have access to information that very few do."

Allegiance to the founding purpose remains consistent. Of the three primary community relations agencies, they are the ones who are still most invested in the issue of antisemitism. Their reputation for being an aggressive agency has helped them build upon this role. Indeed, other agency representatives acknowledge the ADL's central role in fighting antisemitism. "Generally, I would say that because ADL is usually around and identified, people would go to them before coming to us," commented Evan Mendelson, former assistant executive director for the American Jewish Congress.[25] "We are an agency that is unabashed, unafraid to articulate, to be vociferous in its opposition to antisemitism," Tom Neumann summarized. "That manifests itself in action, whether it's legislative, or litigative, or just a utilization of pressure, of public opinion or influence, or whatever the case may be, to impact upon those activities that are detrimental to Jews."[26]

In its *Purposes and Programs* brochure, it is stated that "ADL's prime objective is to counter assaults on the safety, status, rights and images of Jews. Although organized antisemitism has lessened with each passing decade, the roots of antisemitism are deep and far from dead."[27] Images in the booklet include a picture of hooded Ku Klux Klan members in front of a burning cross, with one holding a rifle; snapshots of Nazis and extremist groups; and a cartoon of the United Nations condemning Israel—all of which are used to substantiate ADL's basic approach to dealing with antisemitism. ADL bulletins regularly address issues on extremism and other virulent forms of antisemitism.[28] Publications include a handbook monitoring such phenomena as pro-Arab propaganda in America,[29] and a guide for security for community institutions in dealing with vandalism and bomb threats.[30] The annual audit of antisemitic incidents compiled and distributed by the Anti-Defamation League is used as the primary barometer by the Jewish community to determine whether or not antisemitism has increased or decreased.[31] Clearly, the Anti-Defamation League, more than any other agency or organization, is the most prominent institution in terms of its visibility and the role it plays in defining the place of antisemitism in contemporary American life.

When professionals from the Anti-Defamation League are asked to define what is the single most important problem facing Jews today in the United States, no uniform response is yielded. Despite their affiliation with what is reputed to be the primary agency fighting antisemitism, ADL professionals are as global in their outlook of what issues affect the Jewish community as other communal service organization professionals. However, one feature that characterizes their response is greater emphasis on external difficulties affecting the Jewish people, and less on internal dilemmas such as intermarriage, assimilation, and education. As might be assumed, several members mention antisemitism as the biggest problem because, in the words of one professional, "Whatever the other problems may be, antisemitism will somehow rear its ugly head." However, antisemitism was not the only problem mentioned by ADL professionals.

Other issues that face Jews named by ADL respondents are the position of Israel and American support for the country, intermarriage, assimilation, and Jewish identity issues, intrareligious division, black–Jewish relations, the rise of the radical right, and apathy, especially among Jews under age 35. In addition to the plethora of Jewish-associated difficulties, comments one ADL professional, "Jews in America are faced by the stress and problems faced by all other members of our society: unemployment, finances, raising children."

Both church–state separation and antisemitism are considered very important by ADL professionals. The proportions selecting each problem as primary was approximately equal, while relatively few saw the two issues as integrated. "The virus of antisemitism is alive and well," one respondent stated. Those with the opinion that antisemitism is more of a threat than church–state separation feel that, in the words of this professional, "the church–state issue is seen by many as a limited, irritating, but not dramatic threat." Professionals believing in the continued importance of vigilant church–state separation disagree.

"Because antisemitism is *not* on the rise, the church–state issue, of extreme importance today, will continue to threaten the future of the Jewish community," affirms one. Antisemitism is secondary, comments a second, asserting that separation of church and state is of greater importance because "it could be a result of the First Amendment being dismantled." Those feeling that a breakdown of church–state separation is more important than a rise in antisemitism believe that once the wall of separation begins to crumble, antisemitism will follow. Maintaining church–state separation, then, in their opinion is a preventative measure. Separation of church and state is important because it ensures that the United States will remain a country with no established religion. "Once a religion is 'established,' all nonestablishment groups are endangered," explained one representative. Some fear second-class citizenship, viewing it not only as uncomfortable, but also as potentially dangerous.

When professionals are asked to assess levels of antisemitism today relative to previous time periods, some interesting contradictions emerge. The belief that there is less antisemitism in the United States today than there was prior to World War II and the 1950s is universal among ADL representatives. Jews are seen as more integrated into American society, and Americans as more tolerant. Civil rights acts and antidiscrimination laws are often mentioned as causes of reduced antisemitism. ADL professionals, however, do not uniformly agree on current levels of antisemitism as compared to antisemitism in the 1970s. While many believe that the diminishing trend continues, there are those who feel that antisemitism has increased in the past 15 years. "The Israel factor" is one of the primary reasons for the belief that levels of antisemitism are greater today than previously. Other reasons listed are the economic success of Jews, in tandem with the continued poverty of blacks, and the visibility—politically, socially, and economically—of Jews.

Many respondents feel that there will be more antisemitism in the United States in ten years, or that there easily could be, under the right combination of negative circumstances. The economic stability of the United States and American relations with Israel are causal factors. The growing time span separating us from the Holocaust, mentioned by several respondents, also increases the probability that a rise in antisemitism could recur.

Not a single respondent believed that there would be less antisemitism in ten years. While levels of antisemitism are thought of as relatively stable, the possibility that antisemitism might threaten the security of Jews in the near future still exists for many. However, quite a few think it unlikely. These responses, however, are justified with a variety of explanations. Those believing in a possible rise in antisemitism point to history, changing attitudes and moods in the United States, and the Holocaust. "I do not foresee pogroms or a Holocaust, but we could become quite uncomfortable given the wrong conditions and the wrong national leaders," clarified one professional.

ADL professionals characterized their institution's philosophy of dealing with antisemitism as one of action. "Our prime objective is to counter assaults on the safety, rights, and image of the Jews," prefaced an ADL professional. Direct confrontation is the mechanism for accomplishing this task. In the words of one ADL professional, their organization approaches the problem of antisemitism through "exposure, counteraction, education, use of the law, and positive and constructive community relations." It is this very notion of action that, in the opinion of ADL respondents, distinguishes their organization from all others. Other features that ADL members consider unique are the annual *Audit of Antisemitic Incidents,* which receives a great amount of public exposure, and fact-finding reports on various groups and individuals. These substantive works, supplemented by the ability for swift and direct action, ensures, according to one member, that the ADL is "not given to shooting from the hip, but we are not so contemplative that we cannot act."

According to ADL professionals, the Anti-Defamation League has a great influence on the American Jewish community's perception of antisemitism. "If any single organization is a barometer of antisemitism," writes one respondent, "it is ADL." Others, equally positive, believe, as does this respondent, that "an objective observer would rate ADL as *the* agency to which American Jews turn for reliable information on antisemitism." Again, the annual *Audit of Antisemitic Incidents* is reported as a way in which the ADL influences community perceptions. However, not all respondents are completely positive about how effective they are in influencing the Jewish community's perceptions. "Sometimes I wonder if the majority of the American Jewish community can be influenced," one professional writes. "Through exposing antisemitism to the community, it is our hope that Jews feel more secure."

The majority of ADL professionals believe, almost unanimously, that groups such as the Ku Klux Klan, Posse Comitatus, and neo-Nazi organizations do not have any effect on the way most Americans think about Jews because they are so outside the pale of acceptable American norms. "They are a small segment of social misfits," writes one professional. "Mainstream society views them as 'crazy,' not accepting their ludicrous diatribes." However, there are some who, despite their classification of such groups as "kooks," think they have some effect on American attitudes, although "their influence is limited to a small segment of the population." Others disagree with this assessment of the extent of their effect, claiming that media exposure telecasts their message to millions of Americans, and that some sympathetic individuals are bound to identify with the antisemitic propaganda. Acts of violence are also seen as a potential danger. However, most respondents, while viewing this violence as possibly more dangerous in the future, do not attribute any great significance to such groups in the present. "Although they have a propensity toward violence, I believe they are of little threat if they are monitored closely," states one respondent. This opinion is standard for ADL professionals. Indeed, the ADL does monitor them closely.

ADL professionals are not totally in unison in their assessment of anti-Zionist or anti-Israel statements and whether or not these statements are antisemitic. While the great majority believe that such statements in many cases are antisemitic, this viewpoint is not reflected by all. "It has been my experience that those who speak and write frequently about Israel in a negative manner are merely attempting to mask their antisemitism," writes one professional who thinks that anti-Israel or anti-Zionist statements are usually antisemitic. "Israel is the victim of a double standard, and most often the so-called Israel Lobby is used as a euphemism for 'Jews,'" agrees another respondent. However, not all community relations workers categorize statements in such a way. "Some do, some don't," writes one dissenting professional. "Political statements reflecting valid concerns may not be antisemitic. Yet we must continue to watch for antisemitism in anti-Israel, anti-Zionist remarks."

The American Jewish Congress

Only four members of the American Jewish Congress responded to the survey on antisemitism. Perhaps that is the greatest indicator of the views of the Congress and their direct role in dealing with antisemitism. One of the four respondents mentioned the Christianizing of America as the single most important problem. Not surprisingly, these few respondents view a breakdown in the separation of church and state as more of a problem than a rise in antisemitism, because they feel that the breakdown of such separation will lead to increased antisemitism. Church–state separation is important to Jews because, in the words of one Congress respondent, "it offers Jews the opportunity to be full participants in the community. Less separation creates a feeling of being a guest, and hence less participation in the democracy." However, these few Congress respondents did not feel that antisemitism might threaten the security of Jews in American society in the future. "Not as long as organizations such as the American Jewish Congress, Committee, and ADL are in place and we maintain a healthy economy," is the hopeful outlook of one Congress respondent. "Democracy and civil rights are too basic to the entire fabric of our society," asserts another.

The legal emphasis, according to these few Congress respondents, is what distinguishes the American Jewish Congress from other defense agencies. "We found you could talk, talk, talk; but when the law was on your side you were able to change things eventually, opinions as well, i.e., in housing, the workplace, etc. We still emphasize use of the law and education." Methods relying on a legal foundation are most often suggested by Congress members as a way of combatting antisemitism. "Sometimes, non-action is correct; other times exposure, or legal action," writes one Congress professional. "Bridge building, backed up by legal remedies where possible," suggested another.

Originally, the focus of the American Jewish Congress was on establishing instruments and programs to combat antisemitism. The American Jewish Congress now devotes relatively little of its attention directly to the problems of antisemitism, choosing rather to concentrate on such issues as the separation of church and state, and other civil rights issues for which it was originally founded. According to Phil Baum, associate director of the American Jewish Congress, antisemitism is not an issue with which the Congress is directly involved. "We don't have an organizational position on antisemitism," he said. "We did, some time ago." When asked how he assessed the issue of antisemitism, he responded by saying, "We do not regard antisemitism as a critical and acute problem at the moment for the Jewish community. We do think there are manifestations of antisemitism that occur, and they have to be confronted and dealt with, according to their form."[32]

The American Jewish Congress approaches problems of antisemitism that can be conceptualized as issues concerning church–state separation. "If anything, our way of dealing with it is the way we would deal with any of the issues, through the law," Evan Mendelson, former associate executive director, commented. "If there are ways within the structure of concern about civil liberties, which we have a great deal of concern about, to protect Jews from outright antisemitism, especially kinds of vandalism or whatever, fine. But if it's not something that falls within that broader protection of civil liberties I don't think we would go for it."[33] So the Congress remains, for the most part, on the sidelines of antisemitism issues, acting, when necessary, as the community's lawyer.

The protection and extension of civil rights have come to dominate the agenda of the American Jewish Congress. Antisemitism, to a limited extent, falls under the general rubric of this agenda. In March 1981 an article by Phil Baum appeared in *Congress Monthly*. The article stated the

American Jewish Congress's stance toward antisemitism, and shortly thereafter was adopted by the National Governing Council of the Congress. The article downplayed the threat of antisemitism, declaring that there was no "wave" threatening American Jews.

The Congress more actively involves itself in issues such as apartheid, for example. A request for contributions was mailed in an envelope proclaiming "Apartheid is a Jewish issue."[34] Israel is also utilized as a fund-raising device. Yet another solicitation letter showed a map of the Middle East, minus the state of Israel. The caption asks, "What's missing from this map?"[35] But the primary concentration remains church–state issues, which are still the major emphasis of Congress fund-raising letters. A recent mailer quotes on the outside of the envelope, "Jewish pressure groups should desist in their efforts to strip religion from public life in America," from the Reverend Pat Robertson. Similarly, a recent Congress letter attempted to raise money on the decision of Judge McGarr allowing government-sanctioned display of a religious tableau in Chicago.[36]

Clearly, the Congress views its mission largely as the legal watchdog and activist in dealing with church–state issues. Rounding out the constellation, it can be seen that the Committee sees itself as the expert in intergroup relations, ADL in combatting antisemitism, and the Congress in dealing with church–state issues.

Community Relations Councils

A total of 13 surveys from various Community Relations Councils across the country were returned. Because of their many associations with other agencies, and the tendency to reflect local culture, a distinct CRC profile or flavor is not as identifiable as the other groups. Several respondents identified their organization as CRC/Federation, while one reported that he was employed by the JCRC/ADL.

When asked what they considered the single most important issue facing Jews today in the United States, a large proportion of CRC professionals responded that Jewish identity, in its various forms, was of greatest concern. Underneath the rubric of Jewish identity fell many issues, such as intrareligious division, the question of "who is a Jew?" and the threat to Jewish continuity. Several others were of the opinion that church–state separation problems are the most important, supporting their belief by pointing to the rise of right-wing and Christian Fundamentalist movements. Antisemitism and Israel were also mentioned as the single most important problems facing Jews today in the United States. Intermarriage and assimilation, Jewish education, and lack of communal affiliation were perceived as among the biggest problems.

CRC professionals are virtually unified in their belief that a breakdown in the separation of church and state presents a greater threat than does a rise in antisemitism. The separation of church and state "has been and is the bedrock of our franchise to equal rights and protection," writes one respondent. "Without it, Jews could become de facto second class citizens, allowing a rationale for antisemitism and discriminatory practices toward Jews." Attributing much of the success achieved by Jews in the United States to "constitutional guarantees that have ensured their religious freedom and also their ability to compete in the job market and professions," most respondents see strict separation as a means of holding antisemitism in check. "Do away with the separation of church and state, and we will see a tremendous rise in antisemitism," explains a professional holding this belief. Only one CRC respondent classified a rise in antisemitism as the greater problem. Separation of church and state is important to Jews because, in the words of another, "it protects our 'piece of the pie' as equal members of a pluralistic society. We do not want our Jewishness, however we choose to express it, to be subject to the sufferance of the Christian majority. Less separation implies increasing the 'Judeo-Christian' which becomes the Christian. . . ." The consequences of less separation are, according to yet another professional, "intimidation and a lessening of our individual rights."

"We are at the lowest point of antisemitism in American history," responded one CRC professional, upon being asked to assess levels of antisemitism today compared with previous time periods. "Those (at least in this region) who feel it is increasing are wrong." In his opinion, Jews who feel that antisemitism is increasing are reacting instinctively. "Antisemitic complaints are few and far between," he continued. "Antisemitism has been on a continual decline since World War II. With the guilt of the Holocaust, birth of Israel, strength and involvement of Jews in the American political process, etc., we are in the strongest, safest situation ever in America." This opinion was echoed by many Community Relations Council professionals. Some, however, expressed the belief that there was more antisemitism now than there had been during the 1970s.

In terms of the future prospects for antisemitism, most respondents did not feel they could predict whether there will be more or less antisemitism in the United States in ten years. Incidents such as the Pollard spy case, insider trading scandals, and the Iran-Contra affair were cited as influential events, and reactions to these events used as evidence both that antisemitism was increasing and that it was not on the rise. Many respondents did not believe that antisemitism would threaten the security of Jews in

American society in the future, but quite a few did state that the possibility exists.

No concrete criteria have been established by CRC professionals to determine whether individual incidents are antisemitic. "I do not feel that you can use a specific guideline to rate an act of antisemitism, but you must consider the act in context," explained one respondent. Another respondent echoed this view, saying that there are "no set criteria—you just instinctively know."

Policies that affect Jews negatively are not seen by most CRC professionals as antisemitic. CRC professionals are cautious about jumping on the "antisemitism bandwagon" too quickly. As professional communal workers, however, it is their responsibility to "distinguish between things that are truly antisemitic and things that may simply be negative in effect," explained one CRC professional.

Community Relations Council professionals describe their institution's philosophy of dealing with antisemitism as one that seeks to meld the operations of the various other Jewish organizations. "We seek consensus, drawing upon input of the national agencies and other community based organizations," explained one professional. As a result of this cooperative approach, CRCs are not always involved, after initial discussion, in a particular problem. "There are issues which we feel it is important to become involved with and to express a point of view," explains one professional. "There are other instances where we lend our support, but feel it is adequate to let other Jewish organizations play a major role in dealing with the issue."

This supportive role is reflected in CRC approaches to the problem of antisemitism. "We have strong ties within our community—with other religious groups and with our state and federal legislatures, as well as the press," informed one professional. Ties with other defense agencies are mentioned as well. "We maintain filters for dealing with complaints," explained a professional. "At times we refer them to the ADL and follow up; at other times we follow up and inform ADL." When asked how Community Relations Councils' approach to antisemitism differs from that of other organizations, most respond that they don't, since they are primarily filtering agents rather than primary actors. "It's not different," explained one CRC professional, "because there is a regional ADL office in our community. Most incidents are handled directly by the ADL professional." Others say they hold the middle of the road between the Anti-Defamation League and the American Jewish Committee.

Community Relations Council professionals state that they influence the American Jewish community's perception of antisemitism through community programs and articles in Jewish newspapers. Education, involvement of Jews with non-Jews, and dialogues are the mothods used to combat antisemitism. According to Jerome Chanes, associate director for domestic concerns of the National Jewish Community Relations Advisory Council, local Community Relations Councils are community instruments for the exchange of information and for the coordination of activities among "defense agencies." CRCs are valuable and important tools for mobilizing and coordinating the resources of diverse groups, nationally and locally, in the handling of community relations problems. Local communities are encouraged to undertake their own assessments of antisemitism. Chanes states:

> The NJCRAC convenes a major meeting each December. Before that meeting we ask communities, all the CRCs and federations around the country, each to engage in its own community process aimed at assessing what's going on, what has happened during the course of the past year. We feed these reports, together with our staff judgments, to our national agencies, community reps, and mavens from

the academic world. We feel that the thoughtful delibera-
tions that we conduct can lead to a better annual assessment of the nature and extent of antisemitism in the
United States. The process is still in its infancy, but it could
be an important one.

The effectiveness of Community Relations Councils
depends in large measure on the participation of its constituent groups and on their willingness to accept the CRC
as a coordinating agency. The CRC structure provides
community relations agencies with opportunities to reach
broad segments of the Jewish community at the local level.
CRCs were originally formed as coordinating bodies.
However, for some time they have been initiating and
carrying out community relations programs in their local
communities. Since these are funded primarily through
Federation sources, minimal competition with the national
bodies results.

The National Jewish Community Relations Advisory
Council, as the umbrella instrument for its constituency of
13 national and 113 community Jewish agencies, attempts
to further cooperation between Jews and other groups.
One of the primary roles of the National Jewish Community Relations Advisory Council is to act as a conduit between local community relations agencies and the national
bodies. NJCRAC policy attempts to ensure that national
agencies recognize that local Jewish community relations
committees and councils (CRCs) are central bodies with
primary responsibility for local community relations policy
and programming. Member agencies are responsible for
doing the substantive programmatic work in different
areas, including antisemitism. The National Jewish Community Relations Advisory Council's role is coordinative.

Jerome Chanes explained the function, in addition to
assessment, of the National Jewish Community Relations
Advisory Council regarding antisemitism.

Individuals or groups in a community will come to a CRC with a range of questions on antisemitism. It might be a specific incident that happened, it might be some kind of allegation, it might be an inquiry on a group or organization. Often, I will consult with one of my colleagues at one of the national agencies—usually ADL, because ADL is most into the antisemitism business, so to speak, they're identified with it, and rightly so. If the situation or question involves certain legislative initiatives or judicial proceedings, I'll work closely with professionals at the American Jewish Committee or Congress in addition to those at ADL. NJCRAC also conducts local and regional consultations for our community member agencies."[38]

The National Jewish Community Relations Advisory Council aims to use the availability of Jewish expertise to combat antisemitism, and to use it efficiently.

Through the National Jewish Community Relations Advisory Council process, Jewish community relations policies are formulated with the participation of all agencies and the communities. Differences are debated in this forum, but usually not publicly. Those differences that cannot be reconciled because they rest on fundamental philosophical or ideological disagreements are reduced to the least controversial common denominator. The judgments, appraisals, and recommendations in every plan represent consensus among the constituent organizations. Where there is less than full consensus, dissenting organizations are afforded the right to state their views, which are published as part of the plan.

As with all umbrella organizations that play advisory roles, the ultimate strength or weakness of NJCRAC lies in its ability to persuade and coordinate, rather than to initiate. As a result, the community relations agenda continues to be defined primarily through the other national bodies and then digested into a national program at

NJCRAC. Nevertheless, the individual activities and priorities of the national bodies are a more accurate representation of the institutional views and agendas of American Jews in dealing with antisemitism.

Conclusions

The constellation of community relations agencies fulfills a number of needs for the American Jewish community. First, the organizational approach to combatting antisemitism represents the most efficient means of dealing with continued anti-Jewish beliefs and behavior. Diminishing expression of antisemitic attitudes cannot be divorced from the actions and programs of the community relations agencies themselves. They do their jobs well.

The fact that these agencies have been successful causes some in the Jewish community to question the need for their continued presence. However, these community relations agencies cannot be disbanded because antisemitism is "cured." Physicians are constantly beset by patients who discontinue taking certain kinds of medications because the medicines are working. Patients with high blood pressure, for example, who achieve normal blood pressure levels with medication, may cease to take such pills when they are "all better." Most Jews, of course, are not willing to dismantle the community relations agency network because the Jewish community is feeling better. Jews view the work of these agencies as essential components in the ongoing need for vigilant monitoring of antisemitic behavior and potential antisemitic threats.

The argument is sometimes raised by some within the Jewish community that agencies such as these are self-perpetuating. Henry Feingold, a scholar who has written extensively about community relations issues, commented in a talk given in 1981 for the 75th anniversary of the American Jewish Committee: "There are those who point out that survival of Jewish agencies is neither a mystery nor a blessing. The agencies are, in fact, the bureaucracies or civil service of the Jewish community and, as with all bureaucracies, they develop an autonomous interest in their survival as well as healthy appetites for funds. The problem with bureaucracies is to get them to stop growing."[39] Certainly, the question is not whether or not community relations agencies are necessary, but are they duplicative, and do they respond most effectively to issues of Jewish self-interest?

Together, community relations agencies constitute an effective lobbying force. Often, the agendas of each are substantially different enough to warrant a special place in the institutional constellation. The strategies differ, the extent to which certain issues are dealt with vary, and the need for multiple approaches can therefore be argued effectively. Since institutions do not adjust rapidly, and different times and events call for different responses, the set of community relations agencies can provide multiple approaches to a single problem. One agency may respond quickly when another may not be able to respond so readily. Furthermore, the different approaches and philosophies of the agencies characterize the multiplicity of views on the part of the Jewish public they represent, as well as' the ambivalence and genuine dissent about how much antisemitism exists in the United States and the best ways to deal with it.

Any single organization would be unlikely to be able to incorporate under its institutional portfolio all of the philosophies and approaches that are advocated and supported by different groups of Jews. In short, many agencies exist because there are many differing views. There is no single Jewish view, and therefore no single institution can possibly represent all American Jews about antisemitism. The duplication issue is less salient than the issues of effectiveness and strategy.

Do community relations agencies help to create or promote Jewish anxiety about antisemitism and other issues in order to raise money and legitimate their place in American Jewish society? It would appear that these agencies reinforce what is already known and provide a framework to examine these issues. The agencies help to keep the American Jewish public wary about antisemitism, but they do not create fear. As Jews become increasingly comfortable in American society and are more assertive about their rights and the "inappropriateness" of antisemitism, the approaches of these agencies appeal to a sizable constituency of the American Jewish community.

While cooperative efforts and programming are desirable, it is to be expected that these agencies will jockey more aggressively for members, funding, and influence within the American Jewish community. The creation of the Wiesenthal Center may accelerate some interagency competition. The director of the Wiesenthal Center, Rabbi Marvin Hier, stated that "the worst charge against us is that we are alarmists and overreact to antisemitism. But which is the worst sin: to overreact or underreact?"[40] As a result of its obvious success in raising funds to combat antisemitism, the Wiesenthal Center has basically upped the ante in the Jewish community relations institutional structure. They have demonstrated an ability to tap into a large reservoir of American Jewish concern about antisemitism. It would not be surprising to see the other agencies responding in some way, either through increased programming or through reassertion of the "proper" means to combat antisemitism. It is not likely that the Wiesenthal Center's strategies and tactics will be ignored.

One of the more interesting observations is that some Jewish community relations professionals view the Jewish public as overreacting to the "reality" of antisemitism. As organizational and institutional agendas are devised over the next ten years, it may be that these institutions may have to look inward as well as outward, to determine who is out of touch with whom.

Since Jewish perceptions of antisemitism change over time, the organization roles shift as well. Jews now see antisemitism as related to a wide variety of connected issues. Therefore, organizational and institutional agendas may shift again. Civil rights, programs in Israel, fighting for Soviet Jews, or a multitude of other issues may emerge as the central proprietary role of one or another of these organizations. Organizations will also continue to reflect differing Jewish views of antisemitism. A decade from now it is probable that some readjustments will have been made, and the organizational agendas will shift with the changing mandates provided them by an evolving Jewish public's views of antisemitism.

Like all organizations and institutions, the community relations agencies have taken on a life of their own. They are active with a multitude of issues, events, and programs. In some ways, they are driven by their own success. They are one avenue that Jews use to operate in the political arena. As Jews become more politically active, the strategic questions of when, and where, and how to intervene will become the most critical issues in how Jews deal with antisemitism.

Chapter Six

THE JEWISH PRESS
A WATCHFUL EYE

How the Jewish Press Influences Perceptions

The Jewish press is one of the key components in the Jewish organizational and institutional network. It is the most important medium through which Jewish leaders voice their concerns, Jewish institutions publicize the results of their studies and their agendas, and the Jewish public is made aware of events occurring in the United States and around the world that affect American Jews. The Jewish press both reflects and molds the opinions of its readers.

The Jewish press, in effect, is a middleman of the Jewish community, bridging institutions and the Jewish public. Furthermore, many different sources provide the Jewish press with information: Jewish organizations and institutions of all kinds, Jewish communal leaders and scholars, the general press, and others. In addition, sources under the aegis of the Jewish press, such as the Jewish Telegraphic Agency, play dual roles, both providing and receiving information. This news network helps shape American Jews' perceptions.

As with the general press, the Jewish press consists of various papers staffed by numerous reporters, editors, and contributors. The Jewish press distributes information of social interest, provides information about national issues of importance to American Jews, reports on develop-

ments in Israel, and, in editorials, opinion pieces, and
letters to the editor, presents a running commentary on
current Jewish problems. Antisemitism is among these
prominently covered areas. The Jewish press ensures that
the Jewish public is aware, informed, and continually vigilant about antisemitism in the United States. It is one of
the primary vehicles for constantly keeping the phenomenon of antisemitism in front of the Jewish public.
Jewish newspapers both verify readers' perceptions that
antisemitism still exists and at the same time informs them
about the nature of antisemitism. The Jewish press con-
firms the persistent, if not threatening, character of contemporary antisemitism.

Jewish newspapers and magazines regularly run stories about those areas that they consider to be of most
interest to their Jewish readership. Articles frequently appear about Israel, for example. Areas covered may include
political activity, relationships with Arab neighbors, or
questions of a religious nature, such as "who is a Jew?"
Local stories about community organizations and institutions receive regular exposure. Human interest stories
about local Jewish citizens are common. Stories about Jewish education, assimilation, and intermarriage are frequently canvassed. And antisemitism is within the hier-
archy of critical areas to be covered extensively.

The Jewish press assumes, not without cause, that
Jewish readers want to know about antisemitic events,
research about antisemitism, antisemitic remarks by public leaders, or findings from any study of antisemitism in
the United States or the world. They report a wide variety
of stories that fall under the general rubric of antisemitism.
Coverage ranges from articles on local antisemitic incidents, to court cases involving antisemitic individuals,
groups, or actions, to results of studies and surveys. Editorials, opinion page pieces, and letters to the editor often
address the issue of antisemitism.

The relationship of Jewish newspapers to both the Jewish community and Jewish communal institutions is complex. Jewish newspapers are a combination of many ingredients. They are, in many places, private enterprises that require catchy news so that papers and advertising can be sold. In some places, they are instruments of the Jewish fund-raising structure. Local Federations, which raise and allocate funds for Jewish social services, Israel, and Soviet Jewry, own and/or operate the weekly paper in a growing number of communities. Since Federations require some means of communication, and many papers require subsidy of some form, local Federations have assumed some of the responsibility for, and autonomy over, the weekly publication. Even where the newspapers are independent, cooperative efforts, either between newspapers or with other institutions, are sometimes formal. In the absence of formal ties, editors and reporters often form informal relationships with representatives of Jewish organizations and institutions.

Furthermore, the editors and reporters themselves are members of the Jewish community. They are not dispassionate observers of the events and trends about which they write. As Jews, they are deeply affected and influenced by matters concerning Israel, assimilation, Jewish education, and other major components of Jewish life, including antisemitism. Neither the Jewish newspaper nor the individuals who work for it can be separated from the organizational and institutional networks of which they are an integral part. Like other Jews, their perceptions are colored by their dual identity as Americans and Jews. The coverage of stories about Israel, assimilation, and antisemitism are influenced by the perceptions of the newspaper editors and publishers themselves.

If the Jewish community can be viewed as a totality with component parts, of which organizations and institutions play an integral function, then the Jewish press must be viewed as one of the essential cogs in the institutional machinery. While it is separate, it is not apart. Nor in many ways is it substantially different. The Jewish press reflects the character of the Jewish community because it is a mainstream player.

Stories about antisemitism, whether a single act of vandalism in a local community or a major national story, such as the Nazi march in Skokie, Illinois, receive comprehensive coverage in the Jewish press. Acts of antisemitism or news stories concerning research about antisemitism that are too insignificant for inclusion in the general press often reach Jewish newspapers. The Jewish press is also the purveyor of the many press releases from community relations agencies. It publicizes conferences, meetings, and program planning about antisemitism and the context of each of these. When a major study about antisemitism is completed, the Jewish press reports the findings. If a conference addressing intergroup relations is held, for example, Jewish newspapers cover the gathering, assess its impact, and present the views of the participants.

Coverage surrounding the disbursement of the annual audit of antisemitic vandalism and harassment produced by the Anti-Defamation League of B'nai B'rith exemplifies the relationship between community relations agencies and the Jewish press. Following the release of these studies, Jewish newspapers publish their findings. Editorials on the results and letters to the editor address various aspects of the study. Sometimes spokesmen from other community relations agencies disagree with the findings, and ensuing debate, at both local and national levels, receives attention in the Jewish press.

Ironically, even with stories about the decline of incidents of antisemitism, the subject itself still receives prominent coverage. Furthermore, the debate that follows about the meaning of these audits may negate whatever

positive news is conveyed through the story itself. Regardless of what the audits indicate, whether the number
of incidents are increasing or decreasing, the story affirms
the continued presence of antisemitic incidents. Other stories about antisemitism also appear, often receiving bold
headlines and prominent placement.

The network of Jewish newspapers also creates a
news-sharing process, so that local stories of antisemitism
in one community may appear in another community
newspaper as well. The Jewish Telegraphic Agency picks
up local stories about antisemitism and relays them to
communities throughout the United States. The Associated Press may play the same role. In this way, local stories about antisemitism often receive national readership.

Incidents of antisemitism in other countries around
the world may also appear in local Jewish newspapers.
The specter of worldwide antisemitism reinforces Jewish
perceptions that the problem remains deep-seeded. International stories reaffirm the suspicion that even when
times are good in the United States, the lessons of other
places and other cultures must be considered. Prominent
stories about antisemitism in Argentina or France are not
uncommon. These stories are likely to appear only in the
Jewish press, but nevertheless they are read by hundreds
of thousands of Jewish households.

Jewish press editors and publishers, essential players
in the Jewish communal institutional network, may
choose to run a story or not run a story about antisemitism, depending on how it may affect the workings of
a particular organization. If, for example, a community
relations agency is working on a problem of antisemitism,
the local Jewish press may wait until the appropriate time
for that story to be publicly discussed. The press may assume the role of reassurer, perhaps acting as a calming
influence. Such a role is consistent with the multiple ap-

proaches that are taken within the community relations agencies themselves. That is, there is no universal agreement on how best to deal with antisemitism. Furthermore, it is consistent with the perceptual continuum of denial, wariness, and fear. Some editors, as it will be shown later in this chapter, may choose not to run an article on antisemitism, feeling that coverage would provide more substance and prominence to a particular activity or event that would be better dealt with by downplaying it or avoiding it altogether. In other words, in some cases, an editor may feel that he may not want to fuel what he believes to be overreaction and paranoia on the part of the Jewish public. The constant tension within the Jewish community about how much antisemitism exists, how to deal with it, and what is really antisemitic plays a role in the decision of editors to run particular stories or not to run them. Here, the "pure" journalistic impulses may give way to the biases and beliefs that individual editors and publishers hold as Jews, and not as newspaper people.

In May 1986 the Cohen Center for Modern Jewish Studies at Brandeis University sent a questionnaire consisting of a wide variety of questions about antisemitism and other issues to editors of Jewish newspapers and magazines throughout the United States.[1] Forty surveys were returned, a response rate of 33%.

From an assessment of the surveys, a composite picture emerges that explains why antisemitism is such a well-covered issue in the Jewish press. First, press members believe that their audience cares about antisemitism. Second, the Jewish press is linked to the Jewish institutional network. Third, Jewish editors and reporters themselves are also the audience. Not only do they represent their constituencies; they reflect them as well. Much of the discussion in this chapter therefore focuses on the Jewish press editors. Because of their central role in screening and forming general perceptions of antisemitism, the opinions of Jewish press members themselves are key components in the formation of Jewish views of antisemitism.

The Network of the Jewish Press

The "Jewish" press is something of a misnomer, just as the "press" fails to capture the diversity and conflicting political and social directions of the media in the United States. The Jewish press is by no means a ubiquitous institution. It consists of scores of newspapers and magazines in cities throughout the United States. Nearly every large urban center has at least one, if not multiple, Jewish newspapers. Major metropolitan areas often have a plethora of Jewish publications. According to Robert Cohn, president of the American Jewish Press Association, there are approximately 250 to 300 Jewish magazines, journals, and newspapers in the United States. These range from small newsletters, consisting primarily of local news and information, to major publications providing extensive coverage of national, international, and local items of importance.[2]

The Jewish Press has its own membership organization, The American Jewish Press Association. Organized in 1943, the American Jewish Press Association (AJPA) is a voluntary organization comprising approximately 180 American Jewish newspapers, magazines, and individual journalists in the United States and Canada. Many small papers, and most medium and large papers, are dues-paying members of AJPA. The combined circulation of AJPA publications is over 4.5 million.[3]

The American Jewish Press Association provides a forum for the exchange of ideas and cooperative activities among the Jewish press. Members gather several times a year to discuss important topics and methods of covering significant issues. Such meetings provide cross-fertilization of ideas for Jewish press editors and reporters. The annual meetings are regular exchange mechanisms through which significant issues are canvassed and discussed. If a specific topic is perceived as being of special interest to their readership, Jewish press members assess how better to cover such stories. Antisemitism is one such topic included in this category.

The Readership of the Jewish Press

Jewish newspapers are generally distributed and read by Jews who are more affiliated with Jewish organizations. In some communities, like St. Louis[4] or Cleveland,[5] a large majority of the Jewish households receive a Jewish newspaper. In larger communities such as Philadelphia, the proportion who receive a Jewish newspaper is smaller.[6] Furthermore, many Jewish organizations have their own magazines. These include *Hadassah*, with a circulation of over 500,000, the National Council of Jewish Women, Conservative Judaism, Reform Judaism, B'nai B'rith, the American Jewish Congress with *Congress Monthly*, and scores of others. Jewish community relations agencies, the Anti-Defamation League, and the American Jewish Committee also send regular bulletins, reports, and other publications to their supporters and members. The likelihood that a Jew will receive some form of Jewish publication is very high.

The nature of the readership of a Jewish publication is largely a function of age and life cycle. Individuals between the ages of 21 and 30 are the least likely to receive a Jewish publication. As these individuals marry, have children, and join Jewish organizations, they are much more likely to receive a Jewish publication. If singles under the age of 35 are removed from the denominator, the majority of Jews receive at least one Jewish newspaper, Jewish magazine, or newsletter.

Furthermore, a number of studies have shown that if someone receives a Jewish newspaper, he or she is very likely to read most of it. Certainly, the main stories concerning Israel, church–state events, and antisemitism will attract the reader's attention. Of course, a story about antisemitism often receives a prominent headline. The importance of the subject is emphasized in terms of article positioning and the language of the headline.

The Jewish Telegraphic Agency

Many of the stories of national significance that appear in local Jewish newspapers originate from the Jewish Telegraphic Agency, a wire service that sends stories and information to the Anglo-Jewish press as well as to the general press. The JTA is regarded as "the AP (Associated Press) of the Jewish press."[7]

The JTA serves as a conduit and screening mechanism for the general press and the Jewish press on stories relating to Jewish concerns and, of course, to antisemitism. Jewish newspapers, newsletters, and magazines pick up JTA stories of a national scope for their Jewish audiences. Occasionally, general newspapers will do the same (but less frequently), displaying stories much less prominently.

The JTA helps disseminate stories concerning antisemitism. Many of these stories come from other wire services, and sometimes from a local Jewish newspaper. Jewish papers sometimes call the JTA with stories of potential interest. Additionally, the European bureau and stringers dispersed throughout major cities in Europe contribute stories to the JTA.[8] By picking up stories of local anti-semitism and distributing them nationwide, the JTA elevates the status of such incidents.

Asked about the frequency with which important stories relating to antisemitism occur, Andy Mushin, assistant editor for the JTA, commented, "Unfortunately, there are far too many of them,"[9] suggesting that antisemitic incidents are more frequent than one might expect. Covering antisemitic incidents, bringing them to the attention of the public, is one of the JTA's major roles. "One of our most important purposes is to report them, to make them known," Mushin continued. To ensure that the Jewish community is not the only beneficiary of this knowledge, the JTA not only provides their client newspapers with daily bulletins; they also send them to individuals, congressmen, senators, and the Soviet Union.

Stories about antisemitism are presented differently in the Jewish press than in the general press. Major stories about antisemitism are certainly reported in the general press. Coverage of antisemitic remarks made during Jesse Jackson's bid for the 1984 presidential nomination provides a good example of the different report methods of Jewish and non-Jewish papers. His antisemitic remarks were covered extensively in newspapers and magazines throughout the United States. However, his "Hymietown" slur received even wider coverage in the Jewish press, with bolder headlines and more prominent placement for longer periods of time. Follow-up commentary appeared, and many letters to the editor were printed about the story. However, smaller-scale events, such as desecration of a Jewish cemetery or the release of a new study on antisemitism, may not be covered at all in the general press. It is not unusual to see an event relating to antisemitism appear on the front page of a Jewish newspaper and be totally absent from the general press.

Stories on antisemitism that appear in Jewish news-papers are reported in various ways. Sometimes they are trumpeted as lead stories across the front page, with bold headlines proclaiming the continuing existence of anti-semitism. In other instances, stories on antisemitic inci-dents are placed further inside the paper, not appearing dramatically different from other stories on important is-sues. Placement and layout of stories on antisemitism de-pend to a great extent on the availability of other stories of significance to the Jewish community. However, place-ment is also a distinctly editorial decision and may reflect the editor's own set of denial, wariness, and fear perceptions.

Although not every Jewish newspaper contains an article about or relating to antisemitism in each issue, many papers often do. For example, early in 1987 the ma-jority of Jewish newspapers reported on the overturning of the conviction of noted antisemitic propagandist Ernst Zundel in Canada. Concurrently, the annual *Audit of Anti-semitic Incidents*, published by the Anti-Defamation League, was covered, discussed, and editorialized. An-other poll, which revealed white Protestants' favorable views of Jews, also received extensive coverage in the Jew-ish press. Agency representatives at both the national and the local level were quoted assessing the meaning of these studies for the American Jewish community. During the same time, many Jewish papers also featured occurrences in Cumming, Georgia, site of two civil rights marches within a two-week time span. Pictures of Ku Klux Klan members and riot police appeared in many Jewish papers. Comments of Klan members were juxtaposed with the statements of American Jewish leaders attending the march. A veritable barrage of events, marches, studies, and court cases relating to antisemitism reached the Jew-ish community in early 1987.

Among the articles pertaining to antisemitism that appeared in many Anglo-Jewish papers in the first two months of 1987, were several of international significance, stories on the Neo-Nazi Party in West Germany and appearance of a revival of the infamous book, *The Protocols of the Elders of Zion*, in the Soviet Union. On the local level, the *Jewish Advocate*, Boston's weekly Jewish newspaper, featured lead stories on antisemitism in area universities. LOCAL CAMPUSES GRAPPLE WITH ANTI-SEMITIC ACTS was the front-page heading for two stories: "Swastikas Appear at UMass Boston" and "Mystery Enfolds Tufts Attack."[10] In addition, speakers addressed the topic of antisemitism in locations across the country, and these appearances were publicized in local Jewish papers.

Stories about American Nazis, antisemitic acts on campuses, or pictures of the Ku Klux Klan feed Jewish readers' worst fears. The isolation or infrequency of these events is less important than their continued presence. These stories certainly verify the need for continued institutional monitoring and legal combat to deal with extremist groups.

The Nature of Coverage

The tone of these articles varies a great deal. Many downplay the presence of antisemitism in America, while others, notably those covering incidents of vandalism or defacement, are more inflammatory. However, most stories are not alarmist. In some instances, merely reporting the facts behind a story can be somewhat sensational, given the nature of the subject. The Ernst Zundel issue is a case in point. Many papers reported that Zundel was sentenced in 1985 to 15 months' imprisonment for distributing a booklet entitled "Did Six Million Really Die?"—a denial that the Holocaust occurred. They then proceeded to give the update on the case.[11]

Providing a background of the story before proceeding to the current developments is often a standard journalistic approach. However, owing to the nature of the case, the unexpected overturning of the previous conviction, and the implications of this occurrence, the press conveyed a sense of shock, a feeling of lack of control. "Jews and civil liberty advocates are surprised at the decision of the Ontario Court of Appeals that unanimously reversed the conviction of a German-born anti-Semite in 1985" was the opening line of one story, which appeared in the *Youngstown* (Ohio) *Jewish Times*.[12] This expression of surprise, the unforeseen reversal, and the emphasis placed on the fact that the conviction was unanimously overturned, encourage perceptions that antisemitism may be on the rise.

The *Jewish News* of Detroit ran a story, complete with a picture of a vandalized Yeshiva, under the headline ANTI-SEMITIC INCIDENTS JUMPED IN MICHIGAN.[13] While it did not appear on the front page, it was still in the foresection of the paper. The story focused on increases in antisemitic vandalism in Michigan, as reported in the 1986 annual *Audit of Anti-Semitic Incidents* published by the Anti-Defamation League. The number of incidents in the state that were reported had increased dramatically since 1985. While the story mentioned national decreases in vandalism, bombings, and arson against Jews, it naturally emphasized the position of Michigan relative to the national average. The regional director of the Anti-Defamation League's Michigan division addressed the problem, and the paper reported on accelerated activity by the Michigan region's security committee. This balanced the coverage, resulting in reporting that reflected the middle ground with which most Jews are comfortable.

Similar stories of violence or vandalism on the local level evoke like responses. While they are more alarmist by the very nature of the acts, Jewish papers strive not to be pessimistic or foreboding. These newspapers often rely on other Jewish institutions to place the problem in the proper perspective. The local chapter of the Anti-Defamation League is usually mentioned, as a reassurance to readers, and the director of the regional office quoted. Community relations professionals also act as spokesmen to ensure that the problems of antisemitism are being handled.

Some articles addressing antisemitism are even optimistic. Stories reporting the Anti-Defamation League's annual *Audit of Anti-Semitic Incidents* in 1984, 1985, 1986, and 1987 usually stressed the reduction in actual acts of reported vandalism. Papers also mentioned successful legislation creating anti-bias laws, and the growing cooperation of local police forces. Articles on other surveys, such as the nationwide poll of Evangelical and Fundamentalist Christian attitudes toward Jews, or studies of the attitudes of non-Jews toward Jews, challenged negative assumptions. SURVEY ON CHRISTIAN ATTITUDES CITES POSITIVE FINDINGS was the headline for one paper.[14] FUNDAMENTAL FRIENDS was the heading for another.[15]

Altogether, the coverage of antisemitism in the Jewish press is extensive and tends to be balanced and objective. It is neither hysterical nor overly optimistic. The coverage tends to reflect the way most Jews see antisemitism in the United States.

Coverage in Jewish Press versus General Press

While stories of national significance that concern Jews are widely covered by the general press, day-to-day stories of battles with antisemitism are left to the Jewish press. Such events are sometimes assigned to the Religion section of general papers, where, owing to limited space and the presence of several religious groups, they are often omitted.

Some general newspapers are more likely to consider stories about antisemitism as worthy of coverage in the front half of the paper. This is largely due to the size of the Jewish population in the paper's local market. The *New York Times* is much more likely to run articles on antisemitism than is the *Indianapolis News*. The *New York Times,* with its large Jewish readership, fills the need of an important submarket.

One of the questions in the national survey of Jewish press editors requested respondents to assess how their coverage differed from that of the general press. Members of the Jewish press felt that their investigation was quicker and that stories were covered for longer periods of time, as well as more extensively. Most important, Jewish press members felt that their reporting on antisemitic incidents innately assumed the significance of such stories, a matter that Jewish press members did not feel was always reflected in secular coverage of antisemitic incidents. As one editor of a Jewish weekly responded, "Such incidents that are proved to be antisemitic are not always considered newsworthy by the secular press, as they may appear minor in relation to other news events." Another editor retorted that antisemitism is often not seen as a "sexy" issue, neither new nor daring, by the general press.

Coverage of significant antisemitic incidents and extremist groups sometimes merits the attention of nationally read papers and brings the general public's attention to the continued existence of antisemitism. These magazines and newspapers generally do not address the issue of antisemitism, however, unless it is enmeshed in an exciting, dangerous, or offbeat story, or is part of a more general story regarding racial and ethnic conflict.

While coverage by the general press is often very temporal in nature, when an issue is "hot" it is covered very thoroughly. Several stories of significance to the general American population as well as to the American Jewish population were featured in magazines, newspapers, and on national television during 1985, 1986, and 1987. The farm belt crisis, the popularity of racist demagogues such as Louis Farrakhan, and the significance of attitudes held by Christian Fundamentalists exemplify issues that concerned the entire nation, as well as the more specific Jewish population, and therefore appear in both the general and the Jewish press. Each of these events is discussed below.

Louis Farrakhan

Louis Farrakhan rose to national prominence as a result of his support for Jesse Jackson's 1984 presidential campaign. Threatening a *Washington Post* reporter who divulged Jackson's use of the term *Hymie*, Farrakhan received a forum to trumpet his own antisemitic views and was catapulted into the public eye. In the aftermath of the 1984 election, Farrakhan maintained and even accelerated his attacks against Jews, before ever larger and more enthusiastic audiences.

In October 1985, the *Washington Times* featured a story on the link between Farrakhan and American Nazi Thomas Metzger. The article, written by Tom Braden, a nationally syndicated columnist, was engendered by Farrakhan's recently completed nationwide tour, which drew standing-room crowds in major cities.[16] One week later, *Time* magazine followed up with an essay entitled "The Demagogue in the Crowd."[17] The *New Republic* also cov-

ered Reverend Farrakhan's emergence to national prominence. Fred Barnes, in an article aptly titled "The Farrakhan Frenzy (What's a Black Politician to Do?)" assigns
the media responsibility for ushering Farrakhan to fame.
He goes on to cite the rising volume of Farrakhan coverage, writing that the "Farrakhan hype is in full swing."
Barnes's purpose, one that by this point could be taken to
heart by the general as well as the Jewish press, was to call
for moderation:

> It's not that Farrakhan doesn't warrant coverage; when he
> fills Madison Square Garden beyond capacity, that is a big
> story. What's missing is perspective and clearheaded anal-
> ysis. Farrakhan has spoken in New York dozens of times.
> Why was this appearance significant? Is Farrakhan merely
> a media creation, or is he building grass-roots momentum
> behind his movement? Rather than attempting to answer
> these questions, the press has dwelled relentlessly on a
> single issue: Do you hate Farrakhan or love him?[18]

The article appearing in *Time* magazine, however, did
not focus solely on Farrakhan as hate monger. Rather, the
issue here was the presence of so many supporters of his
racist dogma, and the ambivalence of many black leaders
to denounce him. A demagogue requires support from
others with similar prejudices, Roger Rosenblatt, the author of the piece, asserted:

> People wonder why journalists make so much of Far-
> rakhan. This is one reason why. If Farrakhan were a single
> voice in the wind, little would be risked by letting him
> bellow without notice. But he has accomplices in tens of
> thousands of secret haters who are at least as dangerous as
> their hero because they are anonymous. The press may or
> may not create Farrakhan, but it does not create the silent
> haters.[19]

The Farrakhan story was at this point enlarged to
such a degree that mention of his name was sure to result
in emotionally charged statements by blacks, Jews, and

the press. Farrakhan's skill in exploiting these tensions is only surpassed by his ability to capitalize on media exposure. Fred Barnes explained Farrakhan's success in manipulating the media:

> Louis Farrakhan has figured out the secret of demagoguery. First the posters announcing his appearance go up—"Power at Last Forever," they say—and alarm bells go off in the city's Jewish community. Then pressure is exerted on black officials, not always subtly, to denounce the Black Muslim minister. Next a press conference is called at which Jews and some but not all black leaders criticize Farrakhan. This gets TV and newspaper coverage, but so do comments by other blacks who either defend Farrakhan or complain about being leaned on to attack him. The press, which loves a good rift, now has a running story to cover. Finally, Farrakhan makes his appearance, and he rarely lets anyone down. If his message were confined to black self-help, he'd be ignored by the media. So he performs as expected, peppering his speech with racist and anti-Semitic slurs.[20]

Because of their specific focus, Jewish newspapers were much more likely to introduce the Farrakhan issue differently than the general press. Community relations agencies addressed the issue but placed it in the Jewish perspective. "We've seen his type rise and fall throughout our lives, throughout the lives of our forebears," said Nathan Perlmutter, the former national director of the Anti-Defamation League. Jewish newspapers emphasized the company Farrakhan kept, the unwillingness of black leaders to denounce him, and the antisemitic comments Farrakhan spewed. The Farrakhan phenomenon became an explosive item in the Jewish press. Farrakhan represented the introduction of antisemitic rhetoric into national politics. No aspect of antisemitism, beyond actual expression and violence, is more threatening to American Jews. The views that he expressed called for immediate repudiation on the part of the Jewish publishers and editors. Unlike the general press, the Jewish press found it necessary to emphasize the extensive danger that Farrakhan represented to the Jewish public. In many ways, Farrakhan was not just another story about antisemitism. He was something new in that he was something old—the reappearance, or the threat of the reappearance, of antisemitism in American politics.

The presence of nationally covered stories like those on Farrakhan exacerbates Jews' attitudes and fears regarding the prevalence of antisemitism. No longer was antisemitism the concern of extremists on the fringe. The media granted it national prominence, which in a sense legitimized it. Coverage in Jewish newspapers then snowballed.

By the end of the year, general press attention to Reverend Farrakhan had dwindled. However, Farrakhan was still a topic of concern in the Jewish press, focusing on black–Jewish tensions. The Farrakhan "problem" was also being monitored by community relations agencies, who produced scores of writings. "Look Who's in Farrakhan's Corner," an article that appeared in the December 1985 Anti-Defamation League *Bulletin* and was reprinted in several Jewish newspapers in January 1986, reported on a meeting of Farrakhan and the leaders of several antisemitic organizations such as the Ku Klux Klan, neo-Nazi groups, and other racist organizations.[21] The article, written by the director of the fact-finding department of the Anti-Defamation League's civil rights division, indicated that support for Black Muslim leader Louis Farrakhan was growing among other racist and antisemitic organizations. Although the general press had already discontinued coverage of Farrakhan, considering it "old news," the Jewish press continued to monitor and report about Farrakhan's activities.

Results of a survey of national black leadership,

which determined that Jesse Jackson was viewed by many blacks as their foremost spokesman, appeared in both the general and the Jewish press. However, while the general press assigned primary importance to the position of Jackson, Jewish papers emphasized Farrakhan. The *Washington Post* reported the survey findings under the heading "Jackson Gains Top Ranking as Spokesman for Blacks."[22] Another paper reported the findings under "Jewish Organization Finds Jackson Top Black Spokesman."[23] Jewish newspapers, on the other hand, used the same survey to indicate that Farrakhan's influence was growing. The *Jewish Week* of Washington, D.C., ran an article under the heading "Poll Shows Farrakhan Popularity Increases."[24] The Jewish press was tuning in its readers to the presence of a virulently antisemitic national figure. By emphasizing the position of Farrakhan, rather than headlining generally positive attitudes toward Jews that the study also found, the Jewish press focused on Jewish concerns with antisemitism.

The Farm Crisis

The activities of hate groups attempting to foment antisemitism in the Midwest were covered extensively in both the general and the Jewish press in 1985 and 1986. Antisemitism and the farm crisis were originally covered in early August 1985 by Jewish papers, such as the *New York Jewish Week*, which ran a story titled "Midwest Farm Crisis Sparks Wave of Antisemitism."[25] These stories also announced that a program on the farm crisis would air on the nationally televised program "20/20."

"Seeds of Hate," the "20/20" show, brought the activities of extremist hate groups to the attention of the general public.[26] Right-wing extremists, attempting to exploit the difficult economic times facing farmers, were distributing pamphlets filled with antisemitic dogma, blaming the entire crisis situation on "Jewish bankers" and "the Jewish conspiracy." They were also calling for meetings and advocating legal scams and violence as ways to avoid paying debts. Magazine and newspaper stories covering the existence of these organized hate groups usually mentioned that farmers were often targeted as possible recruits by such right-wing organizations.

The Jewish community responded to the situation in a variety of ways. The Kansas City Jewish Community Relations Bureau (JCRB) began a Farm Crisis Project in April 1985 that received extensive coverage by Jewish newspapers, particularly those located in the Midwest. The project involved over 600 urban Jews in workshops and forums detailing economic and social problems of family farmers.[27] In 1986, 60 members of the Jewish Community Relations Bureau in Kansas City went on a farm tour to Chillicothe, Missouri, in an attempt to transform attitudes of local farmers about Jews. The members visited farms and expressed support for the farmers' struggle. The JCRB achieved a high media profile for its farm tour, which was covered prominently in the Kansas City papers and carried by the Associated Press in newspapers across the country.[28]

Efforts by coalitions of religious and farm leaders have also received widespread attention. In February 1987 the *Rocky Mountain News* ran a commentary piece by a United Press International writer in the Religion Section.[29] "Religious Groups Join to Save Family Farms" concerned the recently held Interreligious Conference on Rural Life. Joint statements and press releases were also issued by member organizations attending the conference, among them the American Jewish Committee, the National Council of Churches, the Rural Crisis Issues Team, the National

Catholic Rural Life Conference, and several other Christian groups and farm advocacy agencies.[30]

Jewish press coverage of the farm crisis differed in several ways from that of the general media. Interestingly enough, the significance of hate groups attempting to attract farm support for antisemitic and racist ideas was debated by Jewish leaders, and this dissonance was reflected in stories printed by the Jewish press. The *Jewish Journal* published a story in March 1986 that reported on the disagreement between representatives of various Jewish agencies as to the relative significance of the farm crisis.[31] The general press, on the other hand, while assigning little political significance to such right-wing extremist groups, did not ever actually call into doubt the importance of the issue. Despite the fact that the Anti-Defamation League declared that actual overt antisemitic incidents had not increased in the farm belt states, antisemitism among farmers continued to be covered in the Jewish press.

Like Farrakhan, the farm crisis received serious attention in the Jewish press. They are watchful of the signs of extremism gaining influence or legitimacy. Therefore, what may seem to be a localized phenomenon, in terms of either region or numbers, takes on special significance for the Jewish press and Jews all over the United States.

Survey of Christian Fundamentalists

The attitudes and beliefs of Christian Fundamentalists have concerned Jews for quite some time. Many Jews fear that the resurgence of evangelical religious fervor might spawn a new wave of antisemitism, because these groups threaten the barriers between church and state. In 1981 the Reverend Bailey Smith, then president of the Southern

Baptist Convention, told a right-wing rally that God "does not hear the prayer of a Jew." His comment served to fuel Jews' fear.

In 1985 the Jewish magazine *Reconstructionist* ran a story by Nathan Perlmutter, former president of the Anti-Defamation League of B'nai B'rith, on Jews and Fundamentalism. Perlmutter claimed that many Jews hold erroneous beliefs about Fundamentalists. Far from being mindlessly militant and antisemitic, Fundamentalists, Perlmutter stated, are "much of the time respectful, even downright reverential toward Jews, and . . . give Israel wholehearted, uncritical admiration."[32] A New York paper, the *Jewish Post and Opinion*, also ran an article reviewing Perlmutter's article.[33]

Early in 1987 the results of a survey of 1,000 white Fundamentalists were published in both the general and the Jewish press. Headlines were generally positive in both, although those of the general press tended to be more optimistic. The *Washington Post* ran the findings under the title "Poll Finds No Rise in Anti-Semitism: Most Evangelicals Reject Jewish Stereotypes."[34] Other optimistic headlines appeared in the *Chicago Tribune*, "Anti-Semitism Fading for Some,"[35] and in the *Chicago Sun-Times*, "Anti-Semitic Views Spurned in Poll."[36]

Headlines in Jewish newspapers, on the other hand, were a bit more conservative: "Evangelical Attitudes Surveyed in Poll" was the story that ran in the *Baltimore Jewish Times*.[37] The Community Relations Committee of the Springfield, Massachusetts, Jewish Federation ran the *Washington Post* article. The story printed by the *Kansas City Jewish Chronicle*, which at the same time had been covering interfaith dialogue addressing the farm crisis situation, was one of the more optimistic articles in a Jewish paper—"Survey on Christian Attitudes Cites Positive Findings."[38]

Discussion of the findings of the Evangelical survey also appeared on editorial pages of several non-Jewish papers. The *Washington Times* ran an editorial under the byline "Catching Up,"[39] while the *Chicago Sun-Times* Commentary section included several paragraphs about the "Heartening Anti-Semitism Poll."[40] Such studies, as with regularly conducted surveys by Louis Harris and other polling agencies, comment on changing attitudes toward Jews. While they are encouraging and optimistic, however, they continue to emphasize the fact that not everyone holds favorable feelings about Jews.

Coverage of such stories in the general and the Jewish press serves several purposes: It assures Jews that such stories are significant, it points out that the United States has become increasingly tolerant of diverse groups within the last few decades, and it also serves to highlight the presence of significant proportions of the population who still adhere to negative stereotypes about Jews.

A Profile of Jewish Press Editors

Jewish press members are much like the American Jewish community. They reflect in microcosm other Jews, demographically, organizationally, and religiously. Furthermore, antisemitism assumes about the same importance for editors as for their readership audience. The range of Jewish press members responding to the questionnaire included independent journalists, managing editors, editors emeritus, publishers, and staff writers. Respondents represented all areas of the country. Place of birth, marital status, number of children, religious affiliation, and secular and Jewish education of those answering the survey are as varied as those of the general Jewish population.

Press representatives surveyed did not appear to be much different from the general population to whom they reported. Survey respondents ranged, for the most part, between the ages of 26 and 65, although 13% are 66 years of age or older. The majority, 84%, were married, and over three-fourths had children. Writers for Jewish newspapers have family compositions similar to their readership. Like the general Jewish population they are a mobile group, with 50% not living in the state in which they were born (see Table 6-1).

Religious affiliation of press respondents generally reflects that of the general Jewish population. The largest proportion of respondents consider themselves Conservative Jews, while "other," a category comprised of secular Jews, non-observant Jews, and those on the border between Orthodox, Conservative, and Reform, had the second highest representation. In most communities, the proportion of Reform Jews is higher than that of other denominations. Reform press respondents, however, accounted for about 16% of those surveyed, and Orthodox members of the Jewish press constituted 11% of all respondents.

Much like the general Jewish population, members of the Jewish press have attained high levels of secular education. The amount and kind of Jewish education they received was varied. Most had attended afternoon Hebrew school or Sunday school; only 11% had attended yeshiva or day school.

Editors assessed the importance of several problems currently facing Jewish people. Among the issues of importance were separation of church and state, programs to combat antisemitism, neighborhoods where Jews can live with other Jews, Jews marrying other Jews, and Jewish children receiving a Jewish education. All are topics that have been covered repeatedly in Jewish newspapers in the recent past. Three of the five issues were considered very important by over three-fourths of the respondents; a small proportion considered any of the issues to be unimportant (see Table 6-2).

Programs to combat antisemitism are considered very important by a majority of members of the Jewish press, but less so than the issues of the separation of church and state, and Jewish children receiving a Jewish education, which were considered very important by over 80% of press respondents. Jews marrying other Jews was viewed as very important by almost three-quarters of those answering the survey. A large majority of Jewish press respondents, 68%, felt that programs to combat antisemitism were very important. This proportion is greater than the share of community relations professionals attributing such importance to antisemitism programs, but lower than that of the general public.

Some other interesting patterns were revealed by the survey. While the greatest share of Jewish press members rated the separation of church and state as very important, Jewish children receiving a Jewish education was considered the single most important issue. Additionally, throughout the survey the prevalence of intermarriage and assimilation are stressed as extremely important problems (see Table 6-3). As with other Jews, achieving the delicate balance of living in two worlds is seen as most important for contemporary American Jews.

Considerable attention is paid to issues regarding the separation of church and state, which in the minds of the editors cannot be separated from the issue of antisemitism. Jewish concern regarding the separation of church and state, as expressed by a number of the editors, goes beyond a theoretical opposition to state-imposed religion. As a Jewish minority in a Christian society, American Jews are concerned with protecting their religious freedom, to be sure. But even more so, they fear that encroachment upon their religious life carries with it a threat of antisemitic behavior. In other words, Jews are not only concerned about their freedom to worship as they please but they feel strongly about the creation of an environment that fosters antisemitic beliefs and behaviors. The establishment of majority rights, which those advocating prayer in school and religious symbols on public property uphold, negates the premise and promise of a pluralistic society, explained several editors. Minorities thus become marginal. To prevent such an atmosphere, Jews concern themselves with maintaining the separation of church and state, which they view as closely linked to antisemitism. Members of the Jewish press fear that any breakdown of separation of church and state is a precursor for increased antisemitism.

How They Cover Stories: Responses from Jewish Press Members

Respondents from the Jewish press were asked their definition of *antisemitism* and *antisemitic incidents*. While no hard-and-fast definition of either term exists, answers are relatively uniform. Derogatory stereotyping, verbal prejudice, vandalism, and discrimination against Jews as a specific group are the most prevalent answers. Antisemitism is described as "a negative bias or expectation based solely on an individual or group's Jewish affiliation." Attributing unusual power, control, or conspiracy to the Jews in general is also classified as antisemitic. Defining an "antisemitic incident" as "an offensive or destructive verbal or physical act that is explainable by reasonable observers as a protest against a person, group, or institution because the person, group or institution is Jewish" allows for the grouping of such varied occurrences as vandalism, stereotyping, and discrimination.

How do Jewish press editors determine if an incident is antisemitic? Various criteria were offered by those members surveyed. "Is it obviously directed against Jews? Is it offensive?" offered one press member as a testing method. Intentions, circumstances and motivation, and language are the most frequently cited criteria for determining whether an incident is portrayed as antisemitic. Who were the parties involved? Is their behavior the result of specific racial or religious prejudice? Is their language slanderous or derogatory? Deciding whether or not to cover a story as antisemitic requires these questions be asked. Otherwise, the story may be a piece of news on vandalism rather than a story of antisemitism. As one respondent wrote: "If the perpetrator communicates a hatred of Jews, the incident is antisemitic. Vandalizing a Jewish home is not antisemitic. Vandalizing a Jewish home with Nazi stickers is antisemitic. Beating up a Jew is not antisemitic. Beating up a Jew while cursing his heritage is antisemitic." Acts directed against Jews with intentional hostility merit consideration as "antisemitic."

Not all incidents of antisemitism are considered suitable for publication. Relatively uniform criteria are used to determine whether or not a particular story is printed: veracity, whether or not the event is controversial and in what ways, ability to document the story, and if publishing the story will be beneficial in any way. The last criterion reflects the role editors play, not only as newspaper professionals but also as Jews. Several respondents stated that in a situation where publishing an antisemitic story would create friction in the community, the article would be held. "Where publicity would damage, perhaps irreparably, inter-community relations, we would elect not to publish the incident," one editor explained. One respondent wrote that newspaper policy avoids fomenting unpleasantness arising from suspected but difficult-to-prove antisemitic incidents: "If an 'event' occurs, we would cover it. If there is an ongoing below-the-surface antisemitism, such as restrictions from private clubs, we will not create controversy as long as laws are not violated." If publicizing restrictions would result in negative feelings, rather than accomplish anything constructive, a Jewish newspaper might not cover the story. Rather, it would leave the incident to the local community relations organizations, reporting the story upon its successul resolution.

In general, most survey respondents wrote that if an incident is truthful and accurate, it is covered. Motivation plays an important role in determining whether or not an incident is considered antisemitic, as is seen in responses to previous questions in the survey. "We try to determine whether an incident was indeed an innocent mistake (as has often happened in the past) or was motivated by a hatred toward Jews and what they represent," answered one press member. This response is the general standard for the majority of press respondents.

Robert Cohn, editor-in-chief of the *St. Louis Jewish Light*, expanded on his paper's criteria of selection:

Is it in the public domain? Then it's covered. For example, there was a Nazi march in South St. Louis, and a Nazi rally and confrontation in Breckenridge Hills, and both were, of course, covered. They also got national publicity. The incidents were phoned in to the JTA.

For other incidents we make different decisions, judgment calls. An example: Swastikas are spray painted on the facade of a temple. Do we cover it, or just report it to the police and don't report it in the paper? In a situation like that we weigh the facts. We have hard evidence. Would covering it be enlightening, or counter-productive?

Who would it help? Would it help the person it happened
to? The Jewish community? We do not try to avoid controversy, and will cover newsworthy events, but we sometimes make a judgment call about whether to cover the
story or not. Is this story going to be helpful, or will publishing it trigger more of that kind of thing? That's the
question usually asked in the vandalism-type cases.[41]

The issue of whether or not to cover certain antisemitic incidents, such as vandalism or desecration of a
Jewish cemetery, is often debated. Sometimes Jewish community relations professionals are reluctant to report incidents to the general public, believing that it might draw
attention to the perpetrators and give them free publicity.
Not wanting to foment "copy-cat" incidents, an occurrence might go unreported to the public. The role that the
Jewish press plays in such incidents is sometimes a function of their relationship with local Community Relations
Council professionals.

Several respondents mentioned that the Jewish Community Relations Council acts as a filtering agent for articles regarding antisemitism, approving stories to be covered. Sometimes a story might seem borderline, very
sensitive. In that case, if relations with other Jewish agencies were open-ended, the editor of the Jewish paper
would check with the community relations agencies. If
they say, "It's at a delicate stage right now," or "We're not
sure of the facts," then the paper often will hold off on
covering the incident. However, if an agency is simply
reluctant to have them cover the story, journalism ethics
prevail, and they cover it anyway. There must be reasons
for postponing the coverage of a valid, important story.

A small number of respondents felt that antisemitism
was overemphasized by the Jewish press. Concern with
antisemitism is equated by these few as paranoia. "In general, the newspaper and the community tend to be overly

sensitive," one said. The personal opinion of a few respondents was that antisemitism is an overplayed concept. "Antisemitism is such a subjective word . . . over-
laid with so much, that it's hard to define what constitutes
antisemitism," explained Arthur Magida, Assistant Editor
of the *Baltimore Jewish Times*.[42] He attributes many claimed
experiences of antisemitism to paranoid, unfounded fears,
assumptions by callers that the world is unfriendly to
Jews. Such feelings, Magida believes, constitute one of the
larger problems facing modern American Jews.

"I personally don't think it's as blatant, virile and nasty, and as 'alive and well' as some people would think it
is."[43] To this end, Mr. Magida wrote a feature story for the
Baltimore Jewish Times in 1986 on Jewish paranoia and antisemitism entitled "Jewish Paranoia." Much to his surprise, he received no response to his article.

The majority of press respondents, however, do not
share his opinion. Rather, they stated that antisemitic incidents are newsworthy events deserving of coverage.
While no respondent relayed information on formal newspaper policy concerning antisemitism, the general consensus was that if it is news, it is printed. Although he personally believes an inordinate amount of credence is given
to incidents of antisemitism, Mr. Magida states that "it is
incumbent upon the press, Jewish and otherwise, to acknowledge that there is a certain level of antisemitism."[44]

Antisemitism is perceived by press correspondents as
a continuing threat, but one that is more dormant than
active. Respondents were asked how much antisemitism
they felt existed in their community: a great deal, a moderate amount, little, or none. Fifty percent of the press members surveyed believe that a great deal or a moderate
amount of antisemitism exists in their community. However, relatively few believe that their area hosts a great
deal of antisemitism, 3%, with the preponderance, 47%,

perceiving a moderate amount of antisemitism in their community. A slightly smaller share, 45%, were of the opinion that there was little antisemitism in their community. None of the press agents surveyed felt that no antisemitism was present.

While less than half of all respondents believed that a moderate amount of antisemitism exists *in their community* (47%), almost three-fourths (74%) were of the opinion that there was a moderate amount of antisemitism *in the United States*. Respondents clearly felt that, while antisemitism may be little felt in their own community, it is more prevalent elsewhere in the United States (see Table 6-4).

Explanations for this differential are many and varied. Because members of the Jewish press interact with other press professionals in various cities, they frequently hear about antisemitic incidents in areas outside of their general locale. They also cover prominent stories in their papers. The very fact that national and international stories on antisemitism run so frequently, more often than the occurrence of actual local incidents, also serves to elevate perceptions of the level of antisemitism in the United States.

Personal Experiences of Antisemitism

Only a marginal proportion of press respondents claim to have experienced no antisemitism in their lifetime. The great majority, 95%, have experienced some, whether it was a little, a moderate amount, or a great deal. Asking press members how much antisemitism they had personally experienced yielded some interesting information. Although the greatest share of respondents believe that a moderate amount of antisemitism exists in both their community and the United States, when asked how much antisemitism they had *personally* experienced in their lifetime, a majority of press members cited experiencing little.

Their reasons for stating that a moderate amount of antisemitism exists when they have personally experienced only a little is revealing. More than half of those surveyed, 58%, have personally experienced a little antisemitism in their lifetime. However, more than a third of Jewish press respondents have personally experienced a great deal or a moderate amount of antisemitism. Over one-fourth of respondents, 26%, have experienced a moderate amount of antisemitism, while 11% have experienced a great deal of antisemitism in their lifetime. Such experiences have an effect on press members, whether implicitly or explicitly. *Only* 5% of those surveyed claim to have personally experienced no antisemitism in their lifetime. Aggregating these figures highlights certain aspects of the question. Of those surveyed, 37% have experienced a great deal or a moderate amount of antisemitism. While 63% have personally experienced little or no antisemitism, the proportion of those who have personally experienced some antisemitism is strikingly high.

Almost a fourth of those surveyed, 24%, reported that they had personally experienced antisemitism in the last 12 months. Incidents ranged from derogatory comments to vandalism, hate mail, and insensitivity on the part of a local PTA, which, despite requests to discuss the issue of separation of church and state, held religious fund-raisers for the school. Comments such as "You don't look like any Jew" were mentioned by several respondents as examples of personally experienced antisemitism.

Members of the Jewish press differ from the Jewish public in one significant way. They report their experiences with antisemitism. Over three-fourths (78%) of those who had personally experienced antisemitism in the

past 12 months reported the incidents. Antisemitic incidents were brought to the attention of the Anti-Defamation League, Jewish Community Relations Councils, the
local police, and, of course, the readership of the Jewish
newspapers (see Table 6-5).

Like the general Jewish community to whom they report, Jewish press representatives believe that a moderate
amount of antisemitism exists in their communities and in
the United States at large. Like their readership also, many
have personally experienced a moderate amount of antisemitism. And furthermore, almost a fourth have personally experienced antisemitism, in one form or another,
over the past year. Members of the Jewish press report to
their readership what they feel is significant and important. But they are not removed or purely objective observers. They are influenced by the same types of incidents
and the same uneasy feelings experienced by the general
Jewish populace. Members of the Jewish press are Jews
first, then editors, writers, or commentators.

Jewish press editors are a microcosm of the institutional network and the Jewish public they serve. In many
ways they are the embodiment of the Jewish press itself.
Jewish newspapers are an essential glue for the Jewish
community. While the variety of Jewish community relations agencies and institutions work in differing formats
with different philosophies to deal with antisemitism,
eventually much of what they do is funneled through the
Jewish press. The Jewish press reflects the dominant approach to antisemitism. Denial and fear are moderated to
wariness, accompanied by aggressive strategies to contain
antisemitism. While direct mailings, organizational newsletters, and conferences are key methods of communicat-
ing with the Jewish public, the Jewish press is the most
critical element linking the organizations and institutions

to the largest proportion of the Jewish population in the United States.

It would be a clear overstatement to say that Jewish perceptions of antisemitism are molded by the Jewish press. In the same way, it would be an overstatement to say that Jewish community relations agencies could not be as effective without this medium. But in a communications loop, American Jewish perceptions about antisemitism are reinforced through the Jewish press, and the work of the agencies becomes more prominent. At some point, the distinction between reflecting and molding Jewish perceptions becomes somewhat blurred. The continued presence of antisemitism in the United States and around the world, in whatever form and to whatever degree, is confirmed for the majority of Jews by the Jewish press, the Jewish community's watchful and wary eye.

Chapter Seven

COMBATTING AND CONTAINING ANTISEMITISM

Except for those who deny the existence of antisemitism, Jews believe that it must be combatted and controlled. They debate how to do that best. Almost all strategies involve a political component. Certainly, the work of the community relations agencies is a critical collective response to antisemitism. While operating in the social and educational realms, developing intergroup dialogue, or a school curriculum about the Holocaust, these agencies are actively involved in a wide variety of political processes.

Combatting antisemitism has evolved along with a broader agenda of promoting civil liberties, separation of church and state, and building political coalitions with other groups that share common interests. Since Jews believe that antisemitism cannot be eradicated, they work feverishly to utilize the political system to contain antisemitism. Political issues, like all other aspects of the American Jewish experience, are assessed through the bifocals that Jews wear because they live in two worlds. Like other Americans, Jews will calculate social and economic costs or the morality of a piece of legislation. But on nearly all issues they will also ask, "Is it good or bad for the Jews?"

Perceptions of antisemitism are part of that evaluation. Certainly, Jews do not operate within the political system only from the particularistic concern of combatting antisemitism. A wide variety of issues obviously concern

215

them as Americans: nuclear energy, the economy, tax structures, and a host of other issues that concern other Americans. But much of Jewish political activity is also concerned with how one outcome or another, one program or another, affects them as Jews.

The organization of ethnic, racial, and religious groups to both protect their civil rights and further their own social and political agendas is an acceptable practice in the American social and political scene. While special interest groups are often referred to in the popular culture with resentment and disdain, there is a normative acceptance of interest group politics. Jews have evolved into a special interest group, as well as a religious-ethnic group. Perhaps no single evolution in American Jewish culture has more significance in terms of dealing with antisemitism than its transformation into a political interest group.

Jews are now well integrated into the American political culture, a process which has been facilitated by the relative absence of political discrimination. The political system itself is utilized to further protect Jews against social, economic, and, ultimately, political discrimination. The community relations agencies are not the only political expression of Jewish political activity. Political action committees for Israel, and public action offices or representatives from a wide variety of Jewish organizations contribute their time, money, and votes to influence political outcomes. The debate about combatting and controlling antisemitism, along with other issues of concern to Jews, then, does not focus on whether or not the political fray should be entered, but when, where, on which issues, and which strategies and tactics to use. Such decisions are made by all special interest groups.

Since most Jews believe that antisemitism must be combatted and controlled, they engage in a wide variety of efforts to achieve that end. Most activities to combat anti-semitism, either group or individual, now include some political component. The use of the media, educational programs, and legislative strategies are all utilized on many varied battlefronts. Political efforts are almost always necessary. For instance, educational programs about the Holocaust require adoption by curriculum committees and school boards. Legislative changes require votes from aldermen, state legislators, or congressmen. Interfaith programs require organizational energy, financial support, and continued efforts to keep the moral issue surrounding antisemitism and other forms of prejudice in the forefront.

Strategies and efforts to control antisemitism within the political arena are increasingly sophisticated, complicated, and expensive. Successfully combatting antisemitism requires a permanent institutional presence to compete in the political arena. The development of community relations agencies and lobbying groups is the most expeditious and efficient means of containing antisemitism within the distinctly American domain of competing interest groups.

Combatting antisemitism requires consideration of such issues as the causes of antisemitism, its origins, and so on. But these are overshadowed by what kinds of coalitions to form, with whom, where financial and human resources should be allocated, and how to manage the best media campaign. For example, since resources are limited in terms of either people or money, careful assessments must be made to ensure that the best political strategies are employed. Jews do not want to waste their time, dollars, or political chips on unsuccessful projects. But neither do they want to shy away from battles because the outcome is assured. Nearly all strategies call for successful coalition building.

But these coalitions can be neither rigid nor single-issue-oriented. Jewish political interests are not replicated by any other group. Social and economic have-nots may make logical partners on some civil rights issues, but not on some economic issues. Blacks and Jews, for example, share a common goal to encourage maximum government protection against employment discrimination on the basis of religion or race. They may, however, disagree sharply about how that protection should be enforced. One may argue for the support of affirmative action programs and the other against. But blacks and Jews may be strongly allied to support legislation that makes violence against a church or synagogue a violation of civil rights.

Looking through their Jewish eyes may cause Jews to look for friends and enemies. The world has often been divided that way for them. But as Americans, and as increasingly sophisticated players in the political system, Jews look less and less for friends or enemies and more and more for allies with mutual interests.

Defining mutual interests is problematic. The equation is complicated by Jewish support for Israel, concern for Soviet Jews, and Jewish perceptions of who is antisemitic and who is not, as well as which antisemitic groups are more or less likely to influence the political system. Jews identify strongly with their fellow Jews in Israel, the Soviet Union, and elsewhere, who are subject to discrimination or are threatened by military foes. American Jews attempt to balance their domestic concerns, including controlling antisemitism, with their concern for Israel and other Jewish communities throughout the world.

Given their national and international agendas, the current political alignment poses serious dilemmas for American Jews. Stronger support for Israel and a stronger anti-Soviet stance can be found to the right of center on the political spectrum, and, therefore, candidates, alliances, and support from the right appeals to Jews on these critical issues. On the other hand, it is the political right that is more likely to advocate prayer in public schools, for example, a political agenda that Jews perceive as a threat to the separation of church and state.

As shown before, Jews perceive the breakdown in separation of church and state as the precursor to anti-semitism. Stronger support for civil liberties is found to the left of center and therefore attracts Jewish support. But the left is also increasingly anti-Israel and advocates some social programs that conflict with many Jews' economic self-interest. Such a configuration leaves no clear road on either side of the political spectrum.

Since friends and enemies are harder to discern and classify, Jewish alliances and allegiances will likely shift more rapidly. Support for Israel, concern for Soviet Jews, economic self-interest, and the protection of religious lib-erties will consequently be weighed more carefully in the political equation.

The transformation of Jews into a special interest group derives partly from a sense among some Jews that they stand alone in dealing with issues that affect them as Jews. Antisemitism is one such issue. Leon Wieseltier, literary editor of the *New Republic* and a former member of the Society of Fellows at Harvard University, believes: "Antisemitism cannot be cured. It can only be fought. And it has been demonstrated many times that Jews are the only people who can be counted upon to fight it."[1]

Most Jews do not share that sentiment. They recog-nize that the political ability of Jews to fight antisemitism or provide support for Israel requires political alliances. Even if most Jews believe that Jews must initiate and lead battles against antisemitism, they do not believe that they have to fight these battles alone. Since political battles are won and lost through coalitions and compromises, most

Jews seek allies and partners. While Jews lead the charge against antisemitism in the political arena, they form coalitions to combat other forms of racial and religious discrimination as well. Thus, the desecration of a synagogue becomes a violation of civil rights, a violation of the law, and not just a random act of vandalism or violence, no matter what the cause or motivation of the perpetrators. And all religious groups are simultaneously protected.

As we move into the 1990s, Jews will become even more active in the political process. Jews have plenty to ante in the political game in terms of dollars, organizational sophistication, and influence. But they do not want to squander their political chips at random. Raising the specter of antisemitism "too often" can be seen by some as alarmist. Inaction can be interpreted as political weakness. Jewish political influence and social and economic success are obvious, and these can be used as tools to combat antisemitism. Jews must be careful not to overplay their hand.

The success of Jews in politics might seem to belie the need to combat antisemitism to some Jews and non-Jews alike. The more successful Jews become, the less obvious becomes the need for programs to combat antisemitism. Yet most Jews still support the need for such programs. For even while Jews are flexing their political muscle, they remain wary.

In discussing the tentativeness of the public's perceptions of antisemitism, Henry Siegman, the executive director of the American Jewish Congress, noted that even though Jews have made it as no other ethnic minority has, "the exquisite fragility of that success in the Jewish psyche" is endemic. "How little it takes to transform the Jewish situation from achievement to disaster. Could it be otherwise for Jews removed by only one generation from the Holocaust?"[2]

Indeed, some successful and integrated Jews are at this exact point in their thinking. It is a strange confluence for American Jews. At the time of their greatest social, political, and economic success and security, they also see signs of the continued persistence of latent antisemitism and growing disenchantment with Israel. But how to resolve this dilemma is confusing, since old friends disappear and new enemies appear, depending on which issue of Jewish concern is being considered.

Antisemitism in the Political Arena

In the wake of the Holocaust, social norms in the United States and elsewhere in the world prohibited most expressions of overt political antisemitism. The constraints from these social norms may be weakening. The marginal acceptability of these expressions is worrisome to Jews. As Steven Rosenfeld has written, "Events have demonstrated growing tolerance of specific expressions of anti-Semitism." He goes on to say that the real danger "is that the texture of public life is becoming coarser. This is no trivial concern."[3]

Jews dread the introduction of antisemitism into the political realm. It is there they feel safest, most secure, and have achieved so much. It is there that expression of antisemitism ought to be "off limits." Antisemitism in politics is the foreboding step to Jews' worst nightmares. Extremist groups are most feared for this reason. They introduce antisemitism into the political dialogue and violate nearly all norms about the acceptability of antisemitic rhetoric.

Attacks on Israel can do the same, and not necessarily from extremists but from the more acceptable liberal left. Attacks on Israel are sometimes thinly veiled antisemitism. This thin veil was removed, and antisemitic sentiments revealed in an article by Gore Vidal appearing in the *Nation*, in which he labeled Israel's Jews "a predatory people" and accused Norman Podhoretz, the editor of *Commentary*, and other American Jews, of being more loyal to Israel than to the United States, his and their "host country."[4] Vidal's writing both exemplified traditional antisemitic stereotypes—while of course denying doing so—and inextricably linked them with anti-Israel criticism. The Vidal attack, for some, adds a touch of legitimacy to antisemitic rhetoric as part of acceptable political discourse. Only more widespread acceptance of extremists could be more disconcerting to American Jews.

Jews wish to keep antisemitism out of the political arena while using the political system to combat antisemitism. They are distinct phenomena, and Jews understand the differences clearly. One has to do with antisemitism as political ideology, the second as a political process to combat it. The former is "un-American," at least in terms of some norms, while the latter is an acceptable part of the political game.

The left as well as the right have recently introduced antisemitism into the political process: Lyndon LaRouche, for example, from the right, and Louis Farrakhan from the left. While most Americans continue to reject the political philosophies of the likes of either Farrakhan or LaRouche, their rhetoric has entered the political dialogue more forcefully than any time since World War II. Many American Jews were more horrified by the failure of many black leaders to openly condemn Farrakhan than by Farrakhan's rhetoric itself. Although many explanations and reasons were given, it took some time for many black leaders to distance themselves from Farrakhan, while others never did.[5] Nevertheless, Farrakhan represented a dangerous breach of the norms that had been established in the post-Holocaust generation. Jewish fears were exacerbated when blatant antisemitism was not condemned or rejected by either leaders or followers.[6]

Other unpleasant realities are also found on the left. Those "soft" on communism are viewed as endangering the well-being of Soviet Jews. Anti-Israel behavior is anathema to Jews, and the political agenda of the far left is seen as too critical of Israel.

Yet Jews remain more suspicious of groups on the right. Jews fear Fundamentalists, for example, for their potential encroachment upon separation of church and state. The results of a study of Fundamentalists, commissioned by the Anti-Defamation League and completed late in 1986,[7] corroborated the suspicions of some Jews. An article that appeared in the *Los Angeles Times* discussed some of the findings, introduced as "some troubling secular attitudes toward Jews,"[8] affirming the doubts of many Jews wary of the rise of the religious right. Jews are concerned about Fundamentalists' views. The ADL study, widely reported in Jewish newspapers, revealed the following: 59% of Fundamentalists believe that Jews could never be forgiven for what they did to Jesus until they accept him as the true savior.[9] This view, coupled with clear conflicts of interest over issues such as prayer in the schools, remain a key concern for most Jews.

As the political agenda of Jews evolves, they will be forced further and further toward the middle of the spectrum by these conflicts. Either extreme threatens their social and economic interests as Americans or their civil and religious liberties as Jews. Israel and other world Jewish concerns enter the equation to push Jews toward the middle because Jews have to play both sides of the political spectrum to find support for both.

Tough choices now face Jewish political activists, contributors, and voters. If American Jewry has come of age, it is because their Americanization has brought them to the unpleasant gray areas of ever-shifting coalitions. The world is neither "them" or "us" nor good for the Jews or bad for the Jews. Now, the "them" is "us" and vice versa, and issues cut both ways for American Jews.

Even the most basic of issues, separation of church and state, is not completely clear-cut for Jews. An opinion poll reproduced in the quarterly *Public Opinion* detailed the differing levels of support for prayer in the schools expressed by the various religious denominations. Nearly four out of five Protestants and Catholics support prayer in schools, as a whole. Fundamentalist support would likely be much higher. However, only 25% of Jews favor prayer in the schools.[10] But on the issue of government support for parochial schools, Orthodox Jews are more likely to agree, since their children attend all-day Jewish schools. Unanimity among Jews on most political issues is evaporating.

While the battle for conservative versus liberal souls will push and pull at Jews, a central issue becomes part of the Jewish response: Who will best control the extremists? Such groups, on either the left or the right, spewing their antisemitic rhetoric and goals, are not likely to gain much of a foothold or following in the United States. Jewish organizations and institutions work effectively through coalitions with other interest groups to keep extremists in check. They have many allies. In a humorous essay in the Sunday *New York Times Magazine*, Russell Baker, in attempting to find nomenclature for extremists said: "Even worse than 'the far right' would be 'right-wing extremists.' Americans hate 'extremists' of all varieties. 'Left-wing extremists,' 'right-wing extremists,' 'moderate extremists'—Americans make no distinction. 'Extremists' are despicable."[11]

And nobody hates them more than Jews. The question then becomes: What political groups will best keep extremists or their sympathizers away from any access to power?

Ultimately, Jews are more likely to fear the right than the left. The left, traditionally, has had less success in the political system in the United States than the right. Jews fear them less as a result. Not only are right-of-center groups successful more often than not, but they are sometimes, in Jewish eyes, difficult to distinguish from extremists. They seem to share too many goals for the comfort of most Jews. And since Jews care most about the protection of their civil liberties and view the right as the greatest threat to the separation of church and state, they will likely continue to align politically with those slightly to the left of center. In other words, Jews will move toward the center but will still lean to the left of center more often than not. But they will not lean very far. Moderates will increasingly appeal to most Jews, as they do to the majority of Americans.

Some analysts argue that since it is the right that supports Israel and since Jews are economically well off, support of left of center violates Jews' own self interest. Through Jewish eyes we have demonstrated that exactly the opposite is the case. The fear of antisemitism continues to motivate Jews in the most fundamental way. The breakdown in the separation of church and state is viewed from Jewish eyes as the forerunner of antisemitism. Thus, as Jews continue to vote predominantly Democratic at the national level, it is precisely their own self-interest that they have in mind. Whether or not they are accurate in their assessment is a moot point, and whether or not these decisions are conscious or well thought-out misses the point.

Through their votes and political support, Jews express their fears of antisemitism, be it the church–state separation or other civil liberties issues. The continued support of the Democrats at the national level is not an old habit. Jews are demonstrating something quite different with their votes. Most Jews continue to distrust Republicans and Conservatives more than Democrats and Liberals because of the association of the right with more dangerous ideologies. Jews' apprehensions about antisemitism, which many fear might become a problem through a breakdown of church–state separation, facilitated by the far right, is enough to produce a response at the polls and in other political activity.

Jewish self-interest is defined more globally than economics or support for Israel alone. Antisemitism continues to play a circuitous role in the political behavior of Jews. For the most part, Jews extract promises of support for Israel from both the right and the left while resisting the social agenda of the political right. It is, of course, a precarious political position. As long as Israel remains America's strongest ally in the Middle East, Jews can afford to combat antisemitism in the United States by staying slightly to the left of center. Thus far, American Jews have not had to choose too often between liberal candidates who do not support Israel and conservative candidates who do support Israel. When such choices occur, they pose terrible dilemmas for American Jews, testing their loyalty to Israel and their fears of antisemitism at home. The issue is even more convoluted in Jewish eyes because anti-Israelism is so linked to antisemitism.

These dilemmas are so critical for Jews because Jews rely so heavily on their political maneuverability and power to combat antisemitism. The political constraints on antisemitism are indeed vital. For as Selznick and Steinberg noted:

> A resurgence of anti-Semitism cannot be ruled out. This study has presented a large body of evidence pointing to the conclusion that cultural resources are more widespread

in American society. The current anti-Semitism of most Americans does not go beyond acceptance of anti-Semitic beliefs and support of mild forms of discrimination. Nor is it a foregone conclusion that political reaction in the United States would be accompanied by anti-Semitism. However, simplistic beliefs and authoritarian attitudes, ignorance and disregard of democratic norms, a low threshhold of tolerance for social and political diversity, insensitivity to the suffering of others—these are tendencies that characterize large numbers of Americans. Given a crisis situation and political leadership, they constitute a potential threat to the democratic order.[12]

Are Jews safe in the United States? As long as democratic institutions are safe, the social and political rights of Jews will be protected, along with those of other minority groups. Such stability cannot be taken for granted. Collectively, Jews are keenly aware of the somewhat precarious restrictions upon racial and religious discrimination. Most Jews remain wary about antisemitism in the United States, wonder about ways to combat it, and are searching for the proper social and political vehicles and alliances to protect their self-interest. Despite their current social, economic, and political stature, Jews remain a minority religious and ethnic group. In the face of this reality, most Jews remain wary, actively expressing their concern throughout the political system. But most Jews perceive antisemitism accurately, and thus far their collective assessment has guided them well.

NOTES

Chapter One

1. The material presented in this book was gathered in a series of surveys conducted between 1981 and 1987. Original research was conducted in telephone interviews in Jewish communities throughout the United States. In addition, mail surveys were conducted among Jewish community professionals, Jewish leadership groups, and Jewish press editors and publishers. Furthermore, personal interviews were conducted with Jewish leaders, members of the Jewish community, and Jewish community relations professionals. These data are presented for the first time in this volume. The surveys used, the methodologies employed, and the statistical findings are included in Appendixes A and B.
2. Ben Halpern, "What is Antisemitism?" *Modern Judaism* 1 (December 1981), pp. 252–253.

Chapter Two

1. Gertrude Selznick and Stephen Steinberg, *The Tenacity of Prejudice: Anti-Semitism in Contemporary America* (New York: Harper & Row, 1969), p. 184.
2. Ibid.
3. Charles H. Stember, "The Recent History of Public Attitudes," *Jews in the Mind of America*, ed. George Salomon (New York: Basic Books, 1966), pp. 310–336.
4. Geraldine Rosenfield, "The Polls: Attitudes toward American Jews," *Public Opinion Quarterly* 46 (1982), 431–443.
5. Ibid., p. 432.
6. Ibid.
7. Geraldine Rosenfield, *Antisemitism in the United States: A Study by*

Yankelovich, Skelly & White, Inc., 1981 (New York: American Jewish Committee, May 1982), p. 2.

8. Gertrude J. Selznick and Stephen Steinberg, *The Tenacity of Prejudice: Anti-Semitism in Contemporary America* (New York: Harper & Row, 1969).

9. Harold Quinley and Charles Glock, *Anti-Semitism in America* (New York: Free Press, 1979).

10. Gertrude J. Selznick and Stephen Steinberg, *The Tenacity of Prejudice: Anti-Semitism in Contemporary America* (New York: Harper & Row, 1969), pp. 26–27.

11. Ibid., pp. 29–30.

12. Gregory Martire and Ruth Clark, *Anti-Semitism in the United States: A Study of Prejudice in the 1980s* (New York: Praeger Publishers, 1982).

13. Ibid., p. 2.

14. Ibid., p. 29.

15. Ibid., p. 25.

16. Ibid., p. 43.

17. Market Facts, Inc., *A National Survey of Black Americans* (Los Angeles: Simon Wiesenthal Center, December 1985).

18. Gregory Martire and Ruth Clark, *Anti-Semitism in the United States: A Study of Prejudice in the 1980s* (New York: Praeger Publishers, 1982), p. 40.

19. Ibid., p. 38.

20. Yankelovich, Skelly & White, *Antisemitism in the United States*, Vol. 2 (New York: American Jewish Committee, 1981), pp. 6–7.

21. The Harris Organization, "Poll Results Contradict Claims That Prejudice Is Increasing," *Harris Survey* (Orlando: Tribune Media Services, Inc., 18 February 1985), p. 2.

22. The Gallup Organization, *Attitudes Concerning the American Jewish Community: The Gallup Poll* (New York: American Jewish Committee, 16 April 1981), p. 1.

23. "Half of U.S. Blacks Are Found to View Jews in Favorable Light," *New York Jewish Week*, 18 January 1985.

24. Louis Harris, *A Study of Anti-Semitism in Rural Iowa and Nebraska* (New York: The Anti-Defamation League of B'nai B'rith, February 1986), p. 7.

25. Press release (New York: Anti-Defamation League of B'nai B'rith, 3 March 1986).

26. Terrance, Hill, Newport & Ryan, *Nationwide Attitudes Survey of Evangelical Christians* (New York: Anti-Defamation League of B'nai B'rith, 1986), pp. 5–7.

27. Marjorie Hyer, "Poll Finds No Rise in Anti-Semitism," *Washington Post*, 10 January 1987.

28. Terrance, Hill, Newport & Ryan, *Nationwide Attitudes Survey of Evangelical Christians* (New York: Anti-Defamation League of B'nai B'rith, 1986), p. 92.

29. Press release (New York: Anti-Defamation League of B'nai B'rith, 8 January 1987).

30. Terrance, Hill, Newport & Ryan, *Nationwide Attitudes Survey of Evangelical Christians* (New York: Anti-Defamation League of B'nai B'rith, 1986), p. 151.

31. Ibid.

32. Ibid., p. 153.

33. Ibid.

34. The Gallup Organization, *Attitudes of the American Public Toward American Jews and Israel: The Gallup Poll, March 1982* (New York: The American Jewish Committee, March 1982), p. 2.

35. David Singer and Renae Cohen, *Probing Public Sentiment on Israel and American Jews: The February 1987 Roper Poll* (New York: American Jewish Committee, 1987).

36. Ibid., p. 3.

37. Ibid.

38. Gregory Martire and Ruth Clark, *Anti-Semitism in the United States: A Study of Prejudice in the 1980s* (New York: Praeger Publishers, 1982), pp. 84–85.

39. Ibid., p. 95.

40. Louis Harris, as quoted in J. Aaron, "Pro-Israel Americans May Not Be Pro-Jewish," *Bergen Jewish News*, 19 June 1986.

41. Ibid.

42. Ibid.

43. "Editor's Chair," *Jewish Post and Opinion*, 8 October 1986.

44. I. A. Lewis and William Schneider, "Is the Public Lying to the Pollsters?" *Current* 245 (September 1982), 25–35.

45. The Anti-Defamation League, *1986 Audit of Anti-Semitic Incidents* (New York: Anti-Defamation League of B'nai B'rith, 1986), pp. 1–4.

46. *The Congressional Record-Senate*, 28 June 1984, pp. S8713–8714.

47. Leonard Zeskind, *Background Report on Racist and Anti-Semitic Organizational Intervention in the Farm Protest Movement* (Atlanta: Center for Democratic Renewal, 1985), p. 1.

48. The Anti-Defamation League, *Extremism on the Right*, An ADL Handbook (New York: Anti-Defamation League of B'nai B'rith, September 1983), p. 15.

49. The Anti-Defamation League, *"Propaganda of the Deed": The Far*

Right's Desperate "Revolution," ADL Special Report (New York: Anti-Defamation League of B'nai B'rith, May 1985), p. 1.

50. Leonard Zeskind, *Background Report on Racist and Anti-Semitic Organizational Intervention in the Farm Protest Movement* (Atlanta: Center for Democratic Renewal, 1985), p. 2.

51. Ibid., p. 3.

52. The Anti-Defamation League, *The American Farmer and the Extremists,* ADL Special Report (New York: Anti-Defamation League of B'nai B'rith, January 1986), p. 6.

53. The Anti-Defamation League, *Extremism on the Right,* An ADL Handbook (New York: Anti-Defamation League of B'nai B'rith, September 1983), p. 44.

54. Ibid., p. 10.

55. The Anti-Defamation League, *Liberty Lobby and the Carto Network of Hate,* ADL Facts, Vol. 27, No. 1 (New York: Anti-Defamation League of B'nai B'rith, 1982), p. 5.

56. Leonard Zeskind, *Background Report on Racist and Anti-Semitic Organizational Intervention in the Farm Protest Movement* (Atlanta: Center for Democratic Renewal, 1985), p. 8.

57. Ibid.

58. The Anti-Defamation League, *Liberty Lobby and the Carto Network of Hate,* ADL Facts, Vol. 27, No. 1 (New York: Anti-Defamation League of B'nai B'rith, 1982), p. 15.

59. Wayne King, "Anti-Semitism Links Violent Groups," *New York Times,* 26 April 1985.

60. Ted Gest, "Sudden Rise of Hate Groups Spurs Federal Crackdown," *U.S. News and World Report,* 6 May 1985, p. 68.

61. "The Pincer Movement," *Instauration,* August 1986, pp. 14–16.

62. Mark Elliott and Michael McClintock, "Holocaust 'Revisionists' and the California Library Association," *Midstream* (April 1986), 36–38.

63. Editorial, *News & Tribune* (Jefferson City, Missouri) 18 May 1986.

Chapter Three

1. The Federation of Jewish Philanthropies of New York, *The Jewish Population of Greater New York: A Profile* (New York: Federation of Jewish Philanthropies of New York, 1984), pp. 25–26.

2. The Jewish Community Federation of Cleveland, *Survey of Cleveland's Jewish Population, 1981* (Cleveland: Jewish Community Federation of Cleveland, 1982), p. 42.
3. Arthur Cohen, "Why I Choose to be a Jew," *Harper's Magazine*, 217 (April 1959), p. 61.
4. Nathan Glazer, *American Judaism* (Chicago: University of Chicago Press, 1972), pp. 141–142.
5. Michael Rappeport and Gary Tobin, *A Population Study of the Jewish Community of MetroWest New Jersey, 1986* (United Jewish Federation of MetroWest, 1987), p. 98.
6. Jonathan B. Woocher, *Sacred Survival: The Civil Religion of American Jews* (Bloomington: Indiana University Press, 1986).
7. Ibid., p. viii.
8. Bruce A. Phillips and Eve Weinberg, *The Milwaukee Jewish Population Study* (Chicago: Policy Research Corporation, 1984), p. iv–16.
9. Bruce A. Phillips and Eleanore Judd, *Supplement to the Denver Jewish Population Study, 1981* (Denver: Allied Jewish Federation of Denver, 1983), p. 3-A.
10. Milton Steinberg, "Current Philosophies of Jewish Life in America," *The American Jew: A Composite Portrait*, ed. Oscar I. Janowsky (New York: Harper, 1942), p. 207.
11. Ben Halpern, "America is Different," *American Jews: A Reader*, ed. Marshall Sklare (New York: Behrman House, 1983), pp. 23–45.
12. Ibid., p. 43.
13. Ibid., p. 39.
14. Charles Liebman, *The Ambivalent American Jew* (Philadelphia: Jewish Publication Society of America, 1973), p. 88.
15. Calvin Goldscheider, *Jewish Continuity and Change: Emerging Patterns in America* (Bloomington: Indiana University Press, 1986).
16. Eugene B. Borowitz, *The Mask Jews Wear: The Self-Deception of American Jewry* (Port Washington, NY: Sh'ma, 1980).
17. Jacob Neusner, *Stranger at Home* (Chicago: University of Chicago Press, 1981).
18. Charles Liebman, *The Ambivalent American Jew* (Philadelphia: Jewish Publication Society of America, 1973), p. 88.
19. Marshall Sklare, *America's Jews* (New York: Random House, Inc., 1971), p. 214.
20. Lucy S. Davidowicz, "American Public Opinion," *The American Jewish Yearbook* 69 (New York and Philadelphia: American Jewish Committee and Jewish Publication Society of America, 1968), p. 205.

Chapter Four

1. Jonathan D. Sarna, "Anti-Semitism and American History," *Commentary* 71 (March 1981), 42–47.
2. Charles Silberman, *A Certain People: American Jews and Their Lives Today*, as quoted in Kenneth L. Woodward, "Jews in a Soulful Debate," Religion Section, *Newsweek* 106 (23 September 1985), p. 77.
3. Ibid.
4. Arthur J. Magida, "Jewish Paranoia," *Baltimore Jewish Times* (7 February 1986).
5. Milton Himmelfarb, "Another Look at the Jewish Vote," *Commentary* 80 (December 1985), 41.
6. Ibid.
7. Benjamin Levitman, "Silberman and Schick Debate Nature of Anti-Semitism," *Palm Beach Jewish World*, 18–24 April 1986, p. 2.
8. Ibid.
9. Meir Kahane, *Never Again! A Program for Survival* (Los Angeles: Nash, 1971), p. 210.
10. Below is a sampling of some ADL publications: *The Populist Party: The Politics of Right Wing Extremism*, Vol. 30, No. 2 (New York: Anti-Defamation League of B'nai B'rith, Fall 1985); *Extremism on the Right: A Handbook* (New York: Anti-Defamation League of B'nai B'rith, 1983); Franz Mintz, *The Liberty Lobby and the American Right* (Westport: Greenwood Press, 1985); *Terrorism's Targets: Democracy, Israel and Jews*, ADL Special Report (New York: Anti-Defamation League of B'nai B'rith, 1981); *Extremism Targets the Prisons*, ADL Special Report (New York: Anti-Defamation League of B'nai B'rith, 1986); *Liberty Lobby and the Carto Network of Hate*, ADL Facts, Vol. 27, No. 1 (New York: Anti-Defamation League of B'nai B'rith, 1982); *"Propaganda of the Deed": The Far Right's Desperate "Revolution"* (New York: Anti-Defamation League of B'nai B'rith, 1985); *Holocaust "Revisionism": A Denial of History*, ADL Facts, Vol. 31, No. 1 (New York: Anti-Defamation League of B'nai B'rith, Winter 1986).
11. "Anti-Semitic 'Literature' Apparently Proliferating," *Baltimore Jewish Times*, 25 October 1985.
12. Ibid.
13. Sylvia Mandelbaum, "Anti-Semitism on the North American Continent," *Jewish Press* (Brooklyn, NY) 1 November 1986, p. 9.
14. Rochelle Saidel Wolk, "Prophecy or Paranoia?" *Lillith* 7 (Fall 1980), 8–10.

15. Abraham H. Foxman, "The Jewish Soul," *B'nai B'rith Record*, December 1983.

16. Ibid.

17. Earl Raab, "Anti-Semitism in the 1980s," *Midstream* 29 (February 1983), p. 11.

18. Ibid., p. 17.

19. Steven M. Cohen, *The Political Attitude of American Jews, 1984* (New York: American Jewish Committee, 1984), p. 30.

20. Ibid., p. 14.

21. Interview with Joel Reck, president of the Jewish Community Relations Council of Boston, Boston, MA, 11 June 1987.

22. Interview with Martin Stein, National Chairman of the United Jewish Appeal, Washington, D.C., 28 April 1987.

23. Interview with Mark Cooper, rabbi at Temple Israel of Natick, Natick, MA, 14 May 1987.

24. Interview with Mitchel Orlik, associate director of the Columbus Jewish Federation, Washington, D.C., 27 April 1984.

25. Ibid.

26. Interview with anonymous respondent, Washington, D.C., 27 April 1987.

27. Interview with Lois Madeson, Newton, MA, 10 June 1987.

28. Interview with anonymous respondent, Washington, D.C., 27 April 1987.

29. Interview with Ruth Fein, campaign chairman for the Combined Jewish Philanthropies of Greater Boston, Boston, MA, 5 May 1987.

30. Ibid.

31. Interview with Rabbi Neil Kominsky, Reform rabbi at Harvard-Radcliffe Hillel, Cambridge, MA 15 May 1987.

32. Interview with Judi Gillman, Waltham, MA, 5 October 1987.

33. Steven M. Cohen, *The Political Attitudes of American Jews, 1984* (New York: American Jewish Committee, 1984), p. 31.

34. Ibid., p. 35.

35. Ibid., p. 6.

36. Ibid., p. 33.

37. Interview with Steven A. Cohen, director of public relations for Brandeis University, Waltham, MA, 10 June 1987.

38. Interview with Alan Goldstein, chairman of the Social Planning and Allocations Committee for the Combined Jewish Philanthropies of Greater Boston, Boston, MA, 8 June 1987.

39. Interview with Martin Stein, National Chairman of the United Jewish Appeal, Washington, D.C., 28 April 1987.

40. Yankelovich, Skelly & White, *Antisemitism in the United States,* Vol. 1 (New York: American Jewish Committee, 1981), p. 27.
41. Gertrude J. Selznick and Stephen Steinberg, *The Tenacity of Preju- dice: Anti-Semitism in Contemporary America* (New York: Harper & Row, 1969).
42. Harold Quinley and Charles Glock, *Antisemitism in America* (New York: Free Press, 1979).
43. For a detailed analysis of one such case, see Rodney Stark and Stephen Steinberg, *It Did Happen Here—An Investigation of Political Anti-Semitism: Wayne, New Jersey, 1967* (Berkeley: Survey Research Center, 1967).
44. Yankelovich, Skelly & White, *Antisemitism in the United States,* Vol. 1 (New York: American Jewish Committee, 1981), p. 30.
45. Ibid.
46. Ibid., p. 70.
47. Ibid.
48. Yankelovich, Skelly & White, *Antisemitism in the United States,* Vol. 2 (New York: American Jewish Committee, 1981), p. 65.
49. Interview with Rabbi Neil Kominsky, Reform Rabbi at Harvard- Radcliffe Hillel, Cambridge, MA, 15 May 1987.
50. Interview with Paul Goldberg, President of the Rochester Jewish Federation, Washington, D.C., 28 April 1987.
51. Interview with Philip Cohen, past president of the Cincinnati, Ohio, Federation, Washington, D.C., 27 April 1987.
52. Interview with Mitchel Orlik, associate director of the Jewish Federation of Columbus, Ohio, Washington, D.C., 27 April 1987.
53. Interview with anonymous respondent, Washington, D.C., 27 April 1987.
54. Interview with Paul Goldberg, President of the Rochester Jewish Federation, Washington, D.C., 28 April 1987.

Chapter Five

1. Henry L. Feingold, *A Jewish Survival Enigma: The Strange Case of the American Jewish Committee* (New York: American Jewish Committee, May 1981), p. 4.
2. The American Jewish Committee, *The American Jewish Committee: An Inside Look* (New York: American Jewish Committee, 1984), p. 10.
3. David Goldstein, Jewish Community Relations Bureau publication (New York: Jewish Community Relations Bureau, 1986).

4. Phillip Baum, *Where We Stand: Antisemitism* (New York: American Jewish Congress, 1981), p. 1.
5. The National Jewish Community Relations Advisory Council, *Joint Program Plan for Jewish Community Relations, 1986–87: Guide to Program Planning of the Constituent Organizations* (New York: National Jewish Community Relations Advisory Council, 1987), p. 29.
6. Gary Rosenblatt, "The Simon Wiesenthal Center: State of the Art Activism or Hollywood Hype?" *Baltimore Jewish Times,* 14 September 1983, p. 68.
7. The Anti-Defamation League of B'nai B'rith, *ADL Charter of 1913* (Chicago: Anti-Defamation League of B'nai B'rith, 1913).
8. Interview with Evan Mendelson, former associate executive, American Jewish Congress, New York, 19 March 1987.
9. Henry L. Feingold, *A Jewish Survival Enigma: The Strange Case of the American Jewish Committee* (New York: American Jewish Committee, May 1981), p. 2.
10. Interview with David Gordis, former executive vice-president, American Jewish Committee, New York, 19 March 1987.
11. The American Jewish Committee, *Summary of Selected Programs and Budget* (New York: American Jewish Committee, November 12, 1986), p. 1.
12. *Background Information:* Below is a profile of community relations professionals responding to the questionnaire. For the corresponding figures, see Table 5-9.

Almost three-fourths of those responding, 74%, are male, while the remaining 26% are female. Most respondents held the title of director or assistant director. The vast majority, 81%, are married, while 13% are divorced, and 4% have never been married. While the age distribution of respondents is quite wide, the greatest proportion are below 44 years of age; 35% are between 35 and 44, while 24% are between the ages of 24 and 35. The remaining 37% consist of older respondents, with 31% between 45 and 64 years of age, and 6% 65 years or older.

Over three-fourths of respondents, 78%, have children. The remaining 22% are childless. In terms of religious identity, the greatest share of community relations professional respondents are Conservative. 36% classify themselves as Conservative, while 26% say they are Reform, 14% are just Jewish, 12% are Other, 6% are Reconstructionist, and 4% are Orthodox.

The secular educational level of Jews is above that of average Americans. Community relations professionals are representative of this fact. Eighty percent have a graduate or professional degree, while the remaining 20% consists of those who have attended and completed college.

In terms of Jewish education, the vast majority have received some form of formal Jewish training. Only 6% say they have received no Jewish education. The remaining respondents have received various kinds of Jewish education. By far the greatest share have attended afternoon Hebrew school or other part-time classes, 59%. An additional 42% have attended Sunday school, often in conjunction with or following afternoon Hebrew school or part-time classes. Twelve percent have attended day school or yeshiva, while 4% list some other form of Jewish education, such as adult education classes or training for the rabbinate. Sixty percent of respondents were enrolled in Jewish education for more than six years, including 28% who say they were enrolled for over ten years.

A substantial proportion of the children of Jewish community relations professionals are receiving formal Jewish education. Again, the greatest proportion, 33%, are enrolled in afternoon Hebrew school or other part-time school, while 26% attend Sunday school. Many respondents indicate that their children attend both forms. Especially significant is the high proportion, 22%, whose children are receiving their Jewish education at a day school or yeshiva. This share is much higher than the equivalent figure for parents, only 12% of whom attended day school or yeshiva. Only 4% reply that their children are receiving no Jewish education, while 32% say the category does not apply, primarily because their children are too young.

When asked how many of their three best friends are Jewish, 81% say that all three are. Thirteen percent say that two of their three best friends are Jewish, while only 1% say that of their three best friends only one is Jewish.

Over half of those responding to the questionnaire, 53%, have been in the field of Jewish community relations for less than 10 years. Twenty-one percent have been community relations professionals for less than 5 years. However, substantial proportions are seasoned community relations professionals. Eighteen percent have been in the field between 11 and 15 years, while 10% have been community relations professionals for 16 to 20 years, and 16% have over 20 years of experience. Despite the large cadre of professionals with many years of experience, by far the greatest proportion of respondents, 65%, have been at their current position for less than 5 years. Sixteen percent have been in their position between 6 and 10 years, while 15% have held their current position longer than 10 years.

13. Interview with Jerome A. Chanes, associate director of Domestic Concerns, National Jewish Community Relations Advisory Council, New York, 6 March 1986.

14. The National Jewish Community Relations Advisory Council, *Joint Program Plan for Jewish Community Relations 1985–86: Guide to Program Planning of the Constituent Organizations* (New York: National Jewish Community Relations Advisory Council, 1986), p. 37.

15. Minutes of the NJCRAC Subcommittee on Assessing Criteria for Measuring Anti-Semitism (New York: National Jewish Community Relations Advisory Council, 19 March 1986).

16. Alisa Kesten, Milton Ellerin, and Sonya Kaufer, *Antisemitism in America: A Balance Sheet* (New York: American Jewish Committee, 30 March 1981).

17. For a report presenting the mission and goals of the American Jewish Committee, see *The Summary of Selected Programs and Budget*, presented to the Large City Budgeting Conference on 12 November 1986.

18. Interview with Dr. David Gordis, former executive vice-president of the American Jewish Committee, New York, 19 March 1987.

19. Interview with Harold Applebaum, special assistant for Anti-semitism and Extremism Programs, American Jewish Committee, New York, 6 March 1987.

20. Interview with Dr. David Grodis, former executive vice-president of the American Jewish Committee, New York, 19 March 1987.

21. The American Jewish Committee, *The Goals of the American Jewish Committee* (New York: American Jewish Committee, 1981).

22. Nathan Perlmutter, "Roundtable discussion with the editors of the *Long Island Jewish World*," reprinted in *Jewish Currents*, September 1985, p. 2.

23. Interview with Tom Neumann, director of intergroup relations, Anti-Defamation League of B'nai B'rith, New York, 18 March 1987.

24. Ibid.

25. Interview with Evan Mendelson, former assistant executive director, American Jewish Congress, New York, 19 March 1987.

26. Interview with Tom Neumann, director of Intergroup Relations, Anti-Defamation League of B'nai B'rith, New York, 18 March 1987.

27. The Anti-Defamation League, *Purposes and Programs* (New York: Anti-Defamation League of B'nai B'rith, 1986).

28. Several examples of *ADL Bulletin* articles are listed below:

Nathan Perlmutter, "Comment: A Year in Retrospect," *ADL Bulletin* (New York: Anti-Defamation League of B'nai B'rith, January 1984), p. 2; Nathan Perlmutter, "Comment: The 10 Most Significant Events," *ADL Bulletin* (New York: Anti-Defamation League of B'nai B'rith, February 1985), p. 2; Alan S. Katchen, "The Station That Broadcast Hate," *ADL Bulletin* (New York: Anti-Defamation League of B'nai B'rith, February 1985), pp. 3–5; Nathan Perlmutter, "Comment: The Year That Was . . ." *ADL Bulletin* (New York: Anti-Defamation League of B'nai B'rith, January 1986), p. 2; Michael Lieberman, "Extremists Try to Exploit Farm Crisis, *ADL Bulletin* (New York: Anti-Defamation League of B'nai B'rith, January 1986), pp. 3–5; Nathan Perlmutter, "Comment: The 10 Most Significant Events," *ADL Bulletin* (New York: The Anti-Defamation League of B'nai B'rith, February 1986), p. 2.

29. The Anti-Defamation League, *Pro-Arab Propaganda in America: Vehicles and Voices—A Handbook* (New York: Anti-Defamation League of B'nai B'rith, 1983).

30. The Anti-Defamation League, *Security for Community Institutions: A Handbook* (New York: Anti-Defamation League, in conjunction with the New York City Police Department, 1984).

31. The Anti-Defamation League of B'nai B'rith, *Audit of Anti-Semitic Incidents* (New York: Anti-Defamation League of B'nai B'rith, 1979–86).

32. Interview with Phillip Baum, associate director, American Jewish Congress, New York, 19 March 1987.

33. Interview with Evan Mendelson, former associate executive director, American Jewish Congress, New York, 19 March 1987.

34. Theodore Bikel, Fund-raising letter (New York: American Jewish Congress, 1986).

35. Theodore Mann, Fund-raising letter (New York: American Jewish Congress, 1986).

36. Henry Siegman, Fund-raising letter (New York: American Jewish Congress, 1986).

37. Interview with Jerome Chanes, associate director of domestic concerns, National Jewish Community Relations Advisory Council, New York, 6 March 1987.

38. Ibid.

39. Henry L. Feingold, *A Jewish Survival Enigma: The Strange Case of the American Jewish Committee* (New York: American Jewish Committee, May 1981), p. 2.

40. Gary Rosenblatt, "The Simon Wiesenthal Center: State-of-the Art

Activism or Hollywood Hype?" *Baltimore Jewish Times*, 14 September 1984, p. 74.

Chapter Six

1. For an explanation of the methodology of the study, see Appendix B.
2. Telephone interview with Robert Cohn, president of the American Jewish Press Association (AJPA) and editor-in-chief, *The St. Louis Jewish Light*, 25 February 1987.
3. The American Jewish Press Association, *Roster of Members, September 1986* (Publication of the American Jewish Press Association, 1986), cover page.
4. Gary A. Tobin, *1982 Demographic and Attitudinal Study of the St. Louis Jewish Population* (St. Louis: Jewish Federation of St. Louis, 1982).
5. The Jewish Community Federation of Cleveland, *Survey of Cleveland's Jewish Population, 1981* (Cleveland: Jewish Community Federation of Cleveland, 1981).
6. William L. Yancey and Ira Goldstein, *The Jewish Population of the Greater Philadelphia Area* (Philadelphia: Federation of Jewish Agencies of Greater Philadelphia, 1984).
7. Telephone interview with Andy Mushin, assistant editor, Jewish Telegraphic Agency, February 1987.
8. Ibid.
9. Ibid.
10. "Swastikas Appear at UMass Boston" and "Mystery Enfolds Tufts Attack," *Jewish Advocate*, 26 February 1987, p. 1.
11. Many Jewish papers ran stories reporting on the Zundel developments. The following are just a few examples: "In Ontario—Court Reverses Conviction of Anti-Semitic Propagandist," *Jewish Advocate*, (Boston) 29 January 1987, p. 1; "Stunning Decision in Ontario," *Atlanta Jewish Times*, 30 January 1987, p. 2; "Ontario Court Reverses Ruling on Zundel," *Baltimore Jewish Times*, 6 February 1987, p. 20; "Canadian Propagandist Free on a Technicality," *Kansas City Jewish Chronicle*, 6 February 1987, p. 4A; "Ontario Court Reverses Anti-Semites Conviction," *Connecticut Jewish Ledger*, 29 January 1987, p. 1; "Propagandist's Conviction Reversed," *Jewish Exponent*, 30 January 1987, p. 6; "Ontario Court Reverses Conviction," *Buffalo Jewish Review*, 30 January 1987, p. 1; "Ontario Court

Reverses Conviction of Anti-Semitic Propagandist," *Sentinel*, 5 February 1987, p. 17; "Ontario Overturns Ruling on Anti-Semite," *American Jewish World*, 6 February 1987, p. 3; "Ontario Court Reverses Conviction of Anti-Semite," *Washington Jewish Week*, 5 February 1987, p. 6; "New Trial for Anti-Semite," *Jewish News*, 6 February 1987, p. 53.

12. "Reverse Conviction of Anti-Semite," *Youngstown Jewish Times*, 13 February 1987.

13. Alan Hitsky, "Anti-Semitic Incidents Jumped in Michigan," *Detroit Jewish News*, 30 January 1987, p. 8.

14. "Survey on Christian Attitudes Cites Positive Findings," *Kansas City Jewish Chronicle*, 6 January 1987, p. 8A.

15. "Fundamental Friends," *Jewish Post & Opinion*, 4 December 1985, p. 1.

16. Tom Braden, "Racists United: Farrakhan and the KKK", *Washington Times*, 11 October 1985.

17. Roger Rosenblatt, "The Demagogue in the Crowd," *Time*, 21 October 1985, p. 102.

18. Fred Barnes, "The Farrakhan Frenzy (What's a Black Politician to Do?)," *New Republic*, 28 October 1985, p. 13.

19. Roger Rosenblatt, "The Demagogue in the Crowd," *Time*, 21 October 1985, p. 102.

20. Fred Barnes, "The Farrakhan Frenzy (What's a Black Politician to Do?)," *New Republic*, 28 October 1985, pp. 13–15.

21. Justin Finger, "Look Who's in Farrakhan's Corner," *ADL Bulletin* (New York: Anti-Defamation League of B'nai B'rith, December 1985), p. 13.

22. Jay Matthews, "Jackson Gains Top Ranking as Spokesman for Blacks—Poll Sought to Assess Farrakhan Influence," *Washington Post*, 21 December 1985.

23. "Jewish Organization Finds Jackson Top Black Spokesman," *New York Voice*, 4 January 1986.

24. Henry Srebrnik, "Poll Shows Farrakhan Popularity Increases," *Jewish Week*, 26 December 1985.

25. Adam Snitzer, "Midwest Farm Crisis Sparks Wave of Anti-semitism," *New York Jewish Week*, 9 August 1985.

26. "Seeds of Hate," *20/20*, 15 August 1985.

27. Walter Ruby, "Sowing the Seeds of Anti-Semitism," *Palm Beach Jewish World*, 9–15 January 1987, p. 20A.

28. Daniel E. Anderson, "Religious Groups Join to Save Family

Farms," *Rocky Mountain News*, 17 February 1987, p. 29; Elizabeth Kaplan, "Crisis Expert Works to Build Ties Between Farmers, Jews," *Kansas City Jewish Chronicle*, 13 June 1986; Andrew H. Malcolm, "Assessing the Crisis on Farms," *New York Times*, 16 February 1987; A. James Rudin, "Farmers in Crisis," *New York Times*, 26 February 1987; Diane Wolkow, "JCRB, ORT Join Forces to Aid Distressed Farmers," *Kansas City Jewish Chronicle*, 16 January 1986, p. 1, p. 21.

29. David E. Anderson, "Religious Groups Join to Save Family Farms," *Rocky Mountain News*, 17 February 1987.

30. "A Declaration on the Rural Crisis," Press release from the Interreligious Conference on Rural Life (New York: American Jewish Committee, 8 February 1987).

31. "Antisemitism Among Farmers in 'Dispute,'" *Jewish Journal*, 21 March 1987.

32. Nathan Perlmutter, "Jews and Fundamentalism," *Reconstructionist*, December 1985, pp. 20–23.

33. "Fundamental Friends," *Jewish Post & Opinion*, 4 December 1985.

34. Marjorie Hyer, "Poll Finds No Rise in Anti-Semitism: Most Evangelicals Reject Jewish Stereotypes," *Washington Post*, 10 January 1987.

35. Bruce Buursma, "Anti-Semitism Fading for Some," *Chicago Tribune*, 9 January 1987.

36. "Anti-Semitic Views Spurned in Poll," *Chicago Sun-Times*, 8 January 1987.

37. "Evangelical Attitudes Surveyed in Poll," *Baltimore Jewish Times*, 16 January 1987, p. 22.

38. "Survey on Christian Attitudes Cites Positive Findings," *Kansas City Jewish Chronicle*, 16 January 1987.

39. "Catching Up," *Washington Times*, 19 January 1987.

40. "Heartening Anti-Semitism Poll," *Chicago Sun-Times*, 11 January 1987.

41. Interview with Robert Cohn, editor-in-chief, *St. Louis Jewish Light*, St. Louis, 25 February 1987.

42. Telephone interview with Arthur Magida, assistant editor, *Baltimore Jewish Times*, 25 February 1987.

43. Ibid.

44. Telephone interview with Arthur Magida, assistant editor, *Baltimore Jewish Times*, 23 September 1987.

Chapter Seven

1. Leon Wieseltier, "Why Anti-Zionism is Antisemitism," *London Jewish Chronicle*, November 1982.
2. Henry Siegman, "Jews and Blacks: Reconciling the Difference," *Congress Monthly*, p. 3.
3. Stephen S. Rosenfeld, "Dateline Washington: Anti-Semitism and U.S. Foreign Policy," *Foreign Policy* (Summer 1982), 172–183.
4. Chris Gersten, "The Chic Anti-Semitism of the Left," *Washington Jewish Week*, 19 June 1986.
5. Interview with Rosalie Zalis, "Koch: Bradley Erred on Farrakhan," *Israel Today*, 31 January 1986.
6. Editorial: "Taking a Stand on Farrakhan," *Long Island Jewish World*, 4–11 October 1985.
7. *Nationwide Attitudes Survey* (New York: Anti-Defamation League of B'nai B'rith, September 1986), conducted by Tarrance, Hill, Newport & Ryan.
8. "Jews Troubled by Fundamentalists' Views," Religion, *Los Angeles Times*, 10 January 1984, p. 4.
9. Ibid.
10. "Opinion Roundup: School Prayers," *Public Opinion* (June/July 1985), pp. 36–7.
11. Russell Baker, "Nuts to Nomenclature," *New York Times Magazine*, 16 August 1987, p. 20.
12. Gertrude J. Selznick and Stephen Steinberg, *The Tenacity of Prejudice: Anti-Semitism in Contemporary America* (New York: Harper & Row) 1969, p. 185.

LIST OF INTERVIEWS

Interviews with Jewish Leaders

Cohen, Philip. Past President of Cincinnati Federation, OH. Quarterly CJF Meeting, 4/27/87.

Cooper, Mark. Rabbi, Temple Israel in Natick, MA, 5/14/87.

Falchuk, Nancy. Past President of the Boston Chapter of Hadassah, 6/10/87.

Fein, Ruth. Past President of CJP (the Combined Jewish Philanthropies of Greater Boston); Campaign Chairman, Past President, American Jewish Historical Society, 6/5/87.

Goldberg, Paul. President Rochester Federation, N.Y. Quarterly CJF Meeting, 4/28/87.

Goldman, Bernard. Board member, Dayton Federation, OH. Quarterly CJF Meeting, 4/27/87.

Goldstein, Alan. Social Planning and Allocations Chair, Combined Jewish Philanthropies, Boston, MA, 6/8/87.

Kominsky, Neil. Rabbi, Harvard-Radcliffe Hillel, Cambridge, MA, 5/15/87.

Levine, Irving B. Lay leader, American Jewish Committee, 6/11/87.

Levine, Phillip. Federation officer, San Francisco. Quarterly CJF Meeting, 4/17/87.

Margolis, Phyllis. Officer of Washington, DC, Federation. Quarterly CJF Meeting, 4/27/87.

Myers, Larry. President, San Francisco Federation. Quarterly CJF Meeting, 4/27/87.

Orlik, Mitchell. Associate Director of Columbus Federation. Quarterly CJF Meeting, 4/27/87.

Parelman, Suzanne. President, Kansas City Federation. Quarterly CJF Meeting, 4/27/87.

Reck, Joel. President, Jewish Community Relations Council of Boston. Boston, MA, 6/11/87.

Schwartz, Alan. Campaign Chairman, Combined Jewish Philanthropies of Greater Boston. Boston, MA, 5/87.

Schwartz, James. Federation officer, Essex County, NJ. Quarterly CJF Meeting, 4/27/87.

Sherman, Joel. President of Combined Jewish Philanthropies, Boston, MA, 6/25/87.

Stein, Martin. National Chairman of United Jewish Appeal. Quarterly CJF Meeting, 4/27/87.

Stern, Saul. Federation Officer, Washington DC. Quarterly CJF Meeting, 4/27/87.

Stone, Deanne. Chairwoman of Combined Jewish Philanthropies of Greater Boston, Women's Division, Brookline, MA, 5/14/87.

Interviews with Jewish Press Members

Barbanel, Howard. Publisher, *Miami Jewish Tribune.* AJPA Conference, 5/20/87.

Cohen, Robert. President of the American Jewish Press Association; Editor-in-Chief, *St. Louis Jewish Light,* 2/25/87.

Horwitz, Arthur. Associate Publisher, *Detroit Jewish News.* AJPA Conference, 5/20/87.

Mushin, Andy. Assistant Editor, Jewish Telegraphic Agency, 2/87.

Magida, Arthur. Assistant Editor, *Baltimore Jewish Times,* 2/87.

Miscellaneous Interviews

Cohen, Steven A. 6/10/87.
Eisen, Robert. 6/87.
Gillman, Judi. 9/17/87.
Gutman, Michelle. 5/87.
Madeson, Lois. 6/10/87.
Nather, Wendy. 4/26/87.
Weingast, Laura. 6/12/87.

Interviews with Community Relations Professionals and Other Institutional Professionals

Applebaum, Harold. Special Assistant, Antisemitism and Extremism Programs, American Jewish Committee, 3/6/87 and 3/19/87.
Baum, Phillip. Associate Director, American Jewish Congress, 3/19/87.
Chanes, Jerome A. Associate Director of Domestic Concerns, National Jewish Community Relations Council, 3/6/87.
Elin, Jennifer. Family Program Coordinator, Jewish Community Center of St. Louis, 2/25/87.
Gad-Harf, David. Executive Director, Community Relations Council of St. Louis, 2/25/87.
Gordis, David. Former Executive Vice-President, American Jewish Committee, 3/19/87.
Kurlander, Harriet. Former Associate Director of the New York Metropolitan Council; New York Regional Director, American Jewish Congress, 3/18/87.
Klugman, Alan. Director of Metropolitan Division Community Campaign, Combined Jewish Philanthropies, Boston, MA, 6/8/87.
Lang, Joseph. Children's worker, Family Program and

Group Service, Jewish Community Center of St. Louis, 2/25/87.

Mendelson, Evan. Former Associate Executive Director, American Jewish Congress, 3/18/87.

Neumann, Tom. Director of Intergroup Relations, Anti-Defamation League of B'nai B'rith, 3/19/87.

Schwartz, Alan. Director, Research and Evaluation Department, Anti-Defamation League of B'nai B'rith, 3/19/87.

Schwartz, Kenneth. Staff member, Jewish Community Center of St. Louis, 2/25/87.

Stern, Marc. Codirector of Commission on Law and Social Action, American Jewish Congress, 3/18/87.

Zoffer, Gayle. Jewish Community Relations Council of St. Louis, 2/25/87.

Appendix A

TABLES

Table 2-1. Non-Jewish Perceptions of American Jewish Loyalty to the United States[a]

NORC[b] and Yankelovich: *Please tell me whether this statement is probably true or probably false. "Jews are more loyal to Israel than to America."*

	NORC (Oct. 1964) Probably true	Yankelovich (Feb. 1981)		
		Probably true	Probably false	Not sure
Total	30%	30%	32%	38%
Race				
White	30	28	34	37
Black	32	36	21	44
Religion				
Catholic	—	25	37	38
Protestant	—	32	29	39
Age				
Under 35	23			
35–54	27			
55+	42			
Under 39	—	30	33	37
40–54	—	25	40	36
55+	—	33	24	43
Education				
Less than high school	46	36	23	41
High school	29	30	27	43
Some college	19	22	43	35
College graduate	12	24	49	27

[a]Geraldine Rosenfield, "The Polls: Attitudes Toward American Jews," *Public Opinion Quarterly* 46 (1982), p. 433.
[b]NORC: the National Opinion Research Center of the University of Chicago, which did the field work for Part Four in the series based on the University of California Five-Year Study of Antisemitism in the United States.

Table 2-2. Distribution of American Respondents by Score on Index
of Antisemitism[a]

Index score[b]	Percent	Number	
0	16	(316)	Least antisemitic third
1	15	(289)	(31%)
2	12	(227)	Middle antisemitic third
3	10	(183)	(32%)
4	10	(192)	
5	8	(156)	
6	6	(125)	
7	7	(130)	
8	6	(108)	Most antisemitic third
9	5	(95)	(37%)
10	3	(58)	
11	2	(34)	
	100 (N) =	(1,913)	

Average score = 3.75

[a]Reproduced from Gertrude J. Selznick and Stephen Steinberg, *The Tenacity of Prejudice: Anti-Semitism in Contemporary America* (New York: Harper & Row, 1969), p. 26.
[b]The index scores and percentages refer to the number of antisemitic statements accepted by respondents as true.

Table 2-3. Trends in Negative Beliefs about Jews among Non-Jews[a,d]

	1964 (%)	1981 (%)	Net difference: 1981–1964 (%)
Probably true			
The movie and television industries are pretty much controlled by Jews.[b]	70	46	−24
Jews have a lot of irritating faults.[b]	48	29	−19
Jews are more willing than others to use shady practices to get what they want.[b]	48	33	−15
The trouble with Jewish businessmen is that they are so shrewd and tricky that other people don't have a fair chance in competition.[b]	40	27	−13
Jews are just as honest as other businessmen.[b]	34	22	−12
International banking is pretty much controlled by Jews.[b]	55	43	−12
Jews always like to be at the head of things.[b]	63	52	−11
Jews should stop complaining about what happened to them in Nazi Germany.	51	40	−10
Jews don't care what happens to anyone but their own kind.[b]	30	22	−8
Jews stick together too much.	58	53	−5
Jewish employers go out of their way to hire other Jews.[b]	60	57	−3
Jews today are trying to push in where they are not wanted.	21	19	−2
Jews are always stirring up trouble with their ideas.	13	14	+1

(continued)

Table 2-3. *(Continued)*

	1964 (%)	1981 (%)	Net difference: 1981–1964 (%)
Jews have too much power in the business world.[b,c]	33	37	+4
Jews are more loyal to Israel than to America.[b]	39	48	+9
Jews have too much power in the United States.[b,c]	13	23	+10

[a]Gregory Martire and Ruth Clark, *Anti-Semitism in the United States* (New York: Praeger, 1982), p. 19.
[b]11-item antisemitism index.
[c]These statements were posed as questions designed to elicit "yes," "no," or "don't know" responses.
[d]Based on those with an opinion.

Table 2-4. Trends in Attitudes toward Jews: Whites versus Blacks among Non-Jews[a,c]

	Total non-Jews			Whites			Blacks		
	1964 (%)	1981 (%)	Net difference: 1981–1964 (%)	1964 (%)	1981 (%)	Net difference: 1981–1964 (%)	1964 (%)	1981 (%)	Net difference: 1981–1964 (%)
Probably true[b]									
Too much power in United States	13	23	+10	13	20	+7	11	42	+31
Care only about own kind	30	21	–9	27	18	–9	49	43	–6
Not as honest as other businessmen	29	22	–7	29	17	–10	28	47	+19
Too much power in business world	33	37	+4	35	35	0	22	51	+29
More loyal to Israel than to United States	39	48	+9	38	45	+7	51	63	+12

Control international banking	56	43	−13	52	40	−12	74	67	−7
Shrewd and tricky in business	40	27	−13	38	24	−12	54	45	−9
Have a lot of irritating faults	48	28	−20	46	28	−18	56	36	−20
Use shady practices to get ahead	47	33	−14	45	30	−15	67	58	−9
Stick together too much	58	53	−5	59	52	−7	52	63	+11
Always like to head things	63	52	−11	62	51	−11	70	64	−6
Mean level of anti-semitism	42.4	35.2	−7.2	40.4	32.7	−7.7	48.5	52.6	+4.1

[a]Gregory Martire and Ruth Clark, *Anti-Semitism in the United States* (New York: Praeger, 1982), p. 42.
[b]Items used in antisemitism index.
[c]Based on those with an opinion.

Table 2-5. Trends in Attitudes toward Jews, by Age[a,b]

	Age							
	1964				1981			
	18–29 (%)	30–39 (%)	40–54 (%)	55 and over (%)	18–29 (%)	30–39 (%)	40–54 (%)	55 and over (%)
Jews have too much power in the United States.	7	9	11	20	16	24	23	31
Jews don't care what happens to anyone but their own kind.	23	23	28	42	18	23	16	31
Jews are just as honest as other businessmen.	25	29	30	35	22	24	17	24
Jews have too much power in the business world.	23	25	30	46	29	35	40	46

Jews are more loyal to Israel than to United States.	30	30	33	53	51	44	39	58
International banking is pretty much controlled by Jews.	34	40	56	77	33	40	36	65
The trouble with Jewish businessmen is that they are so shrewd and tricky that other people don't have a fair chance in competition.	32	33	37	53	23	26	20	39
Jews stick together too much.	51	55	56	66	42	52	54	64
Jews always like to be at the head of things.	62	57	58	73	47	53	47	63
Jews have a lot of irritating faults.	41	41	45	58	22	32	26	37
Jews are more willing than others to use shady practices to get what they want.	41	42	46	59	26	32	26	48

[a] Gregory Martire and Ruth Clark, *Anti-Semitism in the United States* (New York: Praeger, 1982), p. 41.
[b] Based on those with an opinion.

Table 3-1. Jewish Friendship Patterns, by Age

Number of Jewish best friends[a]	Kansas City (%)	Atlantic City, NJ (%)	Baltimore, MD (%)	City			
				Worcester, MA (%)	Rochester, NY (%)	Essex and Morris counties NJ (%)	
Total							
None are Jewish	14	10	7	12	12	5	
One is Jewish	16	9	11	18	19	12	
Two are Jewish	21	15	19	17	21	19	
Three are Jewish	49	64	62	53	45	63	
None are Jewish							
18–24	37	22	19	13	25	13	
25–34	26	26	11	22	29	7	
35–44	17	13	8	17	15	4	
45–54	]4	]5	]3	19	13	5	
55–64				3	2	3	
65+ (65–74)	5	5	3	5	3	8	

One is Jewish						
18–24	17	24	13	32	43	25
25–34	24	11	20	31	22	15
35–44	27	13	11	32	33	13
45–54	]8	]8	]6	13	21	10
55–64				4	8	8
65+ (65–74)	8	4	4	4	4	11
Two are Jewish						
18–24	18	15	31	25	18	31
25–34	26	37	20	15	21	26
35–44	21	11	23	17	24	25
45–54	]18	]9	]17	25	23	15
55–64				18	22	15
65+ (65–74)	20	10	11	13	17	6
Three are Jewish						
18–24	27	39	35	30	14	29
25–34	23	25	47	33	19	52
35–44	35	61	56	35	27	56
45–54	]70	]74	]71	42	38	67
55–64				74	64	72
65+ (65–74)	67	79	79	77	76	74

ᵃSome numbers do not total 100% owing to rounding error.

Table 3-2. Synagogue Membership

City	Percentage of households belonging to a synagogue
Nashville	78
Kansas City	67
St. Louis	66
Cleveland	61
Worcester	60
Milwaukee	56
Baltimore	55
Essex and Morris counties, NJ	53
Atlantic City	51
Denver	47
NJPS (1971)	47
Chicago	44
Boston	41
Washington, DC	40
Miami	38
Phoenix	33
San Francisco	33
Los Angeles	26

Table 3-3. Frequency of Attendance at Religious Services

				City			
Frequency[a]	Washington, DC (%)	Kansas City (%)	Atlantic City (%)	Baltimore, MD (%)	Worcester, MA (%)	Rochester, NY (%)	Essex and Morris counties, NJ (%)
Total							
Never	16	10	15	10	11	17	12
Special times	16	4	9	7	4	7	7
High holidays	14	15	31	22	14	24	18
Few times/year	34	34	20	30	36	32	36
Once a month	10	8	7	13	14	9	NA
Few times/ month	6	8	8	7	9	8	13
Once weekly	3	9	6	9	9	10	6
Several times/ week	—	2	1	2	4	2	2
Not reported	1	11	4	1	—	—	6

[a]Some numbers do not total 100% owing to rounding error.

Table 3-4. Observed Ritual Practices

	Percent responding they "always" or "usually":		
City	Observe Passover seder	Light shabbat candles	Keep kosher[a]
Baltimore (MD)	86%	32%	23%
Essex and Morris counties, (NJ)	78	25	16
Atlantic City (NJ)	80	29	15
Rochester (NY)	80	33	23
Worcester (MA)	82	32	20
Kansas City (MO)	76	27	13
St. Louis (MO)	51	28	16
Washington (DC)	43	21	14

[a]Keep kosher in home, keep two sets of dishes, or eat kosher meat only.

Table 3-5. Current Membership
in Jewish Organizations

City	Percent yes
Kansas City	59
Atlantic City	50
Baltimore	51
Worcester	60
Rochester	47
Boston	28
San Francisco	38
Denver	38

Table 4-1. Jewish Opinions about Extent of Antisemitism
(1984 and 1983)[a,b]

	Agree	Disagree	Not sure
Antisemitism in America may, in the future, become a serious problem for American Jews	77%	10%	14%
1983 NSAJ	69	11	20
Antisemitism in America is currently not a serious problem for American Jews	40	46	14
1983 NSAJ	37	43	20

[a]Steven M. Cohen, *The Political Attitudes of American Jews, 1984* (New York: American Jewish Committee, 1984), Table 6.
[b]Data from the 1983 National Survey of American Jews have been included as well.

Table 4-2. Jewish Perceptions of Antisemitism in Local Community
How much antisemitism would you say there is in your community?

City	Amount of perceived antisemitism				
	Great deal	Moderate	A little	None	Don't know
St. Louis, MO	18%	39%	29%	7%	7%
Washington, DC	8	45	38	4	6
Kansas City, MO	10	42	33	8	7
Atlantic City, NJ	12	36	32	10	9
Baltimore, MD	17	49	26	2	5
Worcester, MA	7	40	39	8	6
Rochester, NY	6	45	42	4	4

Table 4-3. Jewish Perceptions of Personal Experience
with Antisemitism in Lifetime
*How much antisemitism have you personally experienced
in your lifetime?*

City	Amount of personal experience with antisemitism			
	Great deal	Moderate	A little	None
St. Louis, MO	15%	29%	45%	10%
Washington, DC	9	28	51	10
Kansas City, MO	7	24	49	19
Atlantic City, NJ	13	22	43	20
Baltimore, MD	12	30	44	14
Worcester, MA	12	22	52	14
Rochester, NY	11	29	49	11

Table 4-4. Jewish Perceptions of Personal Experience
with Antisemitism in the Past 12 Months
*Have you personally experienced antisemitism in the
past 12 months?*

City	Percent yes
St. Louis, MO	26
Washington, DC	28
Kansas City, MO	23
Atlantic City, NJ	24
Essex and Morris Counties, NJ	17
Baltimore, MD	21
Worcester, MA	22
Rochester, NY	23

Table 4-5. Reporting of Antisemitism

	Atlantic City	Baltimore	Rochester
Percent yes	21	12	12
Percent no	79	88	88
Reasons for not reporting			
Too minor, not important	23	20	NA
Handled personally, considered the source	11	15	NA
Reporting incident would not do any good	6	9	NA
Remark made by customer/patron, could not report it	2	—	NA
Other	28	43	NA

Table 4-6. Jewish Perceptions of Antisemitism among Non-Jewish Groups
"In your opinion, what proportion of each of the following groups in the U.S. is antisemitic? Most, many, some or few?"[a]

	Most or many (%)	Some (%)	Few or not sure (%)
Big business	44	38	18
Union leaders	23	43	34
Hispanics	30	36	33
Blacks	53	33	14
Democrats	7	47	46
Republicans	29	49	22
Liberals	8	32	60
Conservatives	35	42	23
Catholics	41	41	18
Mainstream Protestants	43	39	18
Fundamentalist Protestants	46	28	26
State Department	40	34	26
Pentagon	39	37	24
Media	19	44	36
Police	20	47	33
Is Jesse Jackson antisemitic?	Yes: 74	No: 8	Not sure: 18

[a]Steven M. Cohen, *The Political Attitudes of American Jews, 1984* (New York: American Jewish Committee, 1984), Table 7.

Table 4-7. Awareness of Antisemitic Incidents in Own Area[a]
Have you seen any of following kinds of incidents in your neighborhood or where you work in the last year or two?

	Total (%)	Non-Jews		Jews (%)
		Total (%)	With Jews in neighborhood (%)	
Anti-Jewish remarks where you live or work	13	13	19	40
Anti-Jewish remarks on TV, radio, newspapers	11	11	14	31
Anti-Jewish graffiti on buildings or vehicles	7	6	9	36
Social clubs/groups that restrict Jews	6	5	7	14
Desecration of temples/synagogues	3	3	4	26
Worker passed over for a promotion because he/she is Jewish	2	2	2	10
None	60	61	53	21

[a]Yankelovich, Skelly & White, *Anti-Semitism in the United States*, Vol. 1 (New York: American Jewish Committee, 1981), p. 30.

Table 4-8. Perceived Possibility of an Increase in Antisemitism[a]

	Total (%)	Non-Jews (%)	Jews (%)
Increase in antisemitism is possible:			
In this area	8	7	40
Elsewhere in the country	22	21	67

[a]Yankelovich, Skelly & White, *Anti-Semitism in the United States*, Vol. 1 (New York: American Jewish Committee, 1981), p. 70.

Table 4-9. Feelings about Having a Jew Nominated for President[a]

	Non-Jews (1)(%)	Jews' perceptions (2) of the views held by the majority of non-Jews (%)
If my political party nomi- nated a Jew for president, I would be bothered:		
Very much	9	42
Somewhat	12	36
Very little	14	10
Not at all	59	7
Not sure	6	5

(1) Suppose your political party wanted to nominate a Jew for president of the United States. Would this disturb you very much, somewhat, very little, or not at all? (This question was asked for several groups, not solely about Jews.)

(2) How do you think the majority of non-Jews would feel if their political party wanted to nominate a Jew for president of the United States—do you think this would disturb them very much, somewhat, very little, or not at all? (Jewish version.)

[a]Yankelovich, Skelly & White, *Anti-Semitism in the United States*, Vol. 2 (New York: American Jewish Committee, 1981, p. 65.

Table 5-1. Community Relations Professionals' Attitudes on Jewish-Related Issues

In your opinion, how important is each of the following to the Jewish people?

		Very important	Somewhat important	Not at all important	No response
Separation of church and state	Total[a]	72%	28%	—	—
	AJC	67	33	—	—
	ADL	54	46	—	—
Programs to combat antisemitism	Total[a]	51	46	3%	—
	AJC	44	56	—	—
	ADL	62	38	—	—
Neighborhoods where Jews can live with other Jews	Total[a]	29	58	12	1%
	AJC	22	72	—	6
	ADL	15	54	31	—
Jews marrying other Jews	Total[a]	55	41	4	—
	AJC	61	28	11	—
	ADL	38	54	8	—
Jewish children receiving a Jewish education	Total[a]	61	33	6	—
	AJC	67	28	6	—
	ADL	62	38	—	—

[a]Total includes all survey respondents, including members of the American Jewish Committee, Anti-Defamation League, American Jewish Congress, Federation respondents, and Community Relations Council professionals.
[b]AJC = The American Jewish Committee, ADL = The Anti-Defamation League.

Table 5-2. Community Relations Professionals' Attitudes
on the Most Important Issue Facing American Jews
Which is the single most important?
(Proportion selecting category as most important)

	Selected by		
	Total[a]	AJC[b]	ADL
Jewish children receiving Jewish education	34%	33%	23%
Separation of church and state	29	33	31
Jews marrying other Jews	18	17	8
Programs to combat antisemitism	10	11	15
Neighborhoods where Jews can live with other Jews	6	6	15

[a]Total includes all survey respondents, including members of the American Jewish Committee, Anti-Defamation League, American Jewish Congress, Federation respondents, and Community Relations Council professionals.
[b]AJC = The American Jewish Committee, ADL = The Anti-Defamation League.

Table 5-3. Community Relations Professionals' Attitudes toward Antisemitism

		Amount of antisemitism				
		A great deal	A moderate amount	Little	None	No response
How much antisemitism do you see in your own community?	Total[a]	6%	42%	48%	1%	—
	AJC	6	39	56	—	—
	ADL	23	54	15	—	—
How much antisemitism do you see in the United States?	Total[a]	3	61	30	—	—
	AJC	—	61	28	—	—
	ADL	15	77	—	—	—
How much do you think antisemitism in the United States affects American Jews?	Total[a]	12	33	52	—	—
	AJC	6	39	56	—	3
	ADL	—	69	23	—	—

[a]Total includes all survey respondents, including members of the American Jewish Committee, the Anti-Defamation League, the American Jewish Congress, Federation respondents, and Community Relations Council professionals.
[b]AJC = The American Jewish Committee, ADL = The Anti-Defamation League.

Table 5-4. Community Relations Professionals' Personal Experience with Antisemitism

		Amount of antisemitism				
		A great deal	A moderate amount	Little	None	No response
How much antisemitism have you personally experienced in your lifetime?	Total[a]	4%	46%	48%	—	1%
	AJC	—	56	44	—	—
	ADL	15	38	46	—	—

		Yes	No	No response, not sure
Have you personally experienced any antisemitism in the last 12 months?	Total[a]	38%	61%	1%
	AJC	22	78	—
	ADL	46	46	8
Did you report the incident(s) to anyone?	Total[a]	81	19	
	AJC	50	50	
	ADL	80	20	

[a]Total includes all survey respondents, including members of the American Jewish Committee, the Anti-Defamation League, the American Jewish Congress, Federation respondents, and Community Relations Council professionals.
[b]AJC = The American Jewish Committee, ADL = The Anti-Defamation League.

Table 5-5. Reports of Antisemitism to Community
Relations Professionals

Number of reports	Reported directly to respondent			Brought to attention through organizational and professional networks		
	Total[a]	AJC[b]	ADL	Total[a]	AJC	ADL
None	9%	17%	—	3%	—	—
1–3	42	39	15	16	6	—
4–6	17	28	—	24	28	8
7–10	7	11	—	9	6	8
11–20	23	6	77	19	28	38
21+	—	—	—	25	28	38
No response	—	—	8	—	6	8

[a]Total includes all survey respondents, including members of the American Jewish Committee, the Anti-Defamation League, the American Jewish Congress, Federation respondents, and Community Relations Council professionals.
[b]AJC = The American Jewish Committee, ADL = The Anti-Defamation League.

Table 5-6. Sources of Reports of Antisemitism to Community
Relations Professionals
*How did these incidents come to your attention? What was your main source of
information?*

Source	Brought to professional's attention			Main source		
	Total[a]	AJC[b]	ADL	Total[a]	AJC	ADL
Jewish press	67	72	62	13	17	8
General media	64	83	62	10	22	—
Friends and relatives	41	44	54	4	11	—
Organization bulletin boards	20	—	15	1	—	—
Organization publications	35	56	54	10	6	23
Professional publications	45	28	31	13	6	—
Reported to office	64	78	85	45	33	85
Other	10	—	—	1	—	—
No response	1	—	—	3	6	—

[a]Total includes all survey respondents, including members of the American Jewish Committee, the Anti-Defamation League, the American Jewish Congress, Federation respondents, and Community Relations Council professionals.
[b]AJC = The American Jewish Committee, ADL = The Anti-Defamation League.

Table 5-7. Community Relations Professionals' Attitudes about Antisemitism among Non-Jewish Groups

What proportion of Americans do you feel are actively antisemitic,[a] passively antisemitic,[b] or hold no antisemitic beliefs?

Proportion	Actively antisemitic[a]			Passively antisemitic[b]			Hold no antisemitic beliefs		
	Total[c]	AJC[d]	ADL	Total[c]	AJC	ADL	Total[c]	AJC	ADL
None	—	—	—	—	—	—	1	—	—
1–20%	90%	89%	77%	25%	33%	—	6%	6%	6%
21–40	6	11	15	58	56	69	39	44	54
41–60	1	—	8	10	—	15	16	11	15
61–80	—	—	—	4	—	15	23	17	31
81–100	—	—	—	—	—	—	12	22	—
No response	3	—	—	3	—	—	3	—	—

[a] Those non-Jews whose antisemitic beliefs influence their behavior.
[b] Non-Jews whose antisemitic beliefs do not influence their behavior.
[c] Total includes all survey respondents, including members of the American Jewish Committee, the Anti-Defamation League, the American Jewish Congress, Federation respondents, and Community Relations Council professionals.
[d] AJC = The American Jewish Committee, ADL = The Anti-Defamation League.

Table 5-8. Community Relations
Professionals' Attitudes
about Anti-Israelism
*What proportion of anti-Israel statements do
you think are antisemitic?*

Proportion of statements	Total[a]	AJC[b]	ADL
All	—	—	—
Most	19%	6%	23%
Many	33	39	46
Some	42	56	23
Few	1	—	—
None	—	—	—
No response	4	—	—

[a]Total includes all survey respondents, including
members of the American Jewish Committee, the
Anti-Defamation League, the American Jewish Congress, Federation respondents, and Community Relations Council professionals.
[b]AJC = The American Jewish Committee, ADL =
The Anti-Defamation League.

Table 5-9. Demographic and Religious Profile of Community Relations
Professionals

	Percent		
	Total[a]	AJC[b]	ADL
Age			
25–34	24	22	31
35–44	35	33	31
45–54	16	6	15
55–64	15	22	15
65+	6	6	—
No response	—	6	8
Sex			
Male	74	61	85
Female	26	39	15
Marital status			
Never married	4	—	8
Married	81	72	77
Divorced	13	28	8
No response	1	—	—
Religious denomination			
Orthodox	4	11	—
Conservative	36	17	54
Reform	26	33	23
Reconstructionist	6	6	—
Just Jewish	14	11	8
Other	12	11	8
Secular education level			
Some college	3	11	—
BA/BS	17	6	23
Graduate or professional degree	80	83	77
Type of Jewish education[c]			
Day school	12	14	4
Afternoon Hebrew school	59	38	39
Sunday school	42	48	35
Adult education courses	—	—	—
College courses	—	—	—
None	6	—	—
Other	4	—	13

(continued)

Table 5-9. *(Continued)*

	Percent		
	Total[a]	AJC[b]	ADL
Number of years of Jewish educa-			
tion			
None	6	—	—
1–5	21	28	23
6–10	32	33	31
10+	28	28	31
No response	13	11	8
Number of 3 best friends who are			
Jewish			
3	81	72	78
2	13	22	23
1	1	6	—
None	4	—	—
Number of years in Jewish com-			
munity relations field			
0–5 years	21	17	23
6–10 years	32	44	23
11–15 years	18	6	23
16–20 years	10	6	8
20+ years	16	28	23
No response	3	—	—
Number of years at current posi-			
tion			
0–5	65	50	78
6–10	16	22	8
11–15	4	11	—
16–20	4	6	8
20+	7	11	8

[a]Total includes all survey respondents, including members of the American Jewish Committee, the Anti-Defamation League, the American Jewish Congress, Federation respondents,
and Community Relations Council professionals.
[b]AJC = The American Jewish Committee, ADL = The Anti-Defamation League.
[c]Figures add up to more than 100% because many respondents answered in more than one
category.

Table 6-1. Demographic and Religious Profile of Jewish Press Members

Age	
26–35	26%
36–45	16
46–55	16
56–65	21
66+	13
Not reported	8
Sex	
Male	60
Female	40
Place of birth	
Same as current	26
Different city, same state	13
Out of state	50
Foreign-born	3
Not reported	8
Marital status	
Single	11
Married	84
Divorced	3
Widowed	3
Religious denomination	
Orthodox	11
Conservative	40
Reform	16
Reconstructionist	8
Other	26
Secular education level	
Some college	8
BA/BS	26
Some graduate or professional school	18
Graduate or professional degree	47
Type of Jewish education	
Day school	11
Afternoon Hebrew school	53
Sunday school	47
Adult education courses	37
College courses	32

(continued)

Table 6-1. *(Continued)*

Number of years of Jewish education	
None	5%
1–5	29
6–10	32
Over 10	26
Not reported	5

Table 6-2. Jewish Press Member Attitudes on Jewish-Related Issues
In your opinion, how important is each of the following to the Jewish people?

	Very important	Somewhat important	Not important	No response
Separation of church and state	87%	13%	—	—
Programs to combat antisemitism	68	26	5%	—
Neighborhoods where Jews can live with other Jews	26	61	11	3%
Jews marrying other Jews	74	18	8	—
Jewish children receiving a Jewish education	84	13	3	—

Table 6-3. Jewish Press Members' Attitudes on Most Important Issue Facing Jews
Which of the above is the single most important?

Rank		Selected by
1	Jewish children receiving a Jewish education	53%
2	Separation of church and state	21
3	Jews marrying other Jews	13
3	Programs to combat antisemitism	13
4	Neighborhoods where Jews can live with other Jews	—

Table 6-4. Jewish Press Members' Attitudes toward Antisemitism

| | Amount of antisemitism | | | | |
	A great deal	A moderate amount	Little	None	Not reported
How much antisemitism do you see in your own community?	3%	47%	45%	—	5%
How much antisemitism do you see in the United States?	3	74	21	—	3
How much antisemitism have you *personally* experienced in your lifetime?	11	26	58	5	—

Table 6-5. Jewish Press Members' Personal Experience
with Antisemitism

	Yes	No	Not sure
Have you personally experienced any antisemitism in the *last 12 months*?	24%	74%	3%
Did you report the incident(s) to anyone?	78	22	—

Appendix B

SURVEYS

Survey Methodology

Chapter Three: Jewish Population Studies

All data from Jewish population studies were taken from the following:

James McCann and Debra Friedman, *A Study of the Jewish Community in the Greater Seattle Area* (Seattle, 1979).

Bruce A. Phillips, *Los Angeles Jewish Community Survey Overview for Regional Planning* (Los Angeles, 1980).

Allied Jewish Federation of Denver, *The Denver Jewish Population Study* (Denver, 1981).

Lois Geer, *1981 Population Study of the St. Paul Jewish Community* (St. Paul, 1981).

Lois Geer, *The Jewish Community of Greater Minneapolis 1981 Population Study* (Minneapolis, 1981).

Population Research Committee, *Survey of Cleveland's Jewish Population, 1981* (Cleveland, 1981).

Peter Regenstreif, *The Jewish Population of Rochester, New York* (Rochester, 1981).

Paul Ritterband and Steven M. Cohen, *The 1981 Greater New York Jewish Population Survey* (New York, 1981).

Nancy Hendrix, *A Demographic Study of the Jewish Community of Nashville and Middle Tennessee* (Nashville, 1982).

Policy Research Corporation, *Chicago Jewish Population Study* (Chicago, 1982).

Ira M. Sheskin, *Population Study of the Greater Miami Jewish Community* (Miami, 1982).

Gary A. Tobin, *A Demographic and Attitudinal Study of the Jewish Community of St. Louis* (St. Louis, 1982).

Bruce A. Phillips and William S. Aron, *The Greater Phoenix Jewish Population Study* (Phoenix, 1983–1984).

Jewish Community Federation of Richmond, *Demographic Survey of the Jewish Community of Richmond* (Richmond, 1984).

Bruce A. Phillips and Eve Weinberg, *The Milwaukee Jewish Population Study* (Milwaukee, 1984).

Gary A. Tobin, Joseph Waksberg, and Janet Greenblatt, *A Demographic Study of the Jewish Community of Greater Washington* (Washington, D.C., 1984).

Gary A. Tobin, *A Demographic Study of the Jewish Community of Atlantic County* (Atlantic City, 1986).

Gary A. Tobin, *A Demographic Study of the Jewish Community of Greater Kansas City* (Kansas City, 1986).

Gary A. Tobin, *A Population Study of the Jewish Community of Greater Baltimore* (Baltimore, 1986).

Michael Rappeport and Gary A. Tobin, *A Population Study of the Jewish Community of MetroWest New Jersey, 1986* (MetroWest, 1987).

Gary A. Tobin and Sylvia Barack Fishman, *A Population Study of the Jewish Community of Worcester* (Worcester, 1987).

Gary A. Tobin, Sylvia Barack Fishman, and Sharon L. Sassler, *A Population Study of the Jewish Community of Greater Rochester* (Rochester, 1988).

Gary A. Tobin and Sharon Sassler, *A Demographic Study of the Jewish Community of the San Francisco Bay Area* (San Francisco, 1988).

Gary A. Tobin and Sharon Sassler, *A Demographic Study of New Orleans* (New Orleans, 1988).

The survey methodologies for each study can be found in these reports.

Chapter Four: Methodology for Interviewing Members of the Jewish Community

Approximately 25 interviews with leaders in the Jewish community were conducted between March and July of 1987. Those interviewed included rabbis and volunteers of various Jewish organizations. All had been active participants in Jewish volunteer work for many years, and many were current or former directors, chairmen, or presidents of a host of Jewish organizations and institutions.

About one-third of the interviews were conducted at the quarterly meeting of the Council of Jewish Federations held in Washington, D.C. in April 1987, which brought together highly involved volunteers from all over the country. The majority of the remaining interviews were conducted in the greater Boston area, with representatives from numerous organizations. The interviews were conducted in person, recorded on tape, and later transcribed.

In addition to interviewing lay leaders of the Jewish community, approximately ten Jews randomly selected by age, occupation, or other factors were interviewed.

Chapter Five: Survey of Community Relations Professionals

A survey of community relations professionals was conducted in the spring of 1987. Professionals, those who work for Jewish organizations, representing various agencies, were polled on their opinions about various issues affecting the Jewish community. The questionnaire was designed by Sharon Sassler, Gary Tobin, and Larry

Sternberg, of the Cohen Center for Modern Jewish Studies at Brandeis University, and distributed to branch offices and headquarter locations of Federations, Community Relations Councils, the Anti-Defamation League, the American Jewish Committee, and the American Jewish Congress.

A total of 215 surveys were sent out in April, distributed by the respective agency's representative. A second mailing was repeated in May. Executive directors, regional directors, area directors, and program specialists answered the questionnaire. A total of 73 surveys were returned, a response rate of about 34%. Individual survey respondents are not identified.

Personal interviews were also conducted with key professionals of community relations agencies.

Chapter Six: Methodology for a Survey of Members of the American Jewish Press Association

A survey of members of the American Jewish Press Association was conducted in May 1986. The questionnaire was designed by Gary Tobin and mailed to the president of the AJPA, Robert A. Cohn, for distribution, with a cover letter explaining the nature of the study. A survey was mailed to 114 newspapers and magazines. AJPA members include independent journalists, managing editors, editors emeritus, publishers, and staff writers. A total of 40 surveys were returned, a response rate of over 40%.

Survey Instruments

Chapter Four: Personal Interview Questions

A. Issues Concerning American Jewry
    1. What would you say is the single most important

problem facing Jews in the United States today? Please discuss.

2. What do you think are the biggest problems facing Jews today in the United States? Please discuss.

3. In your opinion, how important is each of the following to American Jews? Is it very important, somewhat important, or not at all important?
   a. Separation of church and state
   b. Programs to combat antisemitism
   c. Neighborhoods where Jews can live with other Jews
   d. Jews marrying other Jews
   e. Jewish children receiving a Jewish education

   Which of the above is the single most important?_____ (Choose a–e)

4. Which do you think presents the greater problem for Jews in the United States—a breakdown of the separation of church and state or a rise in antisemitism? Why?

5. Why is a separation of church and state so important to Jews? What are the consequences of less separation?

B. Assessing Antisemitism

6. Do you think there is more or less antisemitism in the United States today than before WWII? Why?

7. Do you think there is more or less antisemitism in the United States today than in the 1950s? Why?

8. Do you think there is more or less antisemitism in the United States today than in the 1970s? Why?

9. In your opinion, do you think there will be more or less antisemitism in the United States ten years from now than there is today? Why?

10. Do you think that antisemitism might threaten the security of Jews in American society in the future? Why or why not?

C. Addressing Antisemitism

11. What is your definition of *antisemitism.*

12. What methods do you think are the most effective in *combatting* antisemitism?

13. What methods do you think would be the most effective in *completely eliminating* antisemitism?

14. How much antisemitism would you say there is in your own community?
   a. A great deal
   b. A moderate amount
   c. Little
   d. None

15. How much antisemitism would you say there is in the United States?
   a. A great deal
   b. A moderate amount
   c. Little
   d. None

16. Do you think antisemitism in the United States affects American Jews a great deal, some, or not at all?
   a. A great deal
   b. A moderate amount
   c. Little
   d. Not at all

D. Personal Experiences of Antisemitism
    17. How much antisemitism have you personally experienced in your lifetime?
        a. A great deal
        b. A moderate amount
        c. Little
        d. None
    18. To what extent has antisemitism influenced your life?
        a. A great deal
        b. A moderate amount
        c. Little
        d. None
    19. Have you personally experienced any antisemitism in the last 12 months?
        a. Yes   (If yes, please describe.)
        b. No
    20. Did you report the incident(s) to anyone?
    21. If you did report the incident(s), please specify to whom or what organization.
    22. If you did not report the incident(s), why not?

E. Antisemitism in America
    23. What percentage of Americans do you feel are *very* antisemitic—their antisemitic beliefs influence their behavior?
    24. What percentage of Americans do you feel are *somewhat* antisemitic—they hold antisemitic beliefs that do *not* influence their behavior?
    25. What percentage of Americans do you think hold *no* antisemitic beliefs?
    26. Do you think extremist groups like the Ku Klux Klan, Posse Comitatus, and neo-Nazi groups have any effect on the way most Americans think about Jews? Please explain.

27. How much of a threat do these extremist groups pose?

F. American Antisemitism and the Position of Israel
   28. Do anti-Israel/anti-Zionist statements reflect antisemitic beliefs? Please explain.
   29. What proportion of anti-Israel statements do you think are antisemitic? All, most, few, or none?

G. Information Distribution and Antisemitism
   30. What Jewish journals, magazines and newspapers do you receive?
   31. What items interest you the most?
   32. Do stories on antisemitism attract your notice? More so or less so than other stories?

H. Background Information
   1. Age
   2. Sex
   3. Place of birth
   4. Place now residing
   5. Number of years you have lived in your current neighborhood?
   6. Marital status
   7. Do you have children? How many?
   8. In terms of your religious identity, do you consider yourself:
     a. Orthodox
     b. Conservative
     c. Reform
     d. Reconstructionist
     e. Just Jewish
     f. Other
   9. What was the highest level of secular education attained?
   10. What type of Jewish education, if any, did you receive? None, Sunday school, Hebrew school or

other part-time school, day school or yeshiva, other.

11. How many years were you enrolled in Jewish education of any kind?

12. If you have children, what kind of Jewish education, if any, are they receiving?

13. Of your three best friends, how many are Jewish?

Chapter Five: Community Relations Professionals Interview Questions

A. Issues Concerning American Jewry

1. What would you say is the single most important problem facing Jews in the United States today? Please discuss.

2. What do you think are the biggest problems facing Jews today in the United States? Please discuss.

3. In what ways do you think the condition of American Jews in 50 years will differ from what it is now? Please discuss.

4. In your opinion, how important is each of the following to American Jews? Is it very important, somewhat important, or not at all important?

   a. Separation of church and state

   b. Programs to combat antisemitism

   c. Neighborhoods where Jews can live with other Jews

   d. Jews marrying other Jews

   e. Jewish children
      receiving a Jewish
      education
5a. Which of the above is the single most impor-
    tant?_____ (Choose a–e)
5b. Which do you think presents the greater problem
    for Jews in the United States—a breakdown of the
    separation of church and state or a rise in anti-
    semitism? Why?
 6. Why is a separation of church and state so impor-
    tant to Jews? What are the consequences of less
    separation?
B. Assessing Antisemitism
    1. Do you think there is more or less antisemitism in
       the United States today than before World War II?
       Why?
    2. Do you think there is more or less antisemitism in
       the United States today than in the 1950s? Why?
    3. Do you think there is more or less antisemitism in
       the United States today than in the 1970s? Why?
    4. In your opinion, do you think there will be more
       or less antisemitism in the United States in ten
       years than there is today? Why?
    5. Do you think that antisemitism might threaten
       the security of Jews in American society in the
       future? Why or why not?
C. Addressing Antisemitism
    1. What is your definition of *antisemitism?*
    2. What criteria do you use to determine if an inci-
       dent is considered "antisemitic?"
    3. Do you think that policies that affect Jews nega-
       tively are necessarily antisemitic?
    4. How would you characterize your institution's
       philosophy of dealing with antisemitism?

5. How does your organization approach the problem of antisemitism? Please specify.
6. How does your organization's approach to antisemitism differ from other organizations? How is it unique?
7. How does your organization influence the American Jewish community's perception of antisemitism?
8. What methods do you think are the most effective in *combatting* antisemitism?
9. What methods do you think would be the most effective in *completely eliminating* antisemitism?
10. How much antisemitism would you say there is in your own community?
   a. A great deal
   b. A moderate amount
   c. Little
   d. None
11. How much antisemitism would you say there is in the United States?
   a. A great deal
   b. A moderate amount
   c. Little
   d. None
12. Do you think antisemitism in the United States affects American Jews a great deal, some, or not at all?

D. Personal Experiences of Antisemitism
   1. How much antisemitism have you personally experienced in your lifetime?
      a. A great deal
      b. A moderate amount
      c. Little
      d. None

2. To what extent has antisemitism influenced your life?
   a. A great deal
   b. A moderate amount
   c. Little
   d. None

3a. Have you personally experienced any anti-semitism in the last 12 months?
   a. Yes
   b. No

3b. If yes, please describe.

3c. Did you report the incident(s) to anyone?

3d. If you did report the incident(s), please specify to whom or what organization.

3e. If you did not report the incident(s), why not?

4a. How many antisemitic incidents have been reported *directly to you* in the past year?
   (1) None
   (2) One to three
   (3) Four to six
   (4) Seven to ten
   (5) Eleven or more

4b. How many antisemitic incidents have come to your attention through organizational and professional networks in the past year?
   (1) None
   (2) One to three
   (3) Four to six
   (4) Seven to ten
   (5) Eleven to twenty
   (6) Twenty-one or more

4c. How did these incidents come to your attention? Check *all* those that apply.
   (1) Anglo-Jewish Press
   (2) General media

      (3) Friends and relatives
      (4) Organization bulletin boards
      (5) Organization publications
      (6) Professional publications
      (7) Reported to office
      (8) Other (please specify)

    4d. What was your *main* source of information? Check only *one*.
      (1) Anglo-Jewish Press
      (2) General media
      (3) Friends and relatives
      (4) Organization bulletin boards
      (5) Organization publications
      (6) Professional publications
      (7) Reported to office
      (8) Other (please specify)

E. Antisemitism in America

    1a. What percentage of Americans do you feel are *very* antisemitic, i.e., their antisemitic beliefs influence their behavior?

    1b. What percentage of Americans do you feel are passively antisemitic, i.e., they hold antisemitic beliefs that do not influence their behavior?

    1c. What percentage of Americans do you think hold *no* antisemitic beliefs?
      (1) None
      (2) 1–20%
      (3) 21–40%
      (4) 41–60%
      (5) 61–80%
      (6) 81–100%

    2a. Do you think extremist groups such as the Ku Klux Klan, Posse Comitatus, and neo-Nazi groups have any effect on the way most Americans think about Jews? Please explain.

2b. How much of a threat do these extremist groups pose?

3. Do anti-Israel or anti-Zionist statements reflect antisemitic beliefs? Please explain.

4. What proportion of anti-Israel statements do you think are antisemitic?
   a. All
   b. Most
   c. Many
   d. Some
   e. Few
   f. None
   g. Not sure

5. In your opinion, what proportion of each of the following groups *in the United States* is antisemitic?
   (All, most, many, some, few, none, not sure)
   a. Big business
   b. Union leaders
   c. Oil industry
   d. Blacks
   e. Greeks
   f. Hispanics
   g. Italians
   h. Poles
   i. WASPs
   j. Farmers
   k. Urban dwellers
   l. Rural residents
   m. Democrats
   n. Republicans
   o. Liberals
   p. Conservatives
   q. Catholics
   r. Mainstream Protestants

     s. Fundamentalist Protestants
     t. Quakers
     u. Black leaders
     v. State Department
     w. Pentagon
     x. Congress
     y. Media
     z. Police

6. In your opinion, what proportion of each of the following groups *in the United States* is anti-Israel? (All, most, many, some, few, none, not sure)

     a. Big business
     b. Union leaders
     c. Oil industry
     d. Blacks
     e. Greeks
     f. Hispanics
     g. Italians
     h. Poles
     i. WASPs
     j. Farmers
     k. Urban dwellers
     l. Rural residents
     m. Democrats
     n. Republicans
     o. Liberals
     p. Conservatives
     q. Catholics
     r. Mainstream Protestants
     s. Fundamentalist Protestants
     t. Quakers
     u. Black leaders
     v. State Department
     w. Pentagon
     x. Congress

      y. Media

      z. Police

F. The Press and Antisemitism

    1.   What Jewish journals, magazines and news-papers do you receive?

    2.   What items interest you most?

    3.   Do stories on antisemitism attract your notice more or less than other stories? Please explain.

G. Background Information

    1.   Sex

    2.   Marital status

    3.   Age

    4.   Highest level of education completed: some college; college graduate; professional or graduate degree

    5.   Your place of birth

    6a.   Your current primary residence

    6b.   Number of years you have lived in your current neighborhood

    7.   How many children do you have?

    8.   In terms of your religious identity, do you consider yourself:

        a. Orthodox

        b. Conservative

        c. Reform

        d. Reconstructionist

        e. Just Jewish

        f. Other

    9a.   What type of Jewish education, if any, did you receive? None, Sunday school, Hebrew school or other part-time school, day school or yeshiva, other

    9b.   How many years were you enrolled in Jewish education of any kind?

    10.   If you have children, what kind of Jewish education, if any, are they receiving?

11. Of your three best friends, how many are Jewish?

12a. How long have you been in the field of Jewish community relations?

12b. How long have you been at your current position?

13a. Organization

13b. Position

Chapter Six: Jewish Press Survey Interview Questions

1. In your opinion, how important is each of the following to the Jewish people? Is it very important, somewhat important, or not at all important?
   a. Separation of church and state
   b. Programs to combat antisemitism
   c. Neighborhoods where Jews can live with other Jews
   d. Jews marrying other Jews
   e. Jewish children receiving a Jewish education

2. Which of the above is the single most important?_____ (Choose a–e)

3. What would you say is the single most important problem facing Jews in the United States today? Explain.

4. In what ways do you think the condition of American Jews in 50 years will differ from what it is now? Explain.

5. Which do you think is a greater problem for Jews in the United States today—a breakdown of the separation of church and state or a rise in antisemitism? Why?

6. Do you think there is more or less antisemitism in the United States today than 25 years ago? Why?

7. Do you think that antisemitism might become a significant problem for American Jews in the future? Why or why not?

8. What methods do you think are the most effective in *combatting* antisemitism?

9. What methods do you think would be the most effective in *completely eliminating* antisemitism?

10. What is your definition of "antisemitism" or "antisemitic incident?"

11. What criteria do you use to determine if an incident is considered "antisemitic" by your paper?

12. What criteria do you use in deciding whether or not to print a particular story on an incident regarded as antisemitic?

13. In general, do you think your paper treats antisemitic incidents differently than does the non-Jewish press in your community? If so, how?

14. How much antisemitism would you say there is in your community?
    a. A great deal
    b. A moderate amount
    c. Little
    d. None

15. How much antisemitism would you say there is in the United States?
    a. A great deal
    b. A moderate amount
    c. Little
    d. None

16. How much antisemitism have you personally experi-
    enced in your lifetime?
    a. A great deal
    b. A moderate amount
    c. Little
    d. None
17. Have you personally experienced any antisemitism
    in the *last 12 months?*
    a. Yes
    b. No
17a. If you have personally experienced any antisemitic
    incidents in the last year, please describe them
    briefly.
17b. Did you report the incident(s) to anyone?
    (1) Yes
    (2) No
17c. If you did report the incident(s), please specify to
    whom or to what organization(s).
17d. If you did not report the incident(s), why not?
18. In your opinion, what proportion of each of the fol-
    lowing groups *in the United States* is antisemitic?
    (All, most, many, some, few, none, not sure)
    a. Big business
    b. Union leaders
    c. Oil industry
    d. Blacks
    e. Greeks
    f. Hispanics
    g. Italians
    h. Poles
    i. WASPs
    j. Farmers
    k. Urban dwellers
    l. Rural residents
    m. Democrats

n. Republicans
o. Liberals
p. Conservatives
q. Catholics
r. Mainstream Protestants
s. Fundamentalist Protestants
t. Quakers
u. Black leaders
v. State Department
w. Pentagon
x. Congress
y. Media
z. Police

19. In your opinion, what proportion of each of the following groups *in the United States* is anti-Israel?
(All, most, many, some, few, none, not sure)
a. Big business
b. Union leaders
c. Oil industry
d. Blacks
e. Greeks
f. Hispanics
g. Italians
h. Poles
i. WASPs
j. Farmers
k. Urban dwellers
l. Rural residents
m. Democrats
n. Republicans
o. Liberals
p. Conservatives
q. Catholics
r. Mainstream Protestants

    s. Fundamentalist Protestants
    t. Quakers
    u. Black leaders
    v. State Department
    w. Pentagon
    x. Congress
    y. Media
    z. Police

Background Information

20. Age
21. Sex
22. Place of birth (city, state)
23. Marital status
24. Do you have children? Number
25. Do you consider yourself to be:
    a. Orthodox
    b. Conservative
    c. Reform
    d. Reconstructionist
    e. Other (specify)
26. What was the highest level of secular education attained?
    a. Some high school
    b. High school diploma
    c. Some college
    d. BA/BS
    e. Some graduate or professional school
    f. Graduate or professional degree
27a. What type of Jewish education, if any, did you receive? (circle all that apply)
    a. Day school
    b. Afternoon Hebrew school
    c. Sunday school
    d. Adult education courses

     e. College courses
27b. Total number of years enrolled in Jewish education
      of any kind?
28.   Name
29.   Title
30.   Paper

BIBLIOGRAPHY

Books and Articles

ADL Charter of 1913. Chicago: The Anti-Defamation League of B'nai B'rith, 1913.

The Denver Jewish Population Study. Allied Jewish Federation of Denver, Denver: 1981.

Alpern, David M. "Again, Anti-Semitism." *Newsweek* 16 (February 1981): 38–39.

The American Farmer and the Extremists. New York: Anti-Defamation League of B'nai B'rith, 1986.

The American Jewish Committee: An Inside Look. New York: American Jewish Committee, 1984.

Audit of Anti-Semitic Incidents. New York: Anti-Defamation League of B'nai B'rith, 1979–1986.

Barnes, Fred. "The Farrakhan Frenzy (What's a Black Politician to Do?)" *New Republic* 193 (28 October 1985): 13–15.

Bauer, Yehuda. "Anti-Semitism Today—A Fiction or a Fact?" *Midstream* 30 (October 1984): 24–31.

Baum, Phillip. *Where We Stand: Antisemitism.* New York: American Jewish Congress, 1981.

Berger, Marshall J. "A Dissenting Opinion." *Congress Monthly* 53 (January 1986): 5–6.

Borowitz, Eugene. *The Mask Jews Wear: The Self-Deceptions of American Jewry.* Port Washington, NY: Sh'ma, 1980.

Cohen, Arthur. "Why I Choose to Be a Jew." *Harper's Magazine* 217 (April 1959): 61–66.

Cohen, Steven M. "The 1981–82 National Survey of American Jews." *The American Jewish Year Book,* Milton Himmelfarb and David Singer, eds. New York and Philadelphia: American Jewish Committee and the Jewish Publication Society of America, 84(1983): pp. 89–110.

Cohen, Steven M. *The 1983 National Survey of American Jews and Jewish Communal Leaders: Attitudes of American Jews toward Israel and Israelis.* New York: American Jewish Committee, 1983.

Cohen, Steven M. *The Political Attitudes of American Jews, 1984.* New York: American Jewish Committee, 1984.

Cohen, Steven M. *Ties and Tensions: The 1986 Survey of American Jewish Attitudes toward Israel and Israelis.* New York: American Jewish Committee, 1986.

Curtis, Michael, ed. *Antisemitism in the Contemporary World*. Boulder: Westview Press, 1986.

D'Amato, Alfonse M. *The Congressional Record* (June 1984): S8713–8714.

Davidowicz, Lucy S. "American Public Opinion." *The American Jewish Year Book*, Morris Fine and Milton Himmelfarb, eds. New York and Philadelphia: American Jewish Committee and the Jewish Publication Society of America, 69(1968): 198–229.

Dobkowski, Michael N. "American Antisemitism and American Historians: A Critique." *Patterns of Prejudice* 14 (April 1980): 33–43.

Eisen, Arnold M. *The Chosen People in America: A Study in Jewish Religious Ideology*. Bloomington: Indiana University Press, 1983.

Ellerin, Milton, Perlmutter, Nathan, *et al*. "How to Combat Antisemitism." *Patterns of Prejudice* 17 (1983): 3–18.

Elliott, Mark, and McClintock, Michael. "Holocaust 'Revisionists' and the California Library Association." *Midstream* 32 (April 1986): 36–38.

Epstein, Benjamin R., and Forster, Arnold. *Some of My Best Friends . . .* New York: Farrar, Straus and Cudahy, 1962.

Epstein, Benjamin R., and Forster, Arnold. *Report on the John Birch Society*. New York: Vintage Books, 1966.

Extremism on the Right. New York: Anti-Defamation League of B'nai B'rith, 1983.

Extremism Targets the Prisons. New York: Anti-Defamation League of B'nai B'rith, 1986.

Federation of Jewish Philanthropies of New York. *The Jewish Population of Greater New York: A Profile*. New York: Federation of Jewish Philanthropies of New York, 1984.

Feingold, Henry L. *A Jewish Survival Enigma: The Strange Case of the American Jewish Committee*. New York: American Jewish Committee, 1981.

Feingold, Henry L. "Finding a Conceptual Framework for the Study of American Antisemitism." Paper presented at the annual meeting of the Conference of Jewish Social Studies, 6 May 1984.

Forster, Arnold, and Epstein, Benjamin. *Cross-Currents*. New York: Doubleday, 1956.

Forster, Arnold, and Epstein, Benjamin. *Danger on the Right*. New York: Random House, 1964.

The Gallup Organization. *Dramatic Growth in Tolerance during the Last Quarter Century*. Princeton, NJ: Gallup Organization, 1979.

The Gallup Organization. *Attitudes Concerning the American Jewish Community: The Gallup Poll, 1981*. New York: American Jewish Committee, 1981.

The Gallup Organization. *Attitudes of the American Public toward American Jews and Israel: The Gallup Poll, 1982*. New York: American Jewish Committee, 1982.

Garber, David A., ed. *Anti-Semitism in American History*. Chicago: University of Illinois Press, 1986.

Geer, Lois. *1981 Population Study of the St. Paul Jewish Community*. St. Paul, 1981.

Geer, Lois. *The Jewish Community of Greater Minneapolis 1981 Population Study.* Minneapolis, 1981.

Gest, Ted. "Sudden Rise of Hate Groups Spurs Federal Crackdown." *U.S. News & World Report* 6 May 1985: 68.

Glazer, Nathan. *American Judaism.* Chicago: University of Chicago Press, 1972.

Glazer, Nathan. "On Jewish Forebodings." *Commentary* 80 (August 1985): 32–36.

The Goals of the American Jewish Committee. New York: American Jewish Committee, 1981.

Goldscheider, Calvin. *Jewish Continuity and Change: Emerging Patterns in America.* Bloomington: Indiana University Press, 1986.

Halpern, Ben. "What Is Antisemitism?" *Modern Judaism* 1 (December 1981): 251–262.

Halpern, Ben. "America is Different." *American Jews: A Reader*, Marshall Sklare, ed. New York: Behrman House, 1983.

Hamlin, David. *The Nazi/Skokie Conflict.* Boston: Beacon Press, 1980.

Louis Harris and Associates. *A Study of Anti-Semitism in Rural Iowa and Nebraska.* New York: Anti-Defamation League of B'nai B'rith, 1986.

Harris, Louis. "Poll Results Contradict Claims That Prejudice Is Increasing." *The Harris Survey.* New York: Louis Harris and Associates, 18 February 1985.

Hendrix, Nancy. *A Demographic Study of the Jewish Community of Nashville and Middle Tennessee.* Nashville, 1982.

The Heritage Foundation. "A Heritage Roundtable: Anti-Semitism in the Modern World." *The Heritage Lectures*, 28. Washington: Heritage Foundation, 1984.

Herman, Simon N. *Israelis and Jews: The Continuity of an Identity.* Philadelphia: Jewish Publication Society of America, 1970.

Himmelfarb, Milton. "Another Look at the Jewish Vote." *Commentary* 80 (December 1985): 39–44.

Holocaust "Revisionism": A Denial of History, Vol. 31, No. 1. New York: Anti-Defamation League of B'nai B'rith, 1986.

Jewish Community Federation of Cleveland. *Survey of Cleveland's Jewish Population, 1981.* Cleveland: Jewish Community Federation of Cleveland, 1982.

Jewish Community Federation of Richmond. *Demographic Survey of the Jewish Community of Richmond.* Richmond: Jewish Community Federation of Richmond, 1984.

Kahane. Meir, *Never Again! A Program for Survival.* Los Angeles: Nash, 1971.

Katchen, Alan S. "The Station That Broadcast Hate." *ADL Bulletin* 42 (February 1985): 3–5.

Kesten, Alisa, Ellerin, Milton, and Kaufer, Sonya. *Antisemitism in America: A Balance Sheet.* New York: American Jewish Committee, 1981.

Levine, Jacqueline K. "A Changing America and a Changing Jewish Community: Is the Jewish Community Relations Field Responsive?" Address to the NJCRAC Plenary Session, 16 February 1986.

Lewis, I. A., and Schneider, William. "Is the Public Lying to the Pollsters? *Current* 245 (September 1982): 25–35.

Liberty Lobby and the Carto Network of Hate, Vol. 27, No. 1. New York: Anti-Defamation League of B'nai B'rith, 1982.

Liebman, Charles S. *The Ambivalent American Jew*. Philadelphia: Jewish Publication Society of America, 1973.

Lieberman, Michael. "Extremists Try to Exploit Farm Crisis." *ADL Bulletin* 43 (January 1986): 3–5.

Lincoln, C. Eric. *Race, Religion, and the Continuing American Dilemma*. New York: Hill and Wang, 1984.

Loury, G. C. "Behind the Black–Jewish Split." *Commentary* 81 (January 1986): 23–27.

Market Facts, Inc. *A National Survey of Black Americans*. Los Angeles: Simon Wiesenthal Center, 1985.

Martire, Gregory, and Clark, Ruth. *Anti-Semitism in the United States: A Study of Prejudice in the 1980s*. New York: Praeger, 1982.

McCann, James, and Friedman, Debra. *A Study of the Jewish Community in the Greater Seattle Area*. Seattle, 1979.

McClosky, Herbert, and Brill, Alida. *Dimensions of Tolerance: What Americans Believe about Civil Liberties*. New York: Russell Sage Foundation, 1983.

Mintz, Frank P. *The Liberty Lobby and the American Right*. Westport, CT: Greenwood Press, 1985.

Minutes of the NJCRAC Subcommittee on Assessing Criteria for Measuring Antisemitism. New York: The National Jewish Community Relations Advisory Council, March 19, 1986.

National Jewish Community Relations Advisory Council. *Joint Program Plan for Jewish Community Relations 1985–86: Guide to Program Planning of the Constituent Organizations*. New York: National Jewish Community Relations Advisory Council, 1986.

National Jewish Community Relations Advisory Council. *Joint Program Plan for Jewish Community Relations. 1986–87: Guide to Program Planning of the Constituent Organizations*. New York: National Jewish Community Relations Advisory Council, 1987.

Neusner, Jacob. *Stranger at Home*. Chicago: University of Chicago Press, 1981.

Neusner, Jacob. *Israel in America: A Too-Comfortable Exile?* Boston: Beacon Press, 1985.

Perlmutter, Nathan. "Comment: A Year in Retrospect." *ADL Bulletin* 41 (January 1984): 2.

Perlmutter, Nathan. "Comment: The 10 Most Significant Events." *ADL Bulletin* 42 (February 1985): 2.

Perlmutter, Nathan. "Jews and Fundamentalism." *Reconstructionist* (December 1985): 20–23.

Perlmutter, Nathan. "Comment: The Year That Was . . ." *ADL Bulletin* 43 (January 1986): 2.

Perlmutter, Nathan. "Comment: The 10 Most Significant Events." *ADL Bulletin* 43 (February 1986): 2.

Phillips, Bruce A. *Los Angeles Jewish Community Survey Overview for Regional Planning.* Los Angeles, 1980.

Phillips, Bruce A., and Aron, William S. *The Greater Phoenix Jewish Population Study.* Phoenix, 1983–1984.

Phillips, Bruce A., and Judd, Eleanore P. *Supplement to the Denver Jewish Population Study, 1981.* Denver: Allied Jewish Federation of Denver, 1983.

Phillips, Bruce A., and Weinberg, Eve. *The Milwaukee Jewish Population Study.* Chicago: Policy Research Corporation, 1984.

Pogrebin, L. C. "Anti-Semitism in the Women's Movement." *Ms* 10 (June 1982): 45–46.

Policy Research Corporation. *Chicago Jewish Population Study.* Chicago, 1982.

The Populist Party: The Politics of Right Wing Extremism, Vol. 30, No. 2. New York: Anti-Defamation League of B'nai B'rith, 1985.

Prager, Dennis, and Telushkin, Joseph. *Why the Jews?* New York: Simon & Schuster, 1983.

Pro-Arab Propaganda in America: Vehicles and Voices. New York: Anti-Defamation League of B'nai B'rith, 1983.

"Propaganda of the Deed": The Far Right's Desperate "Revolution." New York: Anti-Defamation League of B'nai B'rith, 1985.

Purposes and Programs. New York: Anti-Defamation League of B'nai B'rith, 1986.

Quinley, Harold E., and Glock, Charles Y. *Anti-Semitism in America.* New York: Free Press, 1979.

Raab, Earl. "Anti-Semitism in the 1980s." *Midstream* 29 (February 1983): 11–18.

Rappeport, Michael, and Tobin, Gary. *A Population Study of the Jewish Community of MetroWest, New Jersey, 1986.* New Jersey: United Jewish Federation of MetroWest, 1987.

Regenstreif, Peter. *The Jewish Population of Rochester, New York.* Rochester, 1981.

Reichley, A. James. *Religion in American Public Life.* Washington: Brookings Institution, 1985.

Reinharz, Jehuda, ed. *Living with Antisemitism.* Hanover: University Press of New England, 1987.

Ritterband, Paul, and Cohen, Steven M. *The 1981 Greater New York Jewish Population Survey.* New York, 1981.

Rivkin, Ellis. "A Decisive Pattern in American Jewish History." *Essays in American Jewish History.* Cincinnati: American Jewish Archives (1958): 23–63.

The Roper Organization. *The American Jewish Committee's January 1984 Poll.* New York: American Jewish Committee, 1984.

Rosenberg, M. J. "To Uncle Tom and Other Jews." *Jewish Radicalism: A Selected Anthology,* Jack Nusan Porter and Peter Dreier, eds. New York: Grove Press, 1973.

Rosenblatt, Roger. "The Demagogue in the Crowd." *Time* 26 (21 October 1985): 102.

Rosenfield, Geraldine. *Attitudes of the American Public toward Israel and American Jews: The Yankelovich Findings* (Supplement to Report of December 1974.) An unpublished report of the American Jewish Committee. New York: American Jewish Committee, April 1975.

Rosenfield, Geraldine. *Jewish Concerns Project*. New York: American Jewish Committee, 1978.

Rosenfield, Geraldine. *Attitudes of the American Public toward American Jews and Israel: August 1979; March–April 1980*. New York: American Jewish Committee, 1980.

Rosenfield, Geraldine. "What Do They Think of Us?" *Present Tense* 8 (1981): 8–10.

Rosenfield, Geraldine. "The Polls: Attitudes toward American Jews." *Public Opinion Quarterly* 46 (1982): 431–443.

Rosenfield, Stephen S. "Dateline Washington: Anti-Semitism and U.S. Foreign Policy." *Foreign Policy* 47 (Summer 1982): 172–183.

Roster of Members, September 1986. St. Louis: The American Jewish Press Association, 1986.

Sarna, Jonathan D. "Anti-Semitism and American History." *Commentary* 71 (March 1981): 42–47.

Schuman, Howard, Steeh, Charlotte, and Bobo, Lawrence. *Racial Attitudes in America*. Cambridge: Harvard University Press, 1985.

Security for Community Institutions: A Handbook. New York: Anti-Defamation League of B'nai B'rith, in conjunction with the New York City Police Department, 1984.

"Seeds of Hate." *20/20*, ABC, 15 August 1985.

Selznick, Gertrude, and Steinberg, Stephen. *The Tenacity of Prejudice: Anti-Semitism in Contemporary America*. New York: Harper & Row, 1969.

Sheskin, Ira M. *Population Study of the Greater Miami Jewish Community*. Miami, 1982.

Siegman, Henry. "Jews and Blacks: Reconciling the Difference." *Congress Monthly* 52 (January 1985): 3–4.

Silberman, Charles. *A Certain People: American Jews and Their Lives Today*. New York: Summit Books, 1985.

Silberman, Jeffrey M. "Jewish Responses to Anti-Semitism: A Psychological Overview." *Humanistic Judaism* 11 (1983): 21–29.

Singer, David, and Cohen, Renae. *Probing Public Sentiment on Israel and American Jews: The February 1987 Roper Poll*. New York: American Jewish Committee, 1987.

Sklare, Marshall. *America's Jews*. New York: Random House, 1971.

Sklare, Marshall. *The Jewish Community in America*. New York: Behrman House, 1974.

Sklare, Marshall. *American Jews: A Reader*. New York: Behrman House, 1979.

Sklare, Marshall, ed. *Understanding American Jewry*. New Brunswick: Transaction Books, 1982.

Smith, Tom W., and Dempsey, Glenn R. "The Polls: Ethnic Social Distance and Prejudice." *Public Opinion Quarterly* 47 (Winter 1983): 584–600.

Smith, Tom W., and Sheatsley, Paul B. "American Attitudes toward Race Relations." *Public Opinion* (October/November 1984): 14–53.

Some Survey Data on Jewish Attitudes toward Relationships with Non-Jews. New York: American Jewish Committee, 1961.

Stark, Rodney, and Steinberg, Stephen. *It Did Happen Here—An Investigation of Political Anti-Semitism: Wayne, New Jersey, 1967*. Berkeley: Survey Research Center, 1967.

Steinberg, Milton. "Current Philosophies of Jewish Life in America." *The American Jew: A Composite Portrait*, Oscar I. Janowsky, ed. New York: Harper, 1942.

Stember, Charles H. (ed.). *Jews in the Mind of America*. New York: Basic Books, 1966.

Stillman, Gerald. "Polling American Antisemitism." *Jewish Currents* 36 (July–August 1982): 9–15.

Summary of Selected Programs and Budget. New York: American Jewish Committee, 1986.

Terrance, Hill, Newport and Ryan. *Nationwide Attitudes Survey of Evangelical Christians*. New York: Anti-Defamation League of B'nai B'rith, 1986.

Terrorism's Targets: Democracy, Israel and Jews. New York: Anti-Defamation League of B'nai B'rith, 1981.

Tobin, Gary A. *A Demographic and Attitudinal Study of the Jewish Community of St. Louis*. St. Louis: Jewish Federation of St. Louis, 1982.

Tobin, Gary A. *A Demographic Study of the Jewish Community of Atlantic County*. Atlantic City, 1986.

Tobin, Gary A. *A Demographic Study of the Jewish Community of Greater Kansas City*. Kansas City, 1986.

Tobin, Gary A. *A Population Study of the Jewish Community of Greater Baltimore*. Baltimore, 1986.

Tobin, Gary A. "Jewish Perceptions of Antisemitism and Antisemitic Perceptions of Jews." *Studies in Contemporary Jewry*, Vol. 4, New York: Oxford University Press, 1987.

Tobin, Gary A., and Fishman, Sylvia Barack. *A Population Study of the Jewish Community of Worcester*. Worcester, 1987.

Tobin, Gary A., and Fishman, Sylvia Barack. *A Population Study of the Jewish Community of Greater Rochester*. Rochester, 1988.

Tobin, Gary A., and Sassler, Sharon. *A Demographic Study of the Jewish Community of the San Francisco Bay Area*. San Francisco, 1988.

Tobin, Gary A., and Sassler, Sharon. *A Demographic Study of New Orleans*. New Orleans, 1988.

Tobin, Gary A., Waksberg, Joseph, and Greenblatt, Janet. *A Demographic Study of the Jewish Community of Greater Washington*. Washington, DC, 1984.

Tropp, Robert F. *Measuring Anti-Semitism: Assessing the Criteria*. Paper presented at the NJCRAC Plenary Session, 1985.

Tsukashima, Ronald T. *The Social and Psychological Correlates of Black Anti-Semitism*. San Francisco: R & E Research Associates, 1978.

Velen, Victor A. "Anti-Semitism and the Left." *Midstream* 31 (January 1985): 8–12.

Volkman, Ernest. *A Legacy of Hate: Anti-Semitism in America*. New York: Franklin Watts, 1982.

Weintraub, Ruth G. *How Secure These Rights?* New York: Doubleday, 1949.

Wistrich, Robert. "The Anti-Zionist Masquerade." *Midstream* 29 (August/September 1983): 8–18.

Wolf, Ursula. "The Pincer Movement," *Instauration* (August 1986): 14–16.

Wolk, Rochelle Saidel. "Prophecy or Paranoia?" *Lilith* 7 (Fall 1980): 8–10.

Woocher, Jonathan S. *Sacred Survival: The Civil Religion of American Jews*. Bloomington: Indiana University Press, 1986.

Woodward, Kenneth L. "Jews in a Soulful Debate [views of C.E. Silberman]. *Newsweek* 23 September 1985: 77.

Yancey, William L., and Goldstein, Ira. *The Jewish Population of the Greater Philadelphia Area*. Philadelphia: Federation of Jewish Agencies of Greater Philadelphia, 1984.

Yankelovich, Skelly & White. *1976 Study on Jews, Israel, Middle East*. New York: American Jewish Committee, 1976.

Yankelovich, Skelly & White. *Anti-Semitism in the United States*. 2 vols. New York: American Jewish Committee, 1981.

Zeskind, Leonard. *Background Report on Racist and Anti-Semitic Organizational Intervention in the Farm Protest Movement*. Atlanta: Center for Democratic Renewal, 1985.

Zeskind, Leonard. *Update on Anti-Semitic and Racist Intervention in the Farm Protest Movement*. Atlanta: Center for Democratic Renewal, 1986.

Zweigenhaft, Richard L., and Domhoff, G. William. *Jews in the Protestant Establishment*. New York: Praeger, 1982.

"Antisemitism Today: A Symposium." *Patterns of Prejudice* 16 (1982): 5–53.

Jewish Newspapers

The American Jewish World (Minnesota), 2/6/87.

The Asbury Park Press, 10/21/85.

The Atlanta Jewish Times, 1/30/87.

The Baltimore Jewish Times, 2/7/86, 10/25/85, 1/16/87, 2/6/87, 9/14/84, 8/8/86, 1/3/86, 10/4/85, 3/14/85.

The Bergen Jewish News, (Bergen County, NJ), 2/86.

B'nai B'rith Record, 12/83.

Buffalo Jewish Review, 1/30/87, 1/13/84.

The Connecticut Jewish Ledger, 1/29/87.

The Detroit Jewish News, 1/30/87, 2/6/87.

Israel Today (San Diego, CA), 1/31/86.

The Jerusalem Post, 8/7/85.

The Jewish Advocate (Boston, MA), 1/22/87, 1/29/87, 2/26/87.

The Jewish Exponent (Philadelphia, PA), 1/30/87.
The Jewish Journal (NY), 3/2/87, 2/14/86.
The Jewish Post and Opinion, 12/4/85, 10/8/86, 3/2/83, 7/2/86.
The Jewish Press (Brooklyn, NY), 11/1/86, 1/17/86, 10/18/85.
The Jewish Times (Youngstown, OH), 2/13/87, 3/30/84.
The Kansas City Jewish Chronicle, 1/16/87, 6/13/86, 2/6/87.
The London Jewish Chronicle, 11/82.
The Long Island Jewish World, 10/4–11/85, 7/20–26/84, 10/11–17/85, 12/19/86, 2/27–5/87.
New York Jewish Week, 8/9/85, 1/18/85.
The Northern California Jewish Bulletin, 3/7/86.
Palm Beach Jewish World, 4/18–24/86, 1/9–15/87.
Rocky Mountain News, 2/17/87.
Sentinel (Chicago), 2/15/87.
St. Louis Jewish Light, 5/15/85.
Washington Jewish Week, 6/19/86, 12/26/85, 1/29/87, 2/5/87, 11/20/86, 10/31/85, 11/28/85, 10/3/85, 10/10/85.
The Youngstown Jewish Times, 8/15/86. 1/17/86, 10/11/85, 2/28/86.

General Newspapers

The Boston Globe, 2/18/85.
The Chicago Sun-Times. 1/8/87, 1/11/87.
The Chicago Tribune, 1/8/87.
The Daily News (New York) 9/10 and 11/79.
The Los Angeles Times, 1/10/84.
The News & Tribune (Jefferson City, MO), 5/18/86.
The New York City Tribune, 7/23/86.
The New York Times, 12/2/81, 2/26/87, 2/16/87, 12/2/81, 4/26/85, 8/5/86.
The Washington Post, 12/20/85, 12/21/85, 1/10/87, 10/11/85, 7/26/86.
The Washington Times, 10/11/85, 1/19/87, 11/15/85.

INDEX

317